Nov. 2012

Collected Writings of William Still

Collected
Writings
of William Still

Volume 1: Theological Studies

edited by Nigel M. de S. Cameron and Sinclair B. Ferguson

RUTHERFORD HOUSE BOOKS
Edinburgh

Published by Rutherford House,
17 Claremont Park, Edinburgh EH6 7PJ, Scotland

ISBN 0 946068 38 0

Computer typeset at Rutherford House on Apple Macintosh™

Printed in Great Britain by BPCC Wheatons Ltd, Exeter

CONTENTS

PREFACE

It is our great privilege as editors to introduce this three-volume collection of William Still's writings.

Since 1945, William Still has been minister of Gilcomston South Church, Aberdeen. From there the influence of his ministry has spread all over the world and produced a harvest of fruitful Christians.

William Still entered the ministry of the Church of Scotland when he was already in his thirties, returning to formal education many years after leaving school in his early teens. Throughout his ministry he has been a keen student of Scripture and of whatever literature or conversation might shed further illumination on its message. Believing it to be God's revelation written, he has studied it from cover to cover (and preached through it, and written study notes on it for his congregation several times too). His love for Scripture and his desire to communicate its deep riches are evident in his preaching.

In addition, Mr Still's ministry in public and private is suffused with a love for both God and man. Those who have had the privilege of knowing him agree that these interconnected and inseparable loves have made him human, but with a heavenly spirit; serious, but with a deep note of joy; hard-working, but with a thankful heart; and perhaps most of all, immensely approachable and loveable. He has never pretended to his younger friends and colleagues that he has no weaknesses, although by God's grace he has sought to overcome those that are sinful and compensate for those that are natural. In this, as in many other things, he has been a model to many fragile Christians (which, ultimately, we all are). Something of the richness of his personal spiritual pilgrimage and growth will be sensed in reading the studies contained in this volume.

Pulpit preparation should always be done with a view to the immediate hearers. But the material here presented merits a more permanent form. While the desire to honour one who is greatly esteemed would be sufficient justification for its publication, we believe that the value of the material itself will be widely recognised. Indeed, the manuscripts of Mr Still's preaching and teaching ministry have reminded us of the baskets of fragments which remained after Jesus had fed and satisfied the multitude – there is much here, even in messages preached decades ago, to nourish others in the Christian life.

Collected Writings of William Still will appear in a series of three volumes. Volume One contains studies on some central Christian doctrines and their practical significance. Volume Two will focus on the Christian life, while Volume Three will contain studies on a miscellany of themes. It is impossible for the written word to convey fully the impact of the spoken word. This is particularly true of a unique ministry like William Still's. But we hope these volumes will be read widely and appreciated by those who know the minister of Gilcomston South Church only by reputation, as well as by those who have sat under his ministry in Aberdeen and elsewhere and will be able to 'hear' the familiar cadences of his preaching as they read the printed word.

As those who first heard William Still preach when we were teen-aged students it is difficult for us to believe that our friendships with him now extend over two decades. These volumes will, we trust, give some indication as to why, with multitudes of others in Christian service in Scotland and far beyond, we prize him and his ministry to us.

The bulk of this book derives from two sermon series: *The Cross* was preached in 1967 and *The Holy Spirit* in 1973. *The Devil* is based on addresses given at an IVF (UCCF) conference in 1968, which subsequently appeared (with other material) in booklet form in 1974. *The Second Coming* was first of all a series of addresses at the 1976 Scottish conference of the UCCF, and also appeared as a booklet. *The Lord from Heaven* originated as a series of addresses at the UCCF Welsh Conference, 1974, and *Law and Grace* as a booklet based on earlier material (1981).

We extend special thanks to those who helped Mr Still to gather this material, to Michael Gray and subsequently Vivienne Goddard of the staff of Rutherford House, who have supervised its production, and to Sarah Yorke, who set the type.

Nigel M. de S. Cameron
Sinclair B. Ferguson
January 1990

THE CROSS

1: Death and Resurrection

Isaiah 53:1-10, John 12:20-26.

My own experience has increasingly persuaded me that the concepts of death and resurrection are central to the spiritual life. What aspect of the Christian life is not related vitally to the practicalities of death and resurrection? We must never separate the one from the other. I could have given the title 'The Cross' to sum up simply what I want to say. Yet that is not good enough. It is not the death of Christ – not death as such – but death and resurrection. You cannot hand me one side of a penny. It isn't a coin of the realm unless I have both sides (if you could split it in two!). A great deal that we say in Christian preaching and teaching about *death* and *Christ's death* and *our death* is misunderstood – and is injurious psychologically and spiritually to sensitive souls – because it is too much divorced from its co-relative, *resurrection.*

The outworking of death and resurrection is seen so widely at harvest time. You see it in nature. I cannot go into realms that are almost closed to me (although a cat can look at a king, and I suppose a novice can look at a scientist, and even look over his shoulder and see what he is doing). Do we see this in geology, at all? Do we see it in astronomy? We certainly do in biology, in botany and zoology. We certainly see it in the life of man. We may possibly see it in the life of pure mind, in rationality, in the life and experience of thought itself.

Certainly the Bible, and Christian life itself, are full of death and resurrection. I would go so far as to say this: if you do not understand this about the Bible, and at least begin to understand it in Christian life, then you do not understand anything. You do not know what the Christian faith and the Bible are about, if this idea of death and resurrection is not woven into the very texture of your thought.

Now, greatly daring, but I hope on scriptural grounds, we are going to explore a little. And I want to drive back a little, very reverently and tentatively, into the life and mind of the eternal God, especially the life and mind of the eternal God before the world began.

Before the world was made there was the eternal God subsisting in three Persons – the Father, the Son, and the Holy Spirit – three Persons, one God. And the three Persons in order: the first Person, the second Person and the third Person are co-eternal, are co-equal in power and glory and eternity. The second Person is the Son. He is not the Father. He is *of* the Father, but he is of the Father *eternally*. There never was a time, even in eternity, when there was a Father without the Son. But he is still the Son, the second Person in the Trinity. His filial devotion stretches back beyond creation, and continues in his earthly life, and even in his reigning, seated at the right hand of the Father. He will lay his kingdom at his Father's feet, at the end (1 Cor. 15:28).

Then there is the Holy Spirit. He proceeds from the Father and from the Son, and yet he with the Son is not any less eternal than the Father. The Father, the Son and the Spirit, three Persons – co-equal in power, glory and eternity!

Now here is what I am thinking (we'll get on to more practical things in a moment; be patient if this doesn't appeal to you!): are there any inherent hints of the notion of death and resurrection in the relationships between the different Persons of the Trinity? This is very daring! I don't know. Perhaps what I say in a moment will seem to contradict that, but I do want to say it. And so I begin to probe. Think of the classic statement in Revelation 13:8, which speaks of the Lamb slain from the foundation of the world. There are various renderings of that text. You can put the different parts of it in a different order, but it all comes to the same. 'The Lamb slain from the foundation (or was it from before the foundation?) of the world.'

What does that mean? What does that mean in the mind of God? I only ask the question. I am suggesting this as a text which may shed light on the mind of God in what we will call 'pre' eternity – eternity before the world began. Here is one that may belong to 'post' eternity, either after the consummation, or at it. John says, in Revelation 5:6, that he saw 'in the midst of the throne of God a Lamb, standing as it had been slain.' The hymn 'Crown him with many crowns' expresses the point well. Matthew Bridges and Godfrey Thring speak about Christ's 'Rich wounds yet visible above, in beauty glorified'. I am not thinking of death and resurrection as a fact, but of death as an activity, as a means to an end, a utility; as a serviceability to the end of something blessed and glorious. Paul makes a most striking observation when he says in 2 Corinthians 4:12 that 'Death works'.

How was such an idea first in the mind of God? How, for example, did God see so clearly through the darkness of what is expressed by the prophet in Isaiah 53? The first part deals with the suffering and rejection and uncomeliness of Christ, and then goes on to say that this was not for himself but for us. Then it goes on to describe what was involved for him, not least in his being silent before his accusers, taken from prison and judgment, and cut off, and buried in a grave – and so on.

But then, the 10th verse onwards speaks of God's glorious purpose in Christ's humiliation: 'Yet it pleased the Lord to bruise him; he hath put him to grief: when thou shalt make his soul an offering for sin, he shall see his seed, he shall prolong his days, and the pleasure of the Lord shall prosper in his hand. He shall see of the travail of his soul and be satisfied: by his knowledge shall my righteous servant justify many; for he shall bear their iniquities. Therefore will I divide him a portion with the great and he shall divide the spoil with the strong; because he hath poured out his soul unto death: and he was numbered with the transgressors.' Whenever he first saw the notion of death and resurrection, whether it was simultaneous with his conceptualising of creation or not, he saw it as a unity. This is what I am trying to say. The death and resurrection of Christ was not a kind of subsequent, or contingent, or even opportunist insight. God saw it as something that was integral to his plans. Whether or not it was something integral to his own mind, it was certainly something that came out of his mind.

Consider something else. Why does Paul say, not only that Christ (and Christ's cross) is the power of God, but that he is also the wisdom of God? 'For Christ sent me; not to baptise but to preach the gospel: not with wisdom of words, lest the cross of Christ should be made of none effect. For the preaching of the cross is to them that perish foolishness; but unto us who are being saved, it is the power of God. For it is written, I will destroy the wisdom of the wise and will bring to nothing the understanding of the prudent. Where is the wise? Where is the scribe? Where is the disputer of this world? Hath not God made foolish the wisdom of this world? For after that in the wisdom of God the world by its wisdom knew not God, it pleased God by the foolishness of preaching to save them that believe. For the Jews require a sign, the Greeks seek after wisdom; but we preach Christ crucified, unto the Jews a stumbling block, and unto the Greeks foolishness but unto them which are called, both Jews and Greeks, Christ the power of God and the wisdom of God. Because the foolishness of God is wiser than men; and the weakness of God is stronger than men' (1 Cor. 1:17-25). The wisdom of God! The cross of Christ is the wisdom of God. Was not this something embedded in the mind of the Eternal from the very beginning?

Take another example. Why does Hebrews 12:2 say that it was for the joy that was set before him that Christ endured the cross and despised the shame, and is now seated at the right hand of God, if it wasn't that God saw the whole thing – the ugly thing and the glorious thing – as one in his mind? Even if this was latent in the divine mind before the counsels of eternity, and was only evoked in God's plan of redemption, subsequent to the life of the Trinity, it was still inherent in the divine mind. It came out of the divine mind. The divine, the eternal mind was capable of thinking these thoughts and did think them, whether they were first thought in relation to the counsels of eternity when redemption was first planned or not. They were in, and came forth from, the mind of the eternal God. Yet is it not strange that the eternal being who cannot die, who had no beginning and no ending, should think in these terms – of death and the necessity following it, of resurrection?

Was it, in the counsels of eternity, the intention to create worlds – of natural things, of angels and so on – that evoked the thought of death and resurrection? And had it to do with the divine delegation of authority to creatures that he was to make? And is it all bound up with what would seem to us the danger to God in the creation of man and angels; of granting them a certain authority under him, the authority of free will in fact?

This great hazard of God in creating the worlds, and angels, and men, and giving to Lucifer authority over the creation, and man over the earth seems to me to be no inconsiderable part of the furniture of the divine mind. Is this part of the meaning of the Lamb being slain from the foundation of the world? And was the Lamb standing in the midst of the throne of God as if it had been slain? Although all this may have arisen in the divine mind at the time when creation and redemption were planned, only the Eternal could have thought such thoughts. For, you see, the Eternal, the eternal mind is not static. It is everlasting, but it is not everlastingly stationary. It is not a block of something that has no life in it because it is perfect. The eternal mind is creative, and the very idea of death and resurrection is creative, productive, reproductive, re-creative and surely redemptive indeed!

We see this, do we not, in the re-creative forces working in God's creation, even before sin entered into the world? Do we see it, or is it present in fact, in the life of the astronomical world – constellations, stars and planets? Is there something constantly creative going on in the universe? Is the universe expanding? Certainly we see this principle, this creative activity, in the reproduction of flora and fauna – the plants and animals. Listen to the first chapter of Genesis: 'And God blessed them' – and to created things he 'said, Be fruitful and multiply, and fill the waters and the seas and let fowl multiply on the earth'. And again – 'And God blessed them'. Again, God 'said unto him (man), Be fruitful and multiply and replenish the earth and subdue it and have dominion over the fish of the sea and over the bird of the air and over every living thing that moveth upon the earth'. And again – 'And God said,

Behold I have given you every herb bearing seed, which is upon the face of all the earth, every tree in the which is the fruit of the tree, yielding seed. To you it shall be for meat' (see Gen. 1:20-9). And then notice this – this did not come to pass before sin, but it refers to something that began before sin: 'While the earth remaineth, seed time and harvest (death and resurrection, cold and heat), summer and winter, day and night, shall not cease' (Gen. 8:22).

But perhaps the central text for this theory is in John 12:24. Jesus said, when the Greeks came too late and too early to see him: 'I haven't died yet. They needn't come before I have died. I am no use to them or to anybody before I have died, and been raised from the dead.' That is the context of his statement: 'Except a corn of wheat fall into the ground and die it abideth alone. But if it die, it bringeth forth much fruit.'

Now, Jesus said that primarily of himself; but we know that he desires it to be applied to the life of his disciples, in another sense. And Paul deliberately thus applies it, as we shall see in a moment. Here is the natural order, quite apart, it seems to me, from the question of sin, speaking to us plainly of death and resurrection.

I have been discussing this question with two scientist friends in relation to plant and animal life. They are inclined to think that decay and death, in the plant and animal worlds, are natural, and were natural before the Fall. So in the life of man, as to his animal nature only, decay and death may also be thought of as being quite natural. (We must be careful not to get too hot and bothered about the questions that are asked in this area!) But, while that may be true of man as to his animal nature, God in the creation of man, having breathed the breath of his own life into his clay, into his nostrils, made him a living soul (Gen. 2:7). Presumably that living soul was potentially immortal and undying. Thus man became man as distinct from the plants and the animals. It is interesting to note nevertheless, that although through the Fall man doubtless became mortal, and was destined for natural and spiritual death (God warned that when he partook of the fruit he would surely die, Gen. 2:17), yet man did not die naturally or mortally at once. And you remember that Paul says that sin is *the sting* of death. Mortality has worked progressively through the generations. The early men lived for nearly a thousand years. I wonder if that was the optimum? Methuselah lived to be nearly a thousand. Then as sin wrought into the fibres of their being from generation to generation, men lived shorter, and shorter, and shorter, and shorter – until even in Bible days, the span of the life of man is declared to be seventy years. Mortality did set in, working progressively to the end, in the intention of the enemy, of the second, spiritual, everlasting death – of the soul as well as of the body.

At all events, whatever you think about this, is it not true to say that we see death and resurrection in nature, in the life of man, as well as in the work of redemption?

Now, death is an ugly thing. Nobody really enjoys the time of digging up or replanting, or planting dirty roots in October or November, with scarcely anything to show what they are roots of; or the time of planting bulbs. It is ugly, unattractive and repulsive. But every gardener knows this is absolutely necessary. Really dried roots will not grow. They are dead, or potentially dead, and seeds will not grow, unless they are moistened. Death is necessary.

Think of this in relation to the spiritual life. It is not only necessary but it is beneficent; for it is causative – in its sequence, in its alternation, in its process – of something that is blessed. Notice two things here: first, the process. 'Except a corn of wheat *fall into the ground.*' That is the first thing. Then, the finality. 'Except a corn of wheat fall into the ground *and die.*' It must die. Nothing less than death would lead to new life. This is true in the natural world. The finality of death is necessary to ensure the action of resurrection. There cannot be a resurrection without a death. 'Except a corn of wheat fall into the ground and die, it abideth alone; but if it die, it bringeth forth much fruit.' These are Jesus' words.

Now see this as a spiritual reality in two worlds. First, in the world of those who are not Christians, or who are not *yet* Christians. Those who know not Christ are called to repent. This is a death, nothing less than a death. They have changed their minds absolutely about themselves. They see themselves in God's sight to be hell-deserving sinners. And because they see that, and face the fact that they are undone, that they are dead in trespasses and sins, they cry to God to have mercy on them. When he does and sends his grace, this leads from the death of repentance to the resurrection of the new life.

See it in the world of Christians. It is necessary, as a Christian, to die to many of the blessed, sweet and lovely things that we may enjoy in the Christian life. Many people grow better off as Christians than they ever did as non-Christians. God works in their minds, and in their bodies too, and affects their health and their efficiency, and enables them to do a far better job in the world, and to gain far more skill and efficiency, and get on far better than they did before they knew Christ. It is to those that Jesus says, 'Lay not up treasure on the earth; but lay up treasure in heaven' (Matt. 5:19-20). Which is to say that Christians are called to die many deaths, even to the blessings that God gives them. At the very least, we are to give our firstfruits to the Lord, that we may grow in grace and Christian stature.

Also, in this world, as Paul tells us, we have to die another death, in a sense quite distinct from that. This is a further reach, or range, of the Christian life. We are to die a death in order that the life of Christ may arise in others. These two are spoken of in 2 Corinthians 4:8-11: 'We are troubled on every side, yet not distressed, we are perplexed but not in despair; persecuted but not forsaken; cast down but not destroyed; always bearing about in the body the dying of the Lord Jesus, that the life also of Jesus might be made manifest in our body.'

If Jesus Christ is to shine out of your eyes, it will be by your dying – as the apostle puts it in another place – 'daily'. He says the same thing again in the next verse: 'For we who live are always delivered unto death for Jesus' sake, that the life also of Jesus might be made manifest in our mortal flesh.' 'Always delivered unto death for Jesus' sake'! Dying that we may live! Then in the next verse: 'So then death worketh in us but life in others' (2 Cor. 4:12). This is dying different deaths. Dying that others may live for Christ.

So there are three deaths: first the death of repentance, turning our back on the whole of our old life, and seeing ourselves as in need of the life of Christ. Dying to many of the blessings that come to us because of our faith in Christ. Pruning our lives that they may bear more fruit in Christian character. And lastly, dying deaths that have to be died – these are deeper deaths, sorer deaths – that the life of Christ may arise in others.

The saving power of Christ is in the air just now. It could be, at this very time, at this season in the day of grace, that it is easier, not easy, but easier, to win people. There may be, in Aberdeen – leave the rest of the world aside at the moment – people who are more susceptible to the gospel, and to Christ, and to your interesting them in the gospel, than ever before.

What are you going to do about it? Die a death – whatever that may mean for you.

THE CROSS

2: How Deep is the Fall?

Genesis 3.

God formed man of the dust of the ground. However he did it, he created man in his own image, the pattern image of his own Son who was ultimately to come to the earth as *the* Man. Thus God constituted man a special creation. The opening chapter of Genesis makes this very clear: 'Then God said, Let us make man in our image, after our likeness. . .'. 'So God created man in his own image, in the image of God created he him; male and female created he them' (Gen. 1:26-27).

> Then the Lord God formed man of the dust of the ground and breathed into his nostrils of the breath of life; and man became a living being (or a living soul) (Gen. 2:7).

Not only was man made as a special creation distinct from all other creatures however he was formed of the dust of the ground, but indeed, he was the crown of creation, above the angels. For angels are redeemed man's servants. Man then is a special creation!

This is absolutely essential to a Christian attitude to the Word and to Creation. We know nothing about the creation of the angels – or when that took place, although there may be hints, in Job for instance. But the final and the most glorious act of all creation was of man.

There is no time for us to go over the first two chapters of Genesis and show the grace of God in them – what God created and provided for man. It was all sheer grace and kindness. He lavished upon him, as these two chapters in Genesis show, every conceivable blessing that even the Almighty God himself could have given him; and gave him only one prohibition; and with it the test that the crown of creation, a creature of high rank in God's order of beings needed – one prohibition and one test to put this man, almost drowned in blessings, overwhelmed in divine largesse, on probation. One prohibition!

It is in the light of these two chapters of unexampled grace and goodness, sheer unmitigated grace, that we have the most heinous sin that was ever committed, in the face of all that generosity of God. Man failed in that test. Our father failed in that test. However you may think he has grown, or even perhaps in some sense fallen, upwards as a creature of the earth, let there be absolutely no doubt about his fall, and the utter heinousness of his sin. There is not in the whole of history such an example of base, and horrid, and perverse, and treacherous ingratitude. It is the filthiest, the foulest and vilest thing one could conceive; born of a perverse nature, subtly and yet – paradoxically – openly injected into him.

So I want to ask the question: how serious therefore for man, and for God, is the Fall of man, flying in the face of all this grace?

Well, for one thing (and this is almost the least of it), he being the crown of creation, 'set over the creation as its governor', brought the whole creation crashing in ruins around him. Paul indicates this in Romans 8:18 and the verses that follow: 'I consider that the sufferings of this present time are not worth comparing (or, to be compared with) the glory that is to be revealed in us.' Man is to be an exceedingly glorious creature, far more glorious than any angels. Hence when God came to the earth he did not become an angel, he became a man.

Then this is where he plunges into what we are wanting – 'for the creation (the whole natural creation, not only the earth but the universe) waits with eager longing for the revealing of the sons of God'. In redemption the sons of God are first, and with their full redemption comes (can you credit this?) the redemption of the natural universe. That is the order. Then Paul goes on to explain:

'For the creation was subjected to futility; not of its own will (the natural creation hasn't got a will; but it was *subjected* to futility, it had no option, in that it was under man, and man came down) but by the will of him who subjected it in hope.' God had a purpose. In the Fall he allowed the whole creation to come crashing down, for a purpose of hope that he had in view concerning man.

Then Paul goes on, 'because the creation itself will be set free from its bondage to decay (and disease) and will obtain the glorious liberty of the children of God'. And he adds, 'We know that the whole creation has been groaning in travail together until now.' Is it too poetical to speak of the sighing of the wind and the moaning of the sea? Are these merely subjective to our imaginative minds and ears? 'The whole creation has been groaning in travail together until now; and not only the creation but we ourselves who have the firstfruits of the Spirit, groan inwardly, as we wait for the adoption as sons; indeed for the redemption of our bodies.'

Do you not see that this (and other passages) undoubtedly imply that the fallen state of creation – disease in the plants, disease in animals and all the horrid natural catastrophes – is a result of the Fall of man, creation's governor?

That is almost the least result of the Fall, for the Fall is far more serious than that. That concerns the natural creation, but what concerns man, the crown of creation himself? In Genesis 2:17 the Lord says to Adam, 'You may freely eat of every tree in the garden; but of the tree of the knowledge of good and evil, you shall not eat: for in the day that you do you shall die.' Put another way, put in another word, a more significant word: 'In the day that you disobey me – this is the heinousness of the sin – in the day that you disobey your Benefactor you shall die.' And the fruit of that death lies sprawled across history.

Then, notice the effect upon the man. He hid from God. Now why did God make man? This is difficult. He was undoubtedly perfectly satisfied with the fellowship of the divine Trinity, the Tri-unity of Father, Son, and Holy Spirit – perfectly satisfied. Yet, perhaps we could put it this way. It was for sheer love of the Son that God purposed to make innumerable, myriad sons after his likeness; and it would take an inconceivable number of sons, each unique in himself, to show forth the manifold glories of Christ in redeemed manhood. But I was saying – man hid from God, because of his shame; and when God encountered him he said to him, 'Where are you?' And he said, 'I heard the sound of you in the garden, and I was afraid because I was naked and I hid myself.' These three tell-tale statements! And he said, 'Who told you you were naked? Have you eaten of the tree?' (Gen. 3:10-11). Notice how the Fall begins to take effect. The deceptiveness of the father of lies, Satan, who had infected him, begins to operate instantly. He tried to blame the woman. She was at fault, of course. And so God goes to her. And she seeks to blame the serpent and he was to blame too. They pass it on. Hiding, ashamed, afraid, yet refusing to admit guilt, blaming it on someone else. And although the Devil is to blame, other people are to blame too. His activity does not ever absolve us of our guilt.

So God turned to the serpent first and dealt with him. It is the fifteenth verse here that is important: 'I will put enmity between you and the woman, and between your seed and her seed, he shall bruise your head and you shall bruise his heel.' The condemnation of the man is that the very dust is going to be against him; it is going to be hard, sweaty work to make a living out of the unyielding and unwilling ground. Then the couple were expelled from the Garden, and the flaming sword was set in place to guard the way of the tree of life.

How serious is the Fall? We have only touched on it. Let us put it this way. How deep is the Fall? Paul speaks a lot about this one sin, in Romans chapter 5. This one sin, this parent sin, being itself the offspring of the Devil – this parent sin, with all offspring of sin in every man's life deserved nothing less than death as a penalty. The heinousness of this one sin was so great, gigantically great – vast in its effect. Listen to Paul! 'Therefore sin came into the world through one man and death through sin; and so death spread to all men because all men sinned.'(Rom. 5:12). There must be, in justice, a terrible penalty. 'The soul that sinneth, it shall die' (Ezek. 18:4).

These words are repeated several times in the Old Testament. But it is not mere words that pronounce this death penalty; it is the deed of Christ in dying for us. If you want to know how wicked man is, how much of a sinner he is, you must look at the Cross.

How deep is the Fall? What did it cost the Saviour? This is how deep it is: I give you three statements – three great, classic statements that have rung in my mind and my heart for decades now: 'All we like sheep have gone astray; we have turned every one to his own way; and the Lord (Handel knew something of the depth of the meaning of these words when he suddenly plunged into minor unison!) hath laid upon him (the Father has laid upon the Son) the iniquity of us all.' Take that a stage further in the New Testament. The words of John the Baptist when he saw Jesus, stepping across the arid desert of the Jordan Valley to the river: 'Behold (here again, Handel, I believe that even God himself does not think your notes are unworthy! Oh, these poignant discords!) the Lamb of God that taketh away the sin of the world.' And again, here is another great text. Oh, dear Peter, poor, wayward, sinful Peter, when the Holy Spirit came into him in fullness, what epistles he wrote! Speaking of his Saviour, he says, This is the depth of our sin, this is what it cost the Son of God; this is how deep it is: 'Who himself bore our sins in his own body.' You do not need the 'own' in the Greek. You do not find it in modern translations; but I'm not letting it go because I want it to be as emphatic and personal, yes and poignant, as possible – 'Who himself bore our sins in his own body on the tree' (1 Pet. 2:24).

How deep is the sin of man, one sin in the Fall, and all sins comprehended and encompassed in that sin? The penalty is death for man. Adam must die. He must be punished to death, nothing less. Breath must not be left in his body or – and here is the gospel – his death must be fully, worthily, vicariously substituted by another.

This is only the beginning! I have two other points. How deep is the Fall? Adam was not only to die, or be substituted, because he was guilty of death. Adam must die because he is incurably corrupt. He has not only done wrong things: he has not only committed the sin of sins, but in committing that one heinous, terrible sin, he has made himself through the influence of Satan, a sinner. He is incurably corrupt and cannot be saved. He cannot be converted. You cannot convert that Adam once he is stained and corrupted with sin. The only thing you can do with him is destroy him. That old nature has to be killed out of him. The old nature must die radically before a new nature takes its place. You cannot get spring flowers in the autumn. There must be a death first. And so before there can be any new nature, any resurrection; before the new Adam, and the second or the last Adam can take the place of the old Adam, that first, corrupt, Adam must be slain.

Listen again to Paul: 'Do you not know that all of us that have been baptised into Christ Jesus were baptised into his death? We were buried therefore with him by baptism into death; so that as Christ was raised from the dead by the glory of the Father, we too might walk in newness of life. If we have been united with him in a death like his (if we have been planted together in a death like his) we shall certainly be united with him in a resurrection like his. We know that our old self was crucified with him, so that the sinful body might be destroyed, and we might no longer be enslaved to sin; for he who has died is freed from sin' (that's not a good enough translation: 'for he who has died has been "justified" from sin' is the Greek). 'But if we have died with Christ we believe we shall also live with him; for we know that Christ being raised from the dead will never die again. Death no longer has dominion over him. The death he died, he died to sin once for all, but the life he lives, he lives to God. So you also must consider yourselves dead to sin and alive to God in Christ Jesus. Let not sin therefore reign in your mortal bodies.' In another place, Paul says this to the Colossians – about this death of the Adam in them: 'For you have died (as Christians – you have died – and what are the next words? Read carefully) and your life is hid with Christ in God' (Col. 3:3). Death and resurrection! Christ in his death, viewed as a death distinct from his death as punishment for sins, was punished unto death for Adam's sin and our sin. Here is Christ, the last Adam, dying to destroy the corruption of Adam's nature, and by his Holy Spirit, following his resurrection, he is able to take every man in his regeneration and in his conversion, safely through that death to sin, to arise anew as a new creation.

As to the first point – I said there were three – the penalty is death. As to the second point – the eradication (I am not using this word as some people use it, about sanctification) of the sin principle is also by death. The penalty for our sins is death, the substitutionary death of Christ. But the eradication of the sin principle is also by the death of Christ.

Thirdly, how deep is the Fall? We have looked at *sins*, and what they deserve and have received in Christ. We have looked at *sin*, and what God must do with it to take it away, since it cannot be cured, in order to begin again with a new man, even his man.

Whence the Fall? Satan was to blame, beguiling Eve and Adam. It was a fatal infection. 'An enemy hath done this'. It is vital then that we notice that the very first prophecy of the Saviour in Genesis 3:15 speaks about a deliverer from Satan.

When God gives the first promise of a Saviour, in the very chapter in which the Fall is recorded, he promises a Saviour, to take away man's guilt and penalty, and his innate corruption; but from the source of all the trouble himself – the Devil. 'The seed of the woman (Christ: note in the Revised Standard Version it is 'he', for the seed of the woman *is* Christ) shall bruise the serpent's head.'

Let me give you three other texts here, about Christ's victory over Satan. For when Jesus died, he died to bear the punishment of all the sins of men; he died with the corrupt nature of Adam to take it away; and he died to deal finally with Satan: Christ 'cancelled the bond which stood against us, with its legal demands nailing it to the cross.' Then this: 'He disarmed the principalities and powers and made a public example of them, triumphing over them in it (or in him, or, in Christ he 'disarmed the principalities and powers')' (Col. 2:14-15). Or take another word, Hebrews 2:14: 'Since therefore the children share in flesh and blood, Christ likewise himself partook of the same nature, that through death he might destroy him who has the power of death, that is the Devil.'

If you want to go further than that, think of 1 John 3:8. The reason the Son of God appeared on the earth was to destroy not only the Devil but the works of the Devil. How did he do so? The Devil's apparent triumph over God, whom he envied – poor, miserable creature that he was – was to bring down in ruin God's chief and most glorious creation, man. The victory over Satan in this could be gained only in a man. But there was no man on earth unaffected by the sin. Who could do it? God sent a new man. Jesus lived the thirty-three years of his life, right through his life, sinlessly; at one point he says, 'Satan hath nothing in me' (Jn. 14:30). Although Satan did him to death, death could not hold him, because he died, the only one who ever did, a sinless man. In this sense, the most expected thing in the world is the resurrection. There is nothing surprising in it. It is absolutely inevitable. He *must* rise because he had done no sin. He overcame Satan. He came down and took on Satan on his own ground, in the arena of flesh and blood, and defeated him there, to cast him out. Remember Newman's words:

O wisest love! that flesh and blood,
Which did in Adam fail,
Should strive afresh against the foe
Should strive and should prevail;

O generous love! that he who smote
In Man, for man, the foe,
The double agony in Man,
For man should undergo.

There you see something of the depth, the threefold depth of sin in the Fall of man: its penalty – death, the death of Christ; its eradication – death, the death of Christ; the destruction of the powers and the authority of darkness, the evil powers – the death of a man, a sinless man, even Christ. Three dimensions, dealing with sins – things done; sin – a nature; Satan – a malign, evil being.

But we have said that we must not speak of the death without the resurrection. What of the resurrection in relation to these three? The penalty having been paid by the substitute Christ, he rose from the dead; we are justified, declared by God to be righteous, the death of Adam being complete through the death of Christ. Those who believe in him are alive to God. The very life of God is in their souls. The powers of evil are destroyed, as to their power and authority, and driven out of their kingdom by the death of Christ and by his resurrection – a wonderful extension of Christ's victory on the cross, over Satan. Revelation 12:11 speaks about the victory given to the saints over Satan by Christ's death: 'And they overcame him by the blood of the Lamb and the word of their testimony.'

It takes all these three dimensions of Christ's death, with his resurrection, to deal with your deeds of wrong, your evil infection and your enslavement to the Devil. You need nothing less than a three-dimensional salvation. You!

Yet, although these all belong together, or should do, this is hardly known in the Christian church. But there is no real salvation without these three, because it is only these three that elucidate and expose the depth of what happened in man, when he disobeyed God and gave himself into the clutches of God's enemy, Satan.

A three-fold salvation! And you see, all this salvation is for you. Do you see that the thrill of it is this? When a Christian comes to grips with his enemy, Satan; when he knows that there is a real, live Devil opposed to him in his life, his work, in his home, and he knows that Jesus Christ has given him the right to enjoy victory over him, the depth of peace is quite indescribable. For there are no more foes to conquer. Death, that is called the last enemy, is a mere thing belonging to Satan, and will be thrown out with him. No more foes! We never escape from him entirely in this life, but, 'Each victory will help you', says the hymn, 'some other to win'. And so we enjoy ever deeper and deeper peace in our lives because through Christ we have got to the back of the evil, and have dealt with it; for there is nothing worse than Satan.

THE CROSS

3: The Correction of Sin

Psalm 51.

In the first of these studies we explored the conception of death and resurrection as it existed in the eternal mind before the world began, and speculated a little on the idea of death and resurrection in creation and in nature. Then we went on to consider the depth of the Fall of man, with its results for the world, in relation to the death and resurrection of Jesus Christ.

Let me recall what we were saying then. We see something of the depth of the Fall of man, the rebellion of man against his Maker in what it cost Christ to redeem him on the cross. And in a sense we see that he died three deaths in one. He died bearing the full penalty, suffering the full punishment for the sins of men, as their substitute. Then he not only bore our punishment to the last, but dying he, in a sense, buried our incurably corrupt nature.

Then, thirdly, he wrestled with the author of all this, the 'evil one' who sowed the evil seed in the heart of man that produced such a vile harvest. He wrestled with the Devil on the cross, as he had in Gethsemane, and gained a victory, which had been prophesied almost as soon as Adam sinned (Gen. 3:15). As Paul said, writing to the Colossians, 'he disarmed principalities and powers' (Col. 2:15). Or as the writer to the Hebrews says, 'he took our flesh that he might destroy him that had the power of death, even the Devil'. And to sum up all, from John's epistle: Christ was manifested to destroy not only him that had the power of death, even the Devil, but to destroy his works (1 Jn. 3:8).

You see, it is conceivable that if Christ had merely borne the punishment of men's sins, and taken away their corrupt nature, and had left the Devil, the Devil could have done it again. You know the illustration of the old man who got into a rut, and he always used to cry out in the midst of his prayers, 'Lord, sweep away the cobwebs from my heart.' But the Holy Spirit came to him and gave him a new baptism of light and power. One day, he repeated that several times, and must have realised it was inadequate, for he burst out, 'O Lord, kill the spider.' That is it! 'Kill the spider.' Take away his power to weave cobwebs of sin in the hearts of men.

These, then, are the three dimensions. I shall never tire of saying this. You do not know the gospel unless you know these three, and can distinguish them. The first two alone are inadequate, both biblically and practically.

You may have already come thus far in the Christian life. After much heart-searching and agony, pondering, struggling and searching the Scriptures, you have discovered that Jesus died to take away our sinful nature as well as our sins. He has given that death of his to us – he died it for us. He had no need to die it for himself. He has given that death to us by his Holy Spirit into our hearts, so that we are born crucified (as the title of L.E. Maxwell's book has it – what an inspiration – born crucified!). Yet you find that standing upon that truth still does not enable you to overcome the power of inbred sin in your life. You need to think again. You need to open your eyes and see that there is a real, live Devil working against you. You cannot know a life of victorious sanctification until you have reckoned with the Devil as a person, working in your life, stirring up the old nature as soon as you seek to crucify it.

That is why I stress this third dimension. Do not think that it is something that I have dug out of the depths of my mind, or that I simply enjoy teaching what other people do not teach. No. This works! I have seen it in hundreds, thousands of lives. This works – reckoning with the 'evil one' and gaining victory from him through the death of Jesus Christ day by day, commanding him to go: 'Get thee behind me, Satan.' We saw at the conclusion of the last study that once he is dealt with, there are no more foes. He is the last. When we know that we can deal with him because Christ has fully and finally dealt with him, what dimensions of holy, blessed, experience we may enjoy in our lives! Peace deepens into love, and love deepens and then wells up into joy, and the joy is sometimes so deep and so wonderful that you really think your heart will glow with glory before you get there! Why should this not be so?

You cannot really know the love of Jesus until you know the experience of the death of Christ in your life; you cannot know the peace of God unless you know your sins forgiven; you cannot know the love of Christ unless you know the experience of death to self by his Spirit, not by your strivings; so, I believe, you cannot know the full depth of the joy of the Lord, until you are able to overcome Satan, and keep him down, and say 'You will not spoil my life, you brute.'

I want to go on from that and ask this question: how does the cross of Jesus Christ bring home to us the heinousness of sin, and the enormity of the Fall? The answer is this, first of all: the cross of Jesus Christ is both critical and crucial in bringing home to us the heinousness of sin and the enormity of the Fall, because it reveals to us, as nothing else can do, the enormity, the magnitude of the infamy of sin and the boundlessness of sin's devilry.

Other things reveal human sin very startlingly and very frighteningly. Remember God's death sentence on the generation that he was going to drown in the Flood, saving only eight persons. This speaks of the enormity of the sin of man, that he drowned the lot, a whole generation. The enormity of sin may also be seen in the fact that when the children of Israel refused to go up into the land, God said, 'Listen, you adults who have refused to go up because you fear the giants that I say I'll deal with: because you refuse to go up, every one of twenty years of age and over shall die in the wilderness. I will drive you round and round in circles, round and round in the desert of Sinai for thirty-nine years till every one of you has expired except Joshua and Caleb – because when they went up with the other ten spies to spy out the land they came back and they said, "We can easily take it".' God said, 'Every grown-up but these two shall die. Their carcases shall be spread out in the wilderness.'

After that are you still reticent to speak of a God of anger for sin? Will you stifle this truth before people who get enraged if you dare to speak about the wrath of God? To deny the wrath of God is to tear pages out of the Bible – if you dare to do that! It has been done, but not with impunity. Do you think that God sees people tearing the pages out of his Word (and there are more ways than one of tearing pages out of a Bible), and does nothing about it? Never. Remember the Flood, the carcasses and the story of Korah.

Korah aspired to leadership in the community of Israel in the wilderness, and he began to carp at Moses and Aaron. He presumably thought he could do a better job than they, and so he said, 'You have gone too far; for all the congregation are holy, every one of them and the Lord is among them. Why do you exalt yourselves above the people?' Do you know what Moses, who was the meekest and one of the humblest men who ever lived did then? He did not get angry. He fell flat on his face before God and said, 'See what God thinks about that. Let him be judge, if I am presumptuous in my leadership. Let him be judge. The Lord will show who is his and who is holy and will cause him to come near to him.' And so the Lord whispered in Moses' ear and said, 'Moses, clear out from this whole people. I am going to destroy the whole nation'. 'O God,' said Moses, 'You can't do that.' 'Very well,' said the Lord. There is a danger in arguing with God, but this is a very different kind of arguing, to bring out his mercy. And notice the mercy in the midst of judgment. 'Tell the whole people to clear away from the tents of Korah and all his family.' And then, when everybody had cleared far away from Korah's tents, Moses said: 'We shall know today whom the Lord has sent to do his own work. If these men die the common death of all men, dying quietly in their tents, or if they are visited by the fate of all men, then the Lord has not sent me; but if the Lord creates something new, and the ground opens its mouth and swallows them up with all that belongs to them, and they go down alive into hell, then you shall know that these men have despised the Lord.' And as he finished speaking these words, the ground under them split asunder and the earth opened its mouth and swallowed them up with their household and all the men that belonged to Korah and all their goods (see Numbers 16).

That, you see, exposed sin. You can imagine that the rest of Israel did not lift their finger against Moses again, at least for a long, long time.

Remember Achan as well. God said that everything in the city of Jericho that Israel had taken when they crossed the Jordan was to be devoted to the Lord for destruction, even the most precious things. But Achan spied some precious things in a tent and took them and hid them. And that was why there was defeat at the next battle at Ai. So Moses said, 'There is a sinner among the people and he has caused the whole nation of Israel to suffer defeat.' One man as an individual can bring judgment and distress upon a whole church. So they sought by the aid of the Holy Spirit to find out who had done this, and they came at last unerringly to Achan, who confessed. They took him and all his. I can see the journey they took, from Jericho in the plains right along the bed of the arid Jordan Valley, up by Qumran where the Scrolls were found, into the Valley of Achor. 'And all Israel stoned him with stones. They burned them with fire and stoned them with stones, and they raised over him a great heap of stones that remains to this day. Then the Lord turned from his burning anger. Therefore to this day the name of that place is called the Valley of Achor, the Valley of Trouble' (see Joshua 7).

But although the Flood, the carcasses, Korah and Achan all reveal to men the heinousness of sin and how angry God is with it, this is as nothing to the conviction that the cross of Jesus Christ brings home, as we see from the fact that the New Testament magnifies the death of Jesus Christ absolutely above all. You know the verse that inspired Isaac Watts to write his hymn 'When I survey the wondrous cross': 'God forbid that I should glory, save in the cross of the Lord Jesus Christ' (Gal. 6:14). Never mind the rest, that's enough. 'God forbid that I should glory in anything but' – this is the only thing in the world to glory in. The greatest glory in the whole wide world is due to this – the death of Jesus Christ. There is nothing so great. Says Paul, writing to the Philippians: 'Christ Jesus, though he was in the form of God did not count equality with God a thing to be grasped at, but emptied himself, taking the form of a servant, being born in the likeness of men; and being found in human form, he humbled himself and became obedient unto death, even death on the cross.' That is why God 'has highly exalted him and bestowed on him the name which is above every name' (Phil. 2:5-9). 'The word of the cross is to us who are being saved the power of God' (1 Cor. 1:18). The cross, the power of God!

In the same vein Paul says to the Romans: 'I am not ashamed of the gospel. It is the power of God for salvation to everyone who believes, for in the gospel the righteousness of God is revealed, from faith to faith; for the wrath of God is revealed from heaven against all ungodliness and wickedness of men, who by their wickedness suppress the truth' (Rom. 1:16-18).

The death of Christ shows us, as nothing else can, what a tremendous thing it was that God did, and the absolute necessity for such a tremendous thing; for an awful thing had been done by man. He had rebelled against the grace and lavishness of his Maker.

If, then, it is in the cross that we see how great our sin is, and if it is in and through the cross, interpreted for us by the Holy Spirit, that we may receive true, deep conviction of sin, by which alone we may repent and receive forgiveness, let us look at the cross of Jesus Christ again. I want to consider Christ wrestling with the evil powers. This is what I call the third dimension of the cross.

How tremendous and terrible, how awful and hideous was Christ's struggle with evil, all because he chose to struggle with evil and with the Devil *in human flesh*. As the divine, eternal Son of God he could have wiped the Devil out in a moment, at any time. For the Devil is a mere creature. God could have wiped him away with a flick of his divine finger. But he had to gain the battle where formerly there was defeat. You know Cardinal Newman's hymn:

O loving wisdom of our God!
When all was sin and shame,
A second Adam to the fight
And to the rescue came.

O wisest love! that flesh and blood,

Which did in Adam fail,
Should strive afresh against the foe,
Should strive and should prevail.

O generous love! that he who smote
In Man, for man, the foe,
The double agony in Man,
For man, should undergo.

Now, think what this means. No man who ever lived knows the depth of the vileness, the wickedness, the cruelty and the hatred of Satan against God, because no man has resisted him enough to prove it. The only man who ever resisted Satan to the uttermost, and therefore endured the uttermost agony, travail, and excruciating pain in his whole being, especially his spirit, was Jesus. 'The prince of this world cometh and hath nothing in me' (Jn. 14:30). You see, only a sinless man could discover, in his experience, the awful dastardliness of the Devil, who has stolen the heart of man. What a terrible thing it is, that man has given himself into the hands of Satan by the Fall!

Can you imagine our Lord's wrestling with these evil powers? I think it was Professor R.A. Finlayson who said that you find in the Psalter the autobiography of Christ. In some of the Psalms, the inward sufferings of Christ in redemption are revealed to us in a sense more explicitly than in the New Testament. Psalm 22 is an example:

My God, my God, why hast thou forsaken me? Why art thou so far from helping me, from the words of my groaning?
O my God, I cry by day but thou dost not answer, and by night, but find no rest.
But I am a worm and no man; scorned by men and despised by the people. All who see me mock at me; they make mouths at me; they wag their heads and say, He committed his cause to the Lord; let him deliver him; let him rescue him for he delights in him.
Yet thou art he who took me from the womb; thou didst keep me safe upon my mother's breasts.
Many bulls compassed me; strong bulls of Bashan surrounded me. They open wide their mouths at me, like a ravening and roaring

lion. I am poured out like water, and all my bones are out of joint: my heart is like wax; it melted within my breast.

My strength is dried up like a potsherd; and my tongue cleaves to my jaws; thou dost lay me in the dust of death.

Yea dogs are round about me, a company of evil doers encircle me: they pierced my hands and feet. I may count all my bones: they stare and gloat over me.

They divide my garments among them, and for my raiment they cast lots. But thou O Lord, be not far off. O thou my help, hasten to my aid. Deliver my soul from the sword; my life from the power of the dog.

Save me from the mouth of the lion; my afflicted soul from the horns of the wild oxen.

But the psalm does not end without the resurrection. After all that – it was worth it. But the cost! Are we as bad as to need that? Are we as wicked as to require that of Christ? The facts say, Yes.

I will tell of thy name to my brethren: in the midst of the congregation I will sing praise to thee.

You who fear the Lord, praise him. You sons of Jacob glorify him; and stand in awe of him, all you sons of Israel.

For he has not despised or abhorred the affliction of the afflicted; and he has not hid his face from him, but has heard when he cried to him.

For dominion belongs to the Lord and he rules over the nations. Yea, to him shall all the proud of the earth bow down; before him shall bow all who go down to the dust and he who cannot keep himself alive; posterity shall serve him; men shall tell of the Lord to the coming generation, and proclaim his deliverance to a people yet unborn, that he has wrought it.

That is what we are doing whenever we worship together – and we were certainly unborn when that was written. Consider, further, the words of Psalm 69:

Save me, O God, for the waters have come up to my neck; I sink in deep mire where there is no foothold. I have come into deep waters and the flood sweeps over me. I am weary with my crying. My throat is parched; my eyes grow dim with waiting for my God. More in number than the hairs of my head are those who hate me

without cause. Mighty are those who would destroy me, those who attack me with lies. O God, help me.
Let not those who hope in thee be put to shame through me.
O Lord, God of Hosts, let not those who seek thee be brought to dishonour through me, O God of Israel; for it is for thy sake that I have borne reproach. Shame has covered my face. I have become a stranger to my brethren, an alien to my mother's sons.

O how tellingly true the prophetic psalms are! That is why the librettist of Handel's *Messiah* has given the story of the Saviour mostly from the Old Testament, not from the New.

For zeal for thy house has consumed me, and the insults of those who insult thee have fallen on me. When I humbled my soul with fasting it became my reproach. When I made sackcloth my clothing I became a byword to them, and the talk of those who sit in the gate; and the drunkards made songs about me. But as for me, my prayer is to thee, O Lord. At an acceptable time, O God, in the abundance of thy steadfast love, answer me. Let not the flood sweep over me or the deep swallow me up, or the pit close its mouth over me. According to thy abundant mercy, turn to me; hide not thy face from thy servant.

Can you hear the cry of the Lord on the cross to his Father? The cost, the struggle with Satan – Satan doing his damnedest?
Draw near to me, redeem me, set me free because of mine enemies.

Then this. Here is Messiah:
Thou knowest my reproach and my shame and my dishonour; my foes are all known unto thee. Insults have broken my heart, so that I am in despair. I looked for pity but there was none; and for comforters but I found none. They gave me poison for food, and for my thirst they gave me vinegar to drink.

But it is a victory, not a defeat. Look at what he says through the psalmist by the Holy Spirit; and what seems here to be said against wicked men, for what they did to the psalmist, you apply to the Devil and his demons:
Let their own table before them become a snare; let their sacrificial feasts become a trap; let their eyes be darkened so that

they cannot see and let their loins tremble continually. Pour out thy indignation upon them and let thy burning anger overtake them. May their camp be a desolation; let no one dwell in their tents for they persecute him whom thou hast smitten.

You see Christ is there by the will of God, but the Devil is nonetheless responsible for his evil:
For they persecute him whom thou hast smitten; and him whom thou hast wounded they afflict still more. Add to them punishment upon punishment; may they have no acquittal from thee. Let them be blotted out of the book of the living; let them not be enrolled among the righteous; but I am afflicted and in pain. Let thy salvation, O God, set me on high.

There we find the note of resurrection again:
I will praise the name of God with a song. I will magnify him with thanksgiving. Let the oppressed see it and be glad; you who seek God let your hearts revive; for the Lord hears the needy and will not despise his own that are in bonds. Let heaven and earth praise him, the seas and everything that moves therein, for God will save Zion and rebuild the cities of Judah and his servants shall dwell there and possess it, the children of his servants shall inherit it, and those who love his name shall dwell in it.

Let us consider for a moment the first of my three categories or dimensions: Christ bearing the punishment for our sins. The heart of sin is the pride and presumption of the Devil; you know that. It is expressed (and this is your heart and mine, apart from the grace of God) in the pride that stands over against God. Remember what is spoken of Lucifer, the fallen son of the morning; he says, 'You said in your heart, I will ascend to heaven above the stars of God; I will set my throne on high. I will sit on the Mount of Assembly in the far north (heavenly places), I will ascend above the heights of the clouds. I will make myself like the Most High'. I will, I will, I will, I will! When Jesus hung dying on the cross God was smashing that 'I will' out of man, thrashing it out of him, punishing it out of him. Christ bore all that, every lash it deserved.

Then, before he died, he said it was finished. What was finished – his life? Not at that point. What, then, was finished? It was his wrestling with Satan. You could not say that he was finished with bearing the punishment until he was dead. But what was finished was his battle with the Devil. Then, having gained complete and absolute power over him, having disarmed the principalities and powers, he bowed his head. Note carefully, it did not slump. He 'bowed' his head. There is dignity and absolute control. This most regal person bows his head, and he committed his spirit to God as the King, as the victor he was.

Then the punishment was over, and the diseased body of Adam was ready for the grave. Do you wonder that such cost should inspire awe in those whom the Holy Spirit convicts of sin? Is it to be wondered at? Read the account in Isaiah 6, of Isaiah face to face with the glory of God, and hear him cry, 'Woe is me, for I am undone; for I have seen the glory of God'; or David when the Holy Spirit through Nathan points at him and says, 'Thou art the man – you are now condemned out of your own lips', or the publican, when he stands and beats his breast and says, 'God, be merciful to me a sinner.' Do you think you can repent like that respectably, with dignity? When Peter saw how vile, how wicked, how sinful he was in the sight of his beloved Master, he said 'Lord, go. Depart from me, much as I love you, much as I want to be with you, much as I want your friendship and your presence and your power, and everything, I am not fit for your company. Leave me. Depart from me' (Lk. 5:8).

Have you ever felt like that? Have you ever felt loathsome in the Lord's sight? During the revival in 1859 in Aberdeen, a young boy went down to the Broad Hill on a Sunday night. Many thousands were there at a revival meeting. 'It all happened,' he says, 'because of the sudden death of a fellow workman who had been killed and the remark of another, after we had carried home the dead body, had set my conscience working. I had days of distress and nights of agony from the lashings of an awakened conscience.' Has your conscience ever been wakened up like that? Have you ever seen how bad you really are in the sight of God? He continues: 'While the fear of God haunted me by day and the horror of hell scared me in dreams by night, I frequently awoke drenched in perspiration, and that went on for weeks and months until I was so weakened as to be unable to continue at work, had to see the doctor, take medicine and go to the country for a time. I had recovered somewhat physically but my mind and conscience were still restless and I was trying to quieten the one, and stifle the other, by gaiety, godlessness, and frivolity (never misunderstand people who go mad with that kind of thing, as Saul was mad with the Christians when his conscience was stabbed awake at the martyrdom of Stephen) when I was startled and arrested by that message of the Links.' 'There was a great meeting one Thursday evening, and the Minister, Mr McPhail, gave out his text, after singing and reading and prayer but he never got beyond that. He never got his mouth opened in the way of addressing those present; for the entire meeting broke down. The sound of weeping and sobbing was so loud that no ordinary speaking could have been heard. There were old grey-headed men and women, young men and maidens, weeping and sobbing as if their hearts would break with sorrow, in agony of soul, under conviction of sin and the weight of guilt. The feeling of solemnity was almost overpowering; for the realisation of the presence of the Spirit of God was such as to overawe so much that we did not dare to speak except in whispers, as we tried to point those in agony of soul to the Saviour. You could have no more doubted the presence of the Spirit of God than you could have doubted your own existence.'

This is what happens when the Spirit brings conviction of sin. Here is another example. 'In the Free Church of Airlie a young man listened with close attention to the address, which was of the plainest and simplest kind; the earnest entreaties however were the means of bringing deep trouble into the young man's soul and he sought the retirement of the darkest closet and there tried to solve the problems which appeared to his mind. He had never before doubted the existence of a God, but now he set himself to prove it. Night after night, when the day's work was done he retired to the same room and thought and thought until his brain almost gave way. After some weeks of this dreadful experience a voice seemed to speak aloud and say, "He that cometh unto God must believe that he is and that he is the rewarder of them that diligently seek him." No sooner did this truth awaken him to the real existence of God than sin appeared in its awful enormity, as rebellion against a righteous God. Hitherto he had prided himself on a straight life but now the law of God slew him, and he felt undone. O the awful tension of these days and nights, until it ended in throwing himself bodily down on the floor, crying in the agony of his spirit, "Lord, I give myself away to thee, and if I perish I will perish at thy feet.'"

Yet, there is something much worse than that kind of conviction of sin. It is the blindness and hardness that leads someone not to see himself to be a sinner in God's sight at all. Listen to this: 'The rest of mankind who were not killed by these plagues did not repent of the works of their hands, nor give up worshipping demons, and idols of gold, and wood, and stone which cannot either see, or hear, or walk; nor did they repent of their murders or sorceries or immorality, or their thefts' (Rev. 9:20-1). And this: 'Men were scorched by the fierce heat and they cursed the name of God who had the power over these plagues, and they did not repent and give him glory. The fifth angel poured his bowl upon the throne of the beast and its kingdom was in darkness. Men gnawed their tongues in anguish and cursed the God of heaven for their pains and sores and did not repent of their deeds. . . . Great hailstones, heavy as an hundredweight dropped on men from heaven until men cursed God for the plague of the hail, so fearful was that plague' (Rev. 16:9-11,21). But they did not repent.

Remember, too, the rich man in hell. 'Being in torment he lifted his eyes and saw Abraham and cried, "Father Abraham, have mercy upon me and send Lazarus to dip the end of his finger in water, and cool my tongue for I am in anguish in this flame." But Abraham said, "Son, remember in your lifetime you had your good things and Lazarus his evil things, and now the tables are finally turned.' Then he says, "I beg you send to my father's house, for I have five brothers, and warn them, lest they come to this place of torment." And Abraham said, "They have Moses and the prophets, let them read the Bible." "No, Father Abraham, but if someone went to them from the dead, they would repent." "If they do not hear Moses and the prophets," says Abraham, "neither will they repent or be convinced if someone should rise from the dead" ' (Lk. 16:19-31).

The point is this. The rich man was tormented and sought alleviation, but he did not repent. He could not. It is possible to be beyond the power to repent before we leave the earth. Is it not far better to have known excruciating torments of soul for our sin in God's sight than to remain unmoved in the face of the Crucified?

THE CROSS

4: Repentance

2 Samuel 12:1-15, Psalm 51.

We have been looking at the fall of our first parents, Adam and Eve, and seeking to understand something of the heinousness and enormity of that first sin. And to do so, of course, we have had to see its blackness against the brightness of God's goodness to these two. He made them for his pleasure. They were the highest of his creation, far above angels; angels are only servants. The highest of his creation, beyond all worlds, spheres, and constellations, any ranks of beings – is man. That is proved by the fact that when God came down to the earth he did not come as an angel, or as any other creature, but as man. And so God gave life to these two, and the possibility of fellowship with him. Because he made them for his pleasure that he might have fellowship with them, he set them in this lovely garden, the Garden of Eden, and gave them everything that their hearts could desire naturally, because he loved them and found pleasure in them.

They were the highest creatures he had made. But because he made them for his pleasure, he would expect more pleasure from them than from the beauty of trees, or the sound of rippling water on the rivers, or the glory of a sunset, or the litheness of the leopard, or the beauty of the flowers. So he gave them the right and the power freely to respond to him. Love is something that has to be freely given, or else it is not love. So, before God could have the pleasure and the satisfaction he desired of them, he had to give them a certain amount of what we might call independence – free will if you prefer;

so that they could even turn away if they liked and say, 'No, thank you, God, you have been very generous but I don't particularly want your company. Thank you for life. Thank you for each other. Thank you for the garden. Thank you for everything. But, no thank you for your sovereign lordship over my life.'

They could choose. And they chose to do just that – to turn their back upon him, and listen to his enemy, Satan. It was the dirtiest thing that was ever done. Dirty! Rotten! Can you see that?

We are all infected with that one sin, its fruits and its effects. Its evil, perverse, rebellious will is in every man, woman and child, Christ himself apart. You only need to look round in the world, to hear the daily news, to know your fellows, you only need to look into your own black heart to see that you are a son of Adam and Eve. And yet men do not feel this naturally. Most people do not feel themselves to be sinners at all. You may think I am exaggerating Adam and Eve's sin; but if you have ever given everything you possibly could to somebody, as parents do, and then had them turn their back upon you and despise you, and almost spit in your face, you will have some idea of the heinousness of this dirty trick.

In the previous chapter, we asked how we could possibly bring home to ourselves the awful heinousness of Adam's sin of which we have partaken. We looked at some of the judgments of God recorded in the Old Testament. You can think perhaps of other dire examples of God's terrible judgments. Some people today say that it is all so terrible it cannot be true. So they take the Bible to bits, rejecting what they do not like; not realising that when you take the Bible to bits, and refuse the bits you do not like, you are saying, 'I know better than God. I could write a better Bible than he.' The conceit of it! You see the sin of Adam and of men?

We have seen the heinousness of sin from God's judgments in the Old Testament; but of course, it is in the New Testament we see just how heinous the sin of man is – in the death of Jesus. There never was such a sin as Adam and Eve committed. Yet, the greatest fruit of it, the most dire and terrible fruit of it, was the death of Jesus Christ, even although God himself, in mercy, planned it. So it is ultimately in the cross of Jesus Christ that we see how bad man is.

How do we see it? We see it in three particulars, which can be explained very simply, although they are very profound.

Some would be horrified if they heard me say this, but it is in keeping with the biblical viewpoint: first of all, we see God thrashing Jesus Christ to death for the sins of men – just that – paying the penalty of men's sin, hanging there on that awful cross – the holy Christ, the only perfect man who ever lived. It should be said boldly, but with tremendous reverence: God did that.

Secondly, we see something, in a sense, deeper than that; by dying Jesus took the false, the wicked, the rebellious Adam down into death and buried him. He destroyed him.

Adam and Christ are representative of two orders of manhood: Adam after the fall, this rebellious creature defying his Maker; and the last Adam, Jesus Christ. He comes in human flesh, in the likeness of the flesh of sin – that is very daring to say, isn't it? He was not a sinner. He never sinned, but in taking the likeness of sinful flesh he took upon himself not only the things that wicked men had done wrong, but the nature that did them. He died as Adam should die for his sins, not only bearing the penalty, the punishment for man's sins, but taking away what he was; his evil, sinful, fallen nature. Nor is that all.

Thirdly, in all this Christ was gaining a victory over Satan. It was Satan who led Adam and Eve astray in the garden. But on the cross Jesus gained eternal victory over Satan.

The only way there could be any hope for man to be redeemed was for a man to pass through human life – to be born, to live and to die – without ever having sinned. And if that happened, that man was bound to rise from the dead because there was no sin to keep him in death. Death could not hold him if he was not a sinner. That is why the Devil wanted to keep Christ from the cross, and yet at the same time to put him on it! You see the Devil's dilemma? What a subject it would be for a meditation, or even a holy play. But Christ died because he would not sin. The best of us succumb to Satan far sooner because we lack the strength to resist. We do not know how much the Devil will do to a holy man. Nobody knows how much the Devil would do to a holy man except Jesus, because he was the holy man who alone fully resisted him to death. He died rather than sin. Nobody knows, as he knows, the wickedness of the Devil; for Christ had to undo what Adam had done.

Think of the cost. Think not only of the physical cost – nails through your hands, nails through your feet, a spear through your side, and the long hours of slow death in agony, hanging by your hands from that cross. But there was deeper agony than that. There was the mental, the spiritual pain. It is too, too awful to speak of. But that is the measure of how bad you and I are. It took all that to save one sinner, for you or for me. We need to feel this because these are facts; they are part of history, even if it is more than history.

It is a fact that God made us. It is a fact that we have gone astray and we are all sinners. It is a fact that Jesus died. These are facts; but we do not feel them. So it is that we might be so convicted of our sin, our part in this, that we might want to do something about it, that we must speak in this way.

Repentance, in the Old Testament, means turning from sin to God. It is far more than saying, 'Oh, I'm sorry'. How glibly, how casually, sometimes even contemptuously, we say, 'I'm sorry'. No, this means turning from sin to God. In the New Testament, the word that is used, *metanoia*, means to change your mind. And, of course, it means changing your mind so that you do something about it. That is repentance – to change your mind in the sense of turning round about from sin to God. It is not what Esau, Jacob's brother, thought was repentance. Do you know what the writer to the Hebrews said about Esau? He despised his birthright and sold it to his brother. The writer to the Hebrews says, 'See that no one fails to obtain the grace of God; that no root of bitterness spring up and cause trouble in your heart, as was the case with immoral and irreligious Esau, who sold his birthright for a single meal.' Sold his birthright for a single meal! 'For you know that afterward when he desired to inherit the blessing, he was rejected; for he found no chance to repent though he sought it with tears' (Heb. 12:16-17).

Now scholars discuss what he sought with tears; whether it was the blessing, or a chance to repent. I think we can describe it thus. He was very, very sorry that he lost the blessing; but he was not really sorry that he had grieved God. He wanted the blessing for its own sake, not because it was given by God. He wanted his blessings; as Adam and Eve doubtless wanted to stay in the garden, although they were banished. He despised God, although he still wanted the blessing. And because he despised God, he went too far and could not return.

Remember Lazarus who sat at the rich man's gate to beg for a crust, and the street dogs (which were rather horrible creatures in those days in the East) came and licked his wounds? The semi-wild dogs of the street were kinder to the beggar than the rich man at whose gates he sat! And then both the rich man and Lazarus died. Lazarus went to Abraham's bosom. But the rich man went to hell. In torment he cried, 'Oh, send Lazarus to dip the tip of his finger in water to cool my tongue, for I am tormented'. But he was not sorry for what he had done to Lazarus. It was too late for that. You cannot repent in hell. He was sorry only that he was in torment. He was not repenting any more than Esau was repenting. They were suffering mere remorse because they were in pain and distress at the punishment for their sins. That is not repentance as we know it in the New Testament.

Nor is Judas repentant when he comes back and throws down the thirty pieces of silver after betraying his Master. You remember what it says about Judas in the New Testament? 'When Judas, Jesus' betrayer, saw that he was condemned he repented' (notice it says he repented), and he brought back the thirty pieces of silver to the chief priests and elders saying, 'I have sinned in betraying innocent blood.' They said to him, 'What is that to us? See thou to that!' And he threw down the thirty pieces of silver in the temple, on the floor, and went out and hanged himself. That was not evangelical repentance; that was sheer remorse.

Like Esau and the rich man – but particularly Esau – Judas followed the Devil's way. The Devil makes men think they are very clever, you see. Esau despised his birthright because he was hungry. Judas really despised – nothing less could be true – he despised Christ, although he was one of the twelve apostles; and thought he was far cleverer than the others. You see, it is 'clever' people who come to ruin and disaster. Judas played a dangerous game with his life, and he lost. It was only of *his loss* that he repented. It is very galling, you see, to try to be more clever than God, and then find, as you must find, that you have lost and he has won. That can look very like repentance, but it is just hurt pride that is too proud to live – and goes out and hangs itself.

That kind of thing is what is called 'fruitless sorrow'. There is sorrow in repentance; indeed one of the hymns says, 'With sorrow for sin doth repentance begin'. But it is only *the beginning* of it. The sorrow that is real repentance, change of mind, turning from sin to God, is of a very different sort. This is what Paul says about it: 'For godly grief produces a repentance that leads to salvation' (2 Cor. 7:10). Or what Acts calls, 'repentance unto life' (Acts 11:18). Godly grief produces a repentance that leads to salvation and brings no regret; but worldly grief produces death.

That is exactly what happened in Judas' case because he went and hanged himself. Externally he had no need to hang himself. You might say: why did he do that?   He had to. It was the logical conclusion of what he had done. He had made such a fool of himself. He had shown himself up before the world to be on the wrong side; and some people cannot stand that. There is more to it than that, of course. But this is the nature of remorse, and it has nothing to do with being sorry because you have hurt God and turned against him. You are sorry because you have hurt yourself. That is just pride. Judas perhaps sinned most of all in hanging himself, but he had to do it.

But true, evangelical repentance, gospel repentance, is a sorrow for sin that turns like David and says, 'Oh God I have sinned against thee, thee only. Have mercy' (Ps. 51:1). And it turns to live an absolutely new life. Nothing else is any good. Listen to what Paul said to King Agrippa: 'I have gone everywhere, preaching to Jew and Gentile in Judea, and everywhere I have gone, King Agrippa, I have told people that they should repent and turn to God, and perform deeds worthy of repentance, and make restitution' (Acts 26:20). There are people who if they really repented in God's sight would have to go out tomorrow and put something right with somebody. There are some people, you know, so proud, deep down in their hearts, that it nearly chokes them to give an apology if they do something wrong. They will not admit that they are wrong. But how sweet it is to admit that you are wrong when you really are. And how it endears you to people. Some people cannot have any friends because they are never wrong. I was saying to somebody just the other day, 'The only possibility that we can be friends is that I get to know the worst about you, and you get to know the worst about me'. It is the only possibility of friendship, among Christians. My dearest friends are those who know the blackest about me and love me just the same – not because of the blackness, but because at least with them I have been honest. And if I have turned away from my sins, then they love me for that and want to help me.

Deeds! Paul told Agrippa that he had gone around telling everybody that they should repent and turn to God and perform *deeds worthy of repentance*. If you are sorry for your sins – show it!

Now look at David for a moment. See what evangelical repentance did to him. That man looked at that woman with cold heat. What do I mean by that? He lusted after her, but with cold calculation he actually planned her downfall, godly man though he had been, God's chosen man, the king of Israel. He seemed utterly blind to what he had done, even after he had done it. That is not always the case. Sometimes the Devil blinds us to the heinousness of what we are doing until it is done, and then he turns and laughs and says, 'Do you see what you have done?' He laughs at us, and we are instantly shocked at how deliberately yet blindly we have sinned. But that was not the situation here. David was utterly blind to the heinousness of his sin. But then Nathan the prophet came and told him the story about someone who stole the one ewe lamb that a poor man had. David was furious with that man; but he did not see that it was himself. That is exactly like us. We do not see how bad we are. And we need somebody to tell us. It may be God or it may be somebody from God. Nathan came from God to David: 'You are the man.' And then, David said, 'I have sinned against the Lord.' The baby was born, and it died, as a judgment of God. Then David washed himself, and anointed himself, and went to the temple and worshipped God (2 Sam. 11 and 12).

Look at another who showed his true repentance by his changed life: Simon Peter. He kept protesting to Jesus that he was the best of the disciples. I wonder what Judas thought about this? Poor Peter. He had an inferiority complex, or something of that sort, I am sure. In the end he even dared to say, 'Though all that lot, all these other eleven, desert you, I will not'. And then when the servant maid came and said, 'Do you belong to this lot from Galilee?' he denied it three times and cursed and swore. And then the Devil, who had done this in poor Peter's heart, left him for a time and let him see what he had done; and Peter went out and wept bitterly (Lk. 22:31-34;54-62).

The word that was spoken about Peter came true: after that, when he was truly converted, he went and strengthened his brethren. But you see, these are two classic examples of true, evangelical repentance, that has some action and some fruit. Deeds. If you are repenting in God's sight, then show it. Show it! Because there is no true repentance unless there is something to see.

You cannot repent in your heart and go on being the same, old, wicked, sinful person. Repentance must have lips. It must have hands. It must have feet. If your mind is changed, then show it by your changed way of life.

But you might say, 'Now, what connection has all this with the death of Christ? What's the connection of this with the Cross?' Listen to these verses from the chapter where Paul is addressing the people of Athens, the Oxford (or is it Cambridge?) of ancient Greece: 'As God's offspring we should not think the deity is like gold or silver, or stone; a representation by the art and imagination of man, worshipping idols, statues.' And then Paul goes on: 'The times of ignorance (men worshipping sticks and stones, and silver and gold) God overlooked.' That does not mean that he ignored them 'but he looked beyond them to the one who was to come, even Christ.' God suffered the sins of men, right through the Old Testament days. He put up with them until Christ came and died. 'But now', says Paul, 'God commands all men everywhere to repent; because he has fixed a day on which he will judge the world in righteousness, according to standards of perfect righteousness, by a man (and that man is Christ Jesus, the judge appointed by the Father) whom he has appointed; and of this he has given assurance to all by raising the man that died from the dead. Therefore he commands all men everywhere to repent' (Acts 17:29-31). Christ has judged Satan. He has not only defeated Satan, but he has judged him. And he has judged sin. Sin is judged finally by Jesus on the cross.

Ever since Jesus died and rose, Christians have been living in the last days. The world could go on for hundreds or thousands of years; it could go on, I suppose, for millions of years. But these are still the last days because they come after Christ has done his final deed of judging Satan and sin. 'And so,' says Paul, 'God now, after Christ's death, commands everyone to repent'; because after the day of grace, it is also the day of judgment. The day of grace is the day of judgment. Or put it this way. The day of grace, however long it lasts, is a day of pending judgment. Satan and sin are judged; and at the last day sinners will be judged if they choose to go Satan's way, sin's way, and remain rebellious against God. And that this is to happen is testified by the resurrection. The very fact that Jesus rose from the dead indicates that God means business. Jesus has died and risen. What are you going to do about it?

You say, 'I do not feel that I should do anything about it'. Feelings? What can your feelings do? Think of the early dark nights of winter. Could you change them into the light nights, by feeling that you wanted light nights? What could you do about that? Not a thing. Feelings? Do not judge by your feelings. Don't go by your feelings. It is facts that count. Facts, facts – Jesus died and rose again to judge Satan and sin; your sin and mine.

And what we have got to do, men and women, young men and maidens, is to dissociate ourselves from Satan and sin, and say, 'I'll have none of it. I see myself as a sinner in God's sight and I will not live guilty any longer. I will come to God and cry to him to help me – to have mercy upon my soul; and live the rest of my life changed, turned right about, going in the opposite direction, living an utterly changed life.' That is the only thing to do about it.

I pray with all my heart, since God has now commanded all men everywhere to repent, and that includes you and me, that we will do it. It is no one else's business but yours and God's what you do about it. Then prove it by deeds worthy of repentance.

THE CROSS

5: Forgiveness

Isaiah 53.

God says that if we repent he will forgive us our sins. The forgiveness of sins! It is not primarily forgiveness of sinners – although in certain contexts you can say that quite justly – but the forgiveness of sins.

What is the forgiveness of sins? What is it to forgive? This is the question to which we now turn. What do you think it is to forgive? And what do you think it means to God to forgive? What does he do? What does the word mean? What is the significance of the Bible saying that God is willing to forgive those that will repent?

Here are words that a certain scholar wrote some years ago. I was organist to this man when I was seventeen, in the Methodist Church in Crown Terrace, Aberdeen. He was already quite a scholar, and became a great scholar, first a professor and then the head of a Methodist College – Vincent Taylor, who was one of the best-known New Testament scholars in this country.

He writes – there are qualifications later on but we cannot detail them now: 'It is noteworthy that in none of these passages (he gives a whole lot of passages from the Bible, especially the New Testament, about the forgiveness of sins), is forgiveness represented as the remission, the forgiveness of penalty. It is not punishment that is removed.' He says, 'What is remitted is sin.'

Now you may think that's a quibble, but keep it in mind, and reflect on it.

In another place he says, rather startlingly: 'Forgiveness is not set forth in the Scriptures as the purpose of Christ's death.' Again: 'The true conclusion to be drawn (from the Scriptures he has adduced) is that the absence of a saying of Jesus, directly associating his death with forgiveness, is so far a confirmation of the results gained from our study of apostolic preaching, that the forgiveness of sins is not the primary object of Christ's suffering and death.'

And then, concluding this long chapter on forgiveness, he says 'For the moment we may content ourselves with the statement that the true meaning of the New Testament teaching is that the death of Christ was not necessary to enable God to remit sins.' That – with great respect, and, of course, with affection – is a travesty of the truth.

But Vincent Taylor goes on, as many others do, to remind us, that there are different words in the original Bible languages, especially the New Testament Greek, for 'forgive'. The commonest word, and the word that we are most concerned with, that is translated into our English language 'forgive' means simply 'to remove', 'to remit' or 'send away'. The Old Testament speaks about 'blotting out' and 'putting behind God's back' and 'casting into the depths of the sea'. But quite simply, 'to forgive' in all these references means 'to remove'. There are other words. There is one word in particular, which means not 'to remove' in any sense, because it is not concerned with the sins but with the sinner. It means 'to gratify', to 'show favour to'. An example of its use can be found in Luke 7:41 'A certain creditor had two debtors: one owed five hundred denarii, and the other fifty pence. When he could not pay he forgave them both. Now which of them will love him more? Simon (Peter) answered, The one, I suppose, to whom he forgave more. And Jesus said to him, You have judged rightly.'

Now the word 'forgive' used there twice, is this word 'to gratify', or 'to show favour to': you find the same word, in 2 Corinthians 2:7,10, and 12:13. You also find it in a passage easier to find, and easier to remember perhaps, Ephesians 4:32, and also in Colossians 2:13 and 3:13.

The important thing is this. Here, 'to forgive' is not merely to 'exonerate' and to say, perhaps almost in an off-hand, or cold, or legal, dispassionate way, 'It is all right, I forgive you. Good-bye', but here 'to forgive' is, as it were, 'to reconcile' or 'be reconciled with'; to take the offending one back into your arms. You see there is a full, rich, wonderful content.

But many scholars say this kind of thing – let me read about a sentence each from four or five of them. R. C. Moberly says, 'Forgiveness (and he includes the earlier word, the word for 'removing'), even this barer word, really means the full restoration of delicate personal relations between friends, or between parent and child.'

Archbishop William Temple says: 'To forgive is to restore to the old relationship.'

R. S. Franks says: 'It means the restoration of the sinner to communion with God. It is the breaking down of the barriers between them.' That is a bit nearer the truth.

Then R. N. Flew says: 'God's forgiveness is never a mere passing of the word, a dumb turning of the back, a formal cancelling of a debt. It implies a personal relationship, violated and now restored. Forgiveness means the reception of the sinner into a personal relationship with God, and means too that this relationship is richer than it was before the relationship had been broken.'

And lastly Basil Redlich says: 'Forgiveness is full restoration to fellowship.' Full restoration to fellowship!

Vincent Taylor adduces these men and what they say in support of his idea that we are to think of 'forgiveness' in this fuller, richer, sense.

Now, I often say, very reverently, lest anyone should misunderstand, that the death of Jesus Christ is a means to an end.

It is not the end in itself. And so you might think that I would agree with these men. Let us have the fuller, richer meaning: the gratifying, the showing favour, the taking back, and reconciling and loving. But what if we want the richer concept because we are not very happy about the more elementary one, and, indeed the more elemental one – forgiveness as the removal, the sending away of sins? That is the danger.

Many Scriptures could be cited here, including those that include the concept of redemption, deliverance from the power of evil, and from the fruit of our transgressions. But it is important to underline the simpler meaning, because it is here that we get to the heart of the Christian faith, to the absolute foundation.

This is what is said in Isaiah 53:6: 'All we like sheep have gone astray; we have turned every one to his own way; and the Lord hath laid on him the iniquity of us all.' Notice that expression, 'laid on him'. Christ became our substitute, as the lamb in the Old Testament sacrificial worship became a substitute for the sinner. The man did not die, although the Bible says categorically, in many places, 'The soul that sinneth, it shall die.' So God provides a lamb, and the sinner comes with the lamb, offers it and the lamb is sacrificed as his substitute. This is a picture, undoubtedly, of Christ's redemption and his removal of our sins.

Weigh these words carefully: 'The Lord hath laid on him the iniquity of us all.' When Jesus came to his baptism, to the river Jordan; and in the midst of his open-air preaching John the Baptist saw Jesus coming down the dusty road and said, 'Behold the Lamb of God that taketh away the sin of the world.'

Take these two statements together – 'laid upon' and 'to take away'. Then, turn to what Peter says about this in 1 Peter 2:21. He is speaking about the Christian life and saying to those to whom he is writing: 'For even hereunto were you called (to suffer for righteousness' sake) because Christ also suffered.' The word in the original is 'suffered for us'. In v.24 of the same chapter, Peter says of Christ, 'Who his own self bore our sins in his own body on the tree' – that's the cross, the wood of the cross. So there another word is used. Now, read 1 Peter 3:17: 'For it is better, if the will of God be so, that you suffer for well doing than for evil doing; for Christ also hath once suffered for sins.' The Greek word here translated 'suffered' is not the same word as 'suffered' in 2:21: here it is the word 'died'. Christ once for all died for sins. Then read 1 Peter 4:1-2 'For as much then as Christ has suffered for us in the flesh, arm yourselves likewise with the same mind': here the word is the root of our English words 'patient' and 'pathos'. Then, look at one final statement, in 1 Corinthians 15:3: 'Christ died for our sins, according to the Scriptures.'

Now take all these statements together: 'our iniquities were laid upon him'; 'Behold the Lamb of God that taketh away the sin of the world'; 'He suffered for us,' 'He bore our sins in his own body on the tree'; 'He died for us'; 'He suffered for us'; 'He died for our sins, according to the Scriptures.'

He took our sins away by dying. What does that mean? Did he become a sinner? The Scripture says some very daring things about how near he comes to that in taking sin upon him. Yet he was no sinner, and the proof of that is that he was raised from the dead, on the third day. The sin that he took upon himself never really belonged to him, but he took it upon himself. That is why he appeared to the men in Israel of that day, in Jerusalem and around the cross, to be the criminal, the sinner, suffering for his own sins. He was really, you know, like a dustman. If you do not like to sit next to a dustman in a bus remember that he is not dirty with his own dirt, but with the dirt of others – and maybe with some of yours! That was true of Christ. Although he had no sin of his own, 'he was made sin for us, so that in him we might become the righteousness of God' (2 Cor. 5:21).

The reason we are so sure that he was no sinner, is because death could not hold him. There was no sin to involve him in mortality and in a double death from which he could not emerge. God raised him from the dead on the third day, vindicated him, and thus said to the whole world: 'You crucified him, thinking he was a criminal because you hated him and believed him to be wrong and yourselves right; but God contradicted what you did and raised him from the dead and said, "Look. This is the right one. You are the wrong." ' And so he proved that Christ lived and died as the Holy One.

What then does it all mean? Well, in the first instance, sins, when they are committed, are realities; they exist. They offend and affront God and damage his kingdom and seek to injure him. They are real acts and when they are done it takes something to remove them and their effect. You cannot repair a broken window simply by saying it is all right. It has to be repaired. Sin, and the effect of it, has to be removed.

But how? How does Christ bear our sins? 'The soul that sinneth it shall die.' That is a legal pronouncement; it is a law. There is a punishment, a penalty, for that. Christ bore the punishment, the penalty. He suffered for our sins.

What would you say the Scripture means when it says, 'He suffered for us. He bore our sins. They were laid upon him'? Do not romantically imagine that it was a picnic to die for our sins. A God of wrath who could not look upon sin, cannot be anything else but angry with sin. The God of love cannot ever be anything else but angry with our sins; and angry with those too who will not be separated from them. Crude, you may say. Perhaps, but true nevertheless. A dear, old retired minister, laden with academic honours now sits under a young minister whom I know. The young minister went to him one day and said frankly, 'Now, you have been sitting under my ministry for a year; tell me what you think of it.' That took a bit of courage! 'Well', said the dear man, very kindly, and graciously, for it was a very friendly interview – 'I think your theology is crude.' I think the younger minister might well have said – perhaps he was more polite than I would have been in reply! – 'I think so too; but it is true! Our sin is crude, and it takes something crude to deal with it, even something rude and horrid: in my place condemned he stood.'

And so, if God has begun to give you the spirit of repentance, of a change of mind, of turning from sin to God – if you are really burdened with your sin in his sight, and you see that he bore the penalty, the guilt, and the shame – then you must come to Christ, and receive him. In him you will find removal of your sin. You will discover that he has taken all your punishment, and exhausted it, and satisfied your judge – for God is a judge, no doubt about that. Are we afraid to say that because of modernists? Never! Never in the world! God is a judge. But Christ has satisfied the judge, and along with that – because they all belong together – he has pleased the Father's heart.

There is one thing more to say, and I think it is of great value. The past can haunt us. Is that not so? Does your past sometimes, perhaps even now, haunt you? And are there times when you cannot believe that this holy, just God can possibly forgive and forget and blot out your sins? How thoroughly does he do it? What is the value of what he did? What is the value of his death? The value of his death is the value of his life. The value of his death is the value of who he was, and is. He is God the Son, the second Person of the Trinity. His work on the cross is therefore of infinite and eternal value.

Of course, if you had been able to take his red blood and examine it analytically you would not have found it any different from any other human blood. But that is not the value of his precious blood. Its value lies in the life that he lived; in who he was, and how he lived as a man on the earth. If the value of that life is absolutely infinite; if this is God become man, then the value of what he did in the shedding of his precious blood is of an infinite character, and as the writer to the Hebrews tells us, its efficacy lasts forever.

Here are some biblical texts that spell out the marvel of what he has done: the prophet Isaiah says: 'Lo, it was for my welfare that I had great bitterness; but thou hast held back my life from the pit of destruction; for thou hast cast all my sins behind thy back ' (Is. 38:17).

Or this from Micah: 'Who is a God like thee, pardoning iniquity, and passing over transgression, for the remnant of his inheritance? He does not retain his anger forever because he delights in mercy (steadfast love). He will again have compassion upon us. He will tread our iniquities under foot. Thou wilt cast all our sins into the depth of the sea.' (Mic. 7:18). Have you heard the story of the man who heard that, and was so thrilled by it that he shouted, 'Glory!

Hallelujah!' in the middle of a service, and began to laugh really heartily? And somebody said, 'What on earth's ado with you?' 'I've just been told how deep the sea is around Japan,' he replied!

Here are the words of Jeremiah: 'Behold, the days are coming, says the Lord, when I will make a new covenant with the house of Israel, and with the house of Judah, not like the covenant which I made with their fathers, when I took them by the hand to bring them out of the land of Egypt; my covenant which they broke, though I was her husband, says the Lord. But this is the covenant which I will make with Israel: after those days, says the Lord, I will put my law within them and I will write it upon their hearts; and I will be their God, and they shall be my people. And no longer shall each man teach his neighbour, and teach his brother, saying, Know the Lord; for they shall all know me, from the least to the greatest, saith the Lord; for I will forgive their iniquity and I will remember their sin no more' (Jer. 31:31-34).

These words are twice quoted in the epistle to the Hebrews. 'For I will forgive their iniquity, and I will remember their sins no more' (Heb. 8:12;10:17).

Now, do the guilt and the shame, and the dread of the penalty (what if you were to die tonight?) haunt you? Do they pursue you and terrorise you? Then take hold of God's promises. If you are truly repenting of your sins and turning your back upon them and coming to God through Jesus Christ, he will blot them all out of existence. Somebody else may still rake them up; the Devil himself may dart in and remind you of them; and you have a picture of that dirty thing you did and you say – Oh, God! But I believe, if you were to come to God and say, 'Oh, God, wasn't that awful?' it is quite conceivable that he would say, 'What do you mean? I don't know what you're talking about!'

Because of the value of Christ's death this forgiveness is infinite. It does not matter what you have done. It is infinite – both as to what you have done, and infinite as to the length, the extent of the cancellation. When Christ sits as judge, at the end of the world, he will never bring that up again. Instead he will say: 'Come on, into my arms. Be mine. Be mine. And never refer to it.'

It is a great sin thereafter to go to God and moan about the past and about your past sins. When you start talking about that he might say to you not only that he does not remember what you are talking about, but also: 'That is your silly pride. Forget it, as I have done. Forget it. Blot out the past. You are saved by the blood of Jesus, who bore your punishment.'

This, then, is what God's Word says: 'If we confess our sins, he is faithful and just to forgive us our sins, and to cleanse us from all unrighteousness.' (1 Jn. 1:9). Do you really believe that? And have you experienced it?

THE CROSS

6: Justification

Romans 3:19-26; 4:1-5,13-25; 5:1-2.

God says, 'I will not justify the wicked' (Ex. 23:7). How then can we speak of a Christian and New Testament doctrine of justification by faith and not by works? How then can God, the righteous holy God who cannot look upon sin, justify sinners freely? Yet this is what is said in Romans 3:23,24. But how can God justify the ungodly (Rom. 4:5)? Take these words in. Do you see the contradiction in them? It says first that God will justify sinners freely; and that he will justify the ungodly. The daring of it!

If you ask how this contradiction can be resolved, we first answer boldly, 'Well God does it anyway; that is quite plain.' Scripture makes it perfectly plain that he does justify sinners freely and he does justify the ungodly.

How can a holy, righteous God do that? We shall need some very real explanation before we accept this. But God does do this, says the Scripture, and this is perhaps the most important point about the doctrine of justification by faith. God, the holy, righteous God not only justifies sinners freely and justifies the ungodly, but he shouts it from the ramparts of heaven. He announces it through the courts of high heaven for every angel and every other rank of being there to hear. He shouts it boldly. And here is what he says: 'I now absolve this guilty sinner.' And this is constantly declared. I suppose there was never a day since Christ died and rose again that this has not been shouted in the courts of heaven, with all the amplification necessary for everyone to hear, and the sinner publicly named. 'I now absolve this guilty sinner and declare him to be righteous through his believing in Jesus, my Son.' That is what Romans 5:1 is about: 'being justified by faith we have peace with God through our Lord Jesus Christ.'

Now, notice, this is very objective; I mean it is far beyond us. This is something that is said and done in heaven. The peace that it speaks about is not our peace, but God's peace. In a sense this has nothing to do with us (I mean the declaration). God declares that this guilty sinner is now regarded by him as righteous. He is declared to be righteous through believing in Jesus, and God is therefore at peace with him about his past sins. How wonderful!

This is why, when people come to Jesus Christ and want to follow him we insist that they do not build the Christian life upon anything subjective, like their own feelings. Many of us who have been on the Christian way a long time would confess that if we judged our faith and our possession of Jesus Christ by how we feel, we would be out and in of Christ every day in the week. Out and in, and out and in, and out and in! And if we felt saved now, we would not feel saved tomorrow. Maybe you are not as fitful as that; but perhaps you are more so. It is vital for every Christian to see that our salvation depends on God. It depends upon his character. It depends upon his word. It depends upon his work.

We take these three – his character, his word – the word of this character, and the work of this character through his Son; and we pin our faith to that. It is what God does that makes us Christians, not what we do.

Therefore, if it is all to do with what God does, we must ask this question, before we go on: Why does he not do it more often? Why does he not do it to our friends, and our loved ones, and our fellow workers, and our neighbours? Or, is he doing it more than we know?

The working of God is sovereign, there is absolutely no doubt about that. God will do what he wills, and no one will stop him. He will even set barriers in his own way, to make it harder for him to do what he wants to do, and all to his glory; so that we may say 'Hurrah!' all the more for what God does. He makes it hard *for* himself, and then he has all the glory *to* himself.

The declaration of a sinner's justification is made in heaven before all who may hear. It may not be heard on earth at all. Some people reduce the world to what they can see, and hear, and what they believe to be the case: they will not believe anything beyond their human knowledge. Silly creatures! Some people have never been very far from their birthplace. Although they may see photographs, even moving pictures of other lands and other places, it would be an awful shock to them to be plumped down in the midst of New York, thousands of miles from home, or in Tokyo, or Moscow, or Teheran, or Karachi, and see another world.

In the same way, there are worlds beyond, where Christ has gone, where great things happen constantly in the throne room of the Almighty, and we do not hear or see a thing. It is not on television, so we do not believe in it! What silly, narrow-minded, blinded creatures we are. And this, above all things, happens every day in the courts of heaven: sinners return to God and are declared in heaven to be righteous in Christ.

But we must go into detail, and ask some questions. On what ground does God declare this of any sinner? Is it on the ground of his faith, of his believing in Jesus? Are you following? Is your mind alert? On what ground does God declare this in heaven? Is it on the ground of the believing sinner's faith? The answer is 'No'. Let me state this very boldly, faith does not save us. It is grace that saves, not faith. Am I quibbling with words? Not at all. It is the grace of God that saves. It is God who is our Saviour, not we ourselves, even by our faith. What we and many other people call 'saving faith', is only 'saving faith' because it is a gift of God. God gives a man faith that he might be saved, but it is God who saves, not the faith. It is grace that saves, as Paul says in Romans 3:24. And God's grace saves by providing Christ and the death of Christ as our mercy seat (Rom. 3:25).

What does Scripture mean by describing Christ as the 'mercy seat'? You need to be taken into the wilderness of Sinai to know that, back in time hundreds, even thousands of years ago to the children of Israel in the wilderness, to the Tabernacle. Can you see the Tabernacle with its two compartments, and its courtyard, its enclosure with the brazen altar? Can you see the outer compartment of the Tabernacle with its seven-branched candlestick, its table of the shewbread, and the golden altar of incense? And can you picture behind that great curtain which hides the holiest place of all, the ark in which the two tablets of stone with the ten commandments are laid. Do you see the wooden ark overlaid with gold, and the cherubim at each end overshadowing the Ark of the Covenant? That is God's seat. God dwells there. The High Priest of Israel could enter that place only one day in the year – on the Day of Atonement. God was there, and if any one had gone through that curtain he would have instantly been slain because God's commandment in the Old Testament is not merely ceremonial or symbolic, as these things have become to us, but was vital. If the High Priest had entered any other day of the year other than the Day of Atonement, or if he had entered without blood, he would have died instantly by the judgment of God. The ark was God's seat. God's Shekinah glory dwelt there. The children of Israel saw the holy glory of God hovering above the Tabernacle, and knew his presence to be in that compartment, the holiest place of all. That seat is his judgment seat. Ten words of law, the ten commandments are there and God sits there and says, 'Thou shalt not, and thou shalt.' 'The soul that sinneth one sin shall die.' It spells judgment, judgment, judgment upon the whole guilty world; and not a sinner can be acquitted. God will not justify the wicked!

But on the Day of Atonement (which is a picture of Christ in his redeeming work), the lamb having been slain, in great fear and trembling the High Priest enters the very presence of God and sprinkles the judgment seat with the blood of the lamb. And the judgment seat whence God cannot acquit or justify any sinning soul becomes – to any one who will draw near, any day of the week, any time, in any place – his mercy seat. That is why Paul speaks about Christ being set forth as our 'mercy seat', our propitiation, propitiating the wrath of a holy God for our sins.

But who is it that propitiates God? It is Christ, the righteous one. He is the only man who ever lived who never broke God's law. In his thirty-three years of life he never broke God's holy law once, in thirty-three years of life he never broke God's holy law once, in deed, in word, or thought or intent. He is the perfect lawkeeper. And so because he has not one sin of his own he can take upon his sinless shoulders our sins. No one less could do. If Adam had sought to do this after he had sinned his great, heinous sin, he would have died for that sin and could have done nothing for anyone else. But Jesus, the righteous one – our representative lawkeeper – takes our sins upon his back and dies the death for them and with them, to take them away. He bears the penalty of our sins, and so dies for others.

Then by his resurrection – which is the seal of the effectiveness of what has been done by his death – God claims the right to justify the ungodly, every one who will come and look to his Son. God in fact declares his right to pronounce that guilty sinner righteous, justified.

And this is done, says Paul in the same passage, that God might be just. It is a just thing for God to justify the ungodly on this ground. 'That he might be just', 3:25, 'and that he might be the justifier of him who believes in Jesus', 3:26. Think of that – 'that God might be just; and be the justifier of the ungodly who believes on Jesus.' There. Is that your contradiction resolved? Are you satisfied with that now?

On the one hand God says, 'I will not justify the sinner, the wicked'; yet here his pronouncement in heaven declares that with love, grace and delight he pronounces the guilty sinner 'righteous' in his sight through faith in Jesus. 'That he might be just and, at one and the same time, be the justifier of the ungodly who believe in Jesus.' And so we ask this question, with Paul at the end of Romans chapter three: 'Does God then make void the law?' Does he set it aside? Does he trample upon it? 'God forbid,' says Paul, 'Yea, we establish the law'(Rom.3:31). How does he establish the law? He establishes the law because the man who died had fulfilled it. Notice carefully how he did this: he had fulfilled it in his life. He had fulfilled it perfectly; and then he fulfilled it for us by his death, and made a perfect justification for us.

But, you then want to ask, what is the role of faith in justification? I have said that faith does not save. Saving faith is not saving

What is the role of faith in justification? Look at the Scriptures we have mentioned. It is not a work. It is not something that man may do meritoriously. It is not something that man can do, so that someone can applaud and say, 'Hurrah! Good for you.' Meditate on these Scriptures, as you go over some of them again. The believer in Jesus is justified freely, without any work. He is justified gratuitously. He is justified as a free act of God's grace and mercy (Rom. 3:24).

Again: it is by faith that we are justified, apart from deeds of the law (Rom. 3:28). You see faith is set over against deeds of the law, and faith itself is not a deed of the law, nor a work. Again, Abraham believed the promise that God gave to him, of making him the father of many nations through Isaac, the miracle son of promise; and God counted that faith for righteousness. Abraham simply believed what God said, and God counted that faith for righteousness (Rom. 4:3).

Now, you may ask, does this not mean that faith is equal to righteousness? He who believes receives righteousness. Is that not a work? No! Read it again: 'Abraham believed God and it was counted (reckoned) unto him for righteousness.' What does Paul mean, 'Abraham believed God and it was counted to him for righteousness. Now to him that worketh is the reward not reckoned of grace but of due or debt'? It is not a kindness that your employer does you when he gives you your wages or your salary when you have worked for it. If you had been off sick and he gave you it in full that would be an act of grace; but if you have worked for it, it is your due and you have a right to it.

That is the core of what Paul is saying. Have you got these words? 'But to him that *worketh not* but *believeth* (believing is not a work!) on him that justifieth the ungodly; his faith is counted for righteousness.' The grace of God operating through the exercise of the gift of faith, brings down the righteousness of Christ in his life and in his death, and his rising which seals his righteousness. It is God's work from beginning to end. You have only to hold up your hands for it. But, is that not a work? Not if God lifts your hands! The faith to lift up your hands and say, 'Let me receive', is itself a gift of God. Grace – God's grace – precedes faith, always! Regeneration, the new birth, is the beginning of it. We are born of God before we know it. Every response to God's grace is a sign that the Spirit of God is there. Do you doubt that?

If you were still old-fashioned enough to carry an Authorised Version of the Bible, and you were to turn to the twenty-third chapter of Jeremiah, before you see v.6 you will see four words written in great big capital letters. What are they? THE LORD, OUR RIGHTEOUSNESS. The modern translations do not dignify that passage and these words with capital letters. They may think there is no need to. But those who did, whenever it started, had a conception of the gospel that the modern church just does not have. For those words express the heart of the matter. What God does in justifying us is to give us nothing less than Jesus Christ to be our righteousness; righteousness in his righteous life, and his righteousness in bearing our penalty – the penalty of our sins – in his righteous death. He is our righteousness.

If you were to look up 1 Corinthians 1:30 you would read there, 'It is of (from the grace of) God that Christ is made unto us righteousness.' You see, all that he does, the conviction of sin bringing us to repentance, the receiving of forgiveness, that is the removal of our sins - all this is done because already the Holy Spirit has come to us, unknown to us very likely, and has united us with Christ. In fact the truth of the matter is that we were chosen in Christ before the foundation of the world (Eph.1:4).

It is in Christ, united with him, that we are righteous. That is another story! By this union with Christ there takes place marriage with Christ, the interfusing (but not the confusing) of two spirits, so that they are one forever. By this union what God declares in heaven to be the truth, that we are now justified in Christ, begins to operate on the earth. That is just another way of describing what we call sanctification. When God declares in heaven that we are righteous, that is the objective side of salvation. At the same time, his Spirit comes into our hearts to enable us to believe. And the Spirit that comes to our hearts to enable us to believe enables us to go on believing, until Christ grows in us. I speak very chastely, God knows – Christ grows in us from a seed to a babe, to a man, until he envelops, possesses, and takes the whole of us, and we are able to say like the Apostle Paul, 'For me to live is Christ; and to shuffle off this mortal coil is gain' (Phil. 1:21).

But first – and this is what we are concerned with here – there is the heavenly announcement of grace. There will be announcements in heaven today of sinners returning, repenting and being declared by God to be righteous in Christ – as righteous as Christ, since Christ is their righteousness. The first trumpet sound that may go out today may come from China, or Malaya, or Pakistan, or New York, or London, or perhaps some other building in Aberdeen. Will it sound for someone here? Will your name come over the loudspeakers in heaven today? Let me put it another way. Do you feel (yes, I use the word 'feel' advisedly – how could this happen without you feeling?) – do you feel the arms of love lifting your arms toward him, to receive him?

THE CROSS

7: Reconciliation

Romans 3:19-23, 28-31; 4:1-5; 5:1-11.

We have been considering the Death and Resurrection of Christ in relation to God's pronouncement in heaven that the repentant sinner who trusts wholly in Jesus Christ is righteous in God's sight. The word 'right' is a legal and an exact word. You cannot have a comparative of right, nor a superlative of it. It does not make sense to speak of anything being 'righter', because nothing can be 'righter' or 'rightest'. There is no comparison. If a sum is right it is right, and even the teacher cannot improve on that! Those that are declared righteous in God's sight are accepted by him *in* Jesus Christ, not only through Jesus Christ. They are righteous with the very righteousness of Christ himself, because they are 'in' him.

That does not mean to say that guilty sinners, as soon as they have trusted in Jesus Christ, already live perfect lives, and are perfect in the moral, ethical, even spiritual sense. But, you see, God sees everything telescoped from eternity to eternity. All that he sees, all that he foresees that he will do, all that he purposes to do, he regards in eternity. For eternity is not elongated time, it is a different sphere – there is no past, present and future in eternity. All that God purposes to do is, as far as he is concerned, done. And what he says in heaven about a guilty, repentant and believing sinner, he purposes to do. But he declares it first. The boldness of it! Some of us would not dare to say what we were going to do until we had first tried to, and made sure that we could. But none of that with God! He declares, first of all, that this one he now pronounces, through Christ and in Christ, to be right – let me put it boldly, shockingly – in his sight is as right as Christ.

We have seen the ground of this declaration that God makes in heaven is not our faith; the ground of it is the death of Christ. It is not primarily because we believe that we are justified, but because Christ died. It is through the death of Christ that God comes to us and gives us the gift of faith, and says, 'Here you are, use that, and believe.'

In chapter five, when we spoke of the forgiveness of sins, I quoted some words of Vincent Taylor, the New Testament scholar. Here is more of what he says: 'The question, What is forgiveness? is less easy to answer than one might suppose, especially if one wants to relate the answer to the teaching of the New Testament. In modern theology the distinction between forgiveness and reconciliation is far from clear, and many would affirm that there is not any difference at all between them. Evidence for this statement can easily be found in current definitions of "forgiveness".' And he quotes the five scholars we have quoted already, each with a sentence. For example: 'The full restoration of delicate personal relationships between friends or between parent and child is what is meant by "forgiveness".'

Now, in the chapter on the forgiveness of sins I said that forgiveness is the removal of sins. They are removed by the death of Christ. Bearing the full penalty for men's sins he takes them away from the sight of God. But there is another word in the Greek language which suggests a fuller meaning; not only the removing of the obstacle to friendship with God but the actual act of taking us back into his arms. It is the word *katallagé*, reconciliation.

Strictly speaking – if we want to be strict – when these men say that forgiveness is restoring and taking back, nothing less than reconciling, they are mixing up two words. The word they want is the word which is our subject here. It is reconciliation – restoration, if you like, but reconciliation is the Bible's word; bringing someone back into friendship and fellowship, who has been out of it because of what they have done, because of their sins.

Reconciliation is mentioned in several passages of Scripture. In Romans 5:6-10 Paul says: 'For when we were yet without strength, in due time Christ died for the ungodly.' Here is expressed both our ungodliness and our inability to help ourselves. 'For scarcely for a righteous man will one die, yet peradventure for a good man some would even dare to die. But God commendeth his love toward us, in that while we were (neither right nor good, but wicked) sinners ('enemies' of God, he says in a moment) Christ died for us. Much more then, being now justified by his blood (that is by his death), we shall be saved from wrath through him. For if, when we were enemies, we were reconciled to God by the death of his Son, much more, being reconciled we shall be saved by his life.'

Enemies! This is all I want from this passage at the moment. We were not merely weak, not merely sinners, but *enemies* of God. That is why we needed to be *reconciled* to God, taken back through forgiveness into friendship and fellowship with God, by the blood of his Son. This is what the hymn says:

Jesus sought me when a stranger
Wandering from the fold of God.
He, to rescue me from danger,
Interposed his precious blood.

Why are we enemies by nature? Because we have been infected by the enemy. God has an implacable enemy. Apparently when an angel sins – I suppose especially a great one, or a high one, a resplendent one in great authority, like Lucifer (so the Old Testament suggests, Is. 14, Ezek. 28) – he is unsaveable. There are many fallen angels, waiting in judgment (2 Pet. 2:4). Their leader, the Devil, is implacable and unsaveable. He is destined to burn and suffer torments in hell for ever and ever – the creation of God, a glorious creation of God gone wrong. And it was he who infected man with sin and made Adam a rebel like himself. Now we are all infected; and we are all by nature enemies of God. This is in our blood, our moral and spiritual blood. But we are not unsaveable!

God is able to save his chosen ones, the elect of men who have fallen into Satan's clutches. It is not because they are not responsible, for Adam and Eve fell with their eyes wide open. They deliberately disobeyed God when he had given them everything good. It was a barefaced sin, the first sin, there is no doubt about that. We must not minimise its heinousness. Its heinousness rises to high heaven. But it was masterminded by Satan, the unsaveable enemy. Yet God has mercy on us and says, 'I can save them from his clutches.'

But how can this be when they are tainted with his sin; when because of the sin of Adam, that open, barefaced sin, they partake of his nature and are in a sense, as wicked and sinful, as rebellious and bad as the Devil himself? How can God save men and women who have become like Satan himself, and are his children?

How could God do it? Only by thrashing the enmity out of them. Now, there is much more to it than this, but you cannot say everything every time. Let us stick to one point. He thrashes it out of them in the body of his dearly beloved Son, who never sinned and was never even faintly disobedient to his Father, let alone his enemy. He interposed his precious blood between an angry God and hell–deserving sinners. He thrashed it out of existence in his Son, so that he could say to those who believed in his Son: 'I have no anger against you. I am not at enmity with you any more. I have done *it* away, not you. I have destroyed *it*. I have exhausted my wrath in my Son. And you can come back to me.'

Paul also speaks about reconciliation in Ephesians chapter two. He sets the context in Ephesians 2:11. Paul is writing to the Ephesians, who were largely Gentiles, although there may have been some Jews among them. He wants them to see that they are equal in the sight of God. The issue here was not a matter of colour, but a matter of race; and that can be just as bitter. He wants them to see that they are equal in God's sight through the death of Christ; so he says at the 11th verse, 'Wherefore, remember, that you being in times past Gentiles, in the flesh, who are called uncircumcision by that which is called the circumcision in the flesh made by hands; that at that time, ye were without Christ, being aliens from the commonwealth of Israel, and were strangers from the covenants of promise, having no hope, and without God in the world. But now in Christ Jesus you Gentiles who sometimes were far off are made nigh, (not by becoming Jews but) by the blood of Christ. For he is our (and when he uses the word 'our' here in v.14, that 'our' includes himself, a Jew, and the Ephesians as Gentiles) peace who has made both of us one, and has broken down the middle wall of partition (the barrier) that was between us; having abolished in his flesh the enmity. . . .' Now, notice, he is referring primarily to the enmity between Jew and Gentile: 'Having abolished in his flesh the enmity, even the law of commandments contained in ordinances; for to make in himself of twain one new man (the church, the body of Christ) so making peace (between believing Jew and believing Gentile) in order that he might reconcile both (Jew and Gentile) unto God in one body. (Probably 'in one body' means the one body of Jesus Christ, the church.) And that he might reconcile both in one body through the Cross, having slain the enmity thereby: (the enmity between Jew and Gentile) and came and preached peace to you who were afar off, and to them that were nigh. For through him (Christ) we both (Jew and Gentile) have access (you can run up and into your Father's arms) by one Spirit unto the Father. Now, therefore (he says to the Gentiles), ye are no more strangers and foreigners in this fellowship.'

So the Christian in a church far away from home is always a brother, or sister. Anyone is welcome, but to those who know Christ we can say: You are our brother, you are our sister. You are not a stranger, although we have never spoken to you in our lives before. 'No more strangers and foreigners, but fellow citizens with the saints, and of the household of God.' Now Paul is a Jew writing to Gentiles. Most of us are Gentiles. We are all together 'fellow citizens with the saints and of the household of God, and are built upon the foundation of the apostles and prophets, Jesus Christ himself being the chief cornerstone; in whom all the building fitly framed together groweth unto an holy temple in the Lord.'

So, Jew and Gentile are reconciled and the enmity between them slain. Yet this presupposes the reconciliation, the abolishing of the enmity, between God and the Jew and between God and the Gentile; because if the Gentile is not made friends with God by God, and the Jew is not made friends with God by God, then they can never be true friends with each other. The enmity is abolished by Christ in his death. Only thereby can Jews and Gentiles, and all other repentant, believing sinners be reconciled to God and to one another.

Nor is this all. If you turn to Colossians 1:20 you will see that the reconciliation strangely enough goes even beyond that: 'And having made peace through the blood of his cross, (by Christ) God reconciles all things unto himself; by him I say, whether they be things in earth, or things in heaven. And you, that were sometime alienated and enemies (notice 'enemies' again) in your minds by wicked works yet now hath he reconciled.'

Note that where the word 'reconciliation' or 'reconciled' is, you usually find the word 'enemy' or 'enemies' too. What is in view is the reconciliation of enmity. But by Christ's cross he has not only reconciled men but also 'things'. What does that mean? Are things, natural things, worlds, reconciled with God through the death of Christ? Well, look at Romans 8:18-23. Here is an exciting passage! Paul says, 'For I reckon that the sufferings of this present time are not worthy to be compared with the glory which shall be revealed in (to) us. For the earnest expectation of the creation is waiting for the manifestation of the sons of God.' That is to say, through the death and resurrection of Jesus Christ there is to be a great outshining of the results of Christ's work. We are going to see the redemption of worlds and of men. But the men come first because men are the most important creatures God has made, far more than angels. Angels are only servants. They are mighty and great in many ways, but they are only servants. They cannot be saved by the blood of Christ.

And so, first, the sons of God will be shown forth in their glory, and then the natural creation. There will be no more foot and mouth disease if you like, or potato blight. That is what we are talking about, the fruits of sin in the world. Adam and Eve brought the whole creation round them in ruin. For, says Paul, the creation was made subject to futility (or vanity, emptiness) not of its own will, (you see what he is saying? The trees did not choose to rebel against God, nor the leopards, nor the rivers, nor the mountains, nor the fish) not willingly but by reason of God's purpose who had subjected the natural creation to futility (or unproductiveness) in hope because the creation itself also shall be delivered from the bondage of corruption into the liberty of the glory of the sons of God. For we know that the whole creation groaneth and travaileth in pain together until now. (We catch a sense of this when there is a tidal wave or a volcano erupts). And not only the natural creation, but ourselves also who have the firstfruits of the Spirit; even we ourselves groan within ourselves waiting for the full adoption (being taken right into the Father's heart, taken home to glory as he puts his arms round us and says 'My bairn, you're home'), for the adoption, namely the redemption (the buying back from evil) of the body (which will decay in dust and yet be reconstituted in the Spirit at the coming of Jesus Christ).

But, somebody says, that must mean that all men are going to be saved. How do you make that out? The natural creation did not fall; it was dragged down by Adam and Eve; and God purposes to redeem, and reconcile, indeed forgive, and justify whom he will. But the whole of the natural creation – the whole of the natural creation, whatever that means, will be redeemed. I do not know what all this means, I am not expected perhaps to know, but it's in the Bible!

Look back to Romans 5:11. I have just two points. 'Now', says Paul here, having spoken about our enmity being done away so that we are reconciled to God, having been enemies, we are now saved by his life; 'not only so, but we also boast in God.' Now look back, just for a moment. This word 'boast' is the same word translated 'rejoice' in verse two: 'By whom also we have access by faith into this grace wherein we stand and "boast" in hope of the glory of God.'

Now verse 3, 'And not only so, but we glory (again, the same Greek word 'boast'), we boast in tribulations also.' Then he adds in v.11: 'And not only so but we also boast in God, through our Lord Jesus Christ by whom we have now received the reconciliation.'

What God has done through Christ in so thrashing the enmity out of us in him until there is no enmity any longer, until his wrath is exhausted and extinguished and he takes us back into his heart and takes back the whole of the creation that was ruined by Adam and Eve, is something to shout about and boast about, glory in and exult in, you see!

This leads us on to the last passage which is 2 Corinthians 5:16-18. Paul says, 'Wherefore, henceforth know we no man after the flesh: yea, though we have known Christ after the flesh, yet now henceforth know we him as such (as a mortal man) no more.' He says that our fellowship in the Christian church is not merely with persons who have human bodies: (every living person has!) but our fellowship is with people who are sanctified by the Holy Spirit of Jesus Christ and are already immortal. Their bodies are not immortal, but they will be one day by the resurrection. What Christ has sown in my heart – his Spirit interlocked with my spirit in my heart – will never die. I cannot die. 'They shall never die,' said Jesus about those who believe in his resurrection. That is what he means. Well then, 'If any man be in Christ he is a new creation; old things are passed away (and the old things that are passed away are the enmity with all its fruit), behold all things are become new. And all things are from God (faith is a gift. We do not work our passage; we do not earn our salvation. We get it from God as a gift). All things are from God who hath reconciled us to himself by Jesus Christ and hath given unto us the ministry of reconciliation. 'Out' he says 'into the world, and boast about what God has done in Christ. Boast about it; that God has thrashed the enmity of man out of him in the body of his Son. For God was in Christ reconciling the world unto himself, bearing the punishment (taking the thrashing), not imputing their trespasses unto them; and has committed unto us the word, the ministry, the preaching, the sounding out of the good news of reconciliation. Now then, we are ambassadors for Christ as though God did beseech you by us, using our lips as his mouthpiece and speaking to men through us; be ye, we pray you in Christ's stead – as if Christ were here in visible manifestation – we pray you in Christ's stead, speaking as his mouthpiece, be ye reconciled to God.'

Go out into the world and tell your workmates that tomorrow. We do not all do it in the same way and in the same language – that is not the point. The news needs to get out. Even although many so-called professing Christians will laugh at the news; the news needs to get out that God has thrashed the enmity of man out of him in his Son and is waiting to take those who believe that into his arms, and say to them, 'My bairn, you're back home where you belong, by my grace.'

So, here are two messages: one to you for yourself – if you need it – and one to you for others – and we all need that.

THE CROSS

8: Adoption

Romans 8:1-24.

We are going to consider the subject of adoption from three New Testament passages.

1. Romans 8:14-17. 'For as many as are led by the Spirit of God they are the sons of God; for ye have not received the spirit of bondage again to fear; but ye have received the Spirit which places you in Christ as sons, whereby we cry Abba, Father. The Spirit himself beareth witness with our spirit (for they are joined together indissolubly. They will never be unjoined – his Spirit and our spirit, never! The divine, the creator, redeemer Spirit, of course, is always distinct from the created spirit, but yet the two are joined) that we are the born-ones of God; and if born-ones heirs, heirs of God and joint heirs with Christ if so be that we suffer with him, that we may be also glorified together.'

2. Galatians 4:1-6. 'Now, I say that the heir, as long as he is a child (think of anyone who has an inheritance, perhaps a title. Think of the Prince of Wales!) differeth nothing from a servant though he be lord of all, but is under tutors and governors until the time appointed of the father. Even so we (believing Jews before the coming of Christ. Notice this carefully), when we were children were in bondage under the elements of the world. But when the fulness of the time was come, God sent forth his Son, made of a woman, made under the law to redeem them that were under the law, that we might receive the adoption of sons. And because ye are sons, God

---

hath sent forth the Spirit of his Son into your hearts crying, Abba, Father.'

3. Ephesians 1:3-6. 'Blessed be the God and Father of our Lord Jesus Christ who hath blessed us with all spiritual blessings in heavenly places in Christ according as he hath chosen us in him before the foundation of the world that we should be holy and without blemish before him, in love (or that we should be holy, without blemish before him; in love) having predestinated us unto the adoption of children (placing as sons – it is not bairns here but sons) by Jesus Christ to himself, according to the good pleasure of his will, to the praise of the glory of his grace wherein he made us accepted in the beloved – engraced us, I think we said last time we read Ephesians – in the beloved.'

When we bring Paul's words in Romans and Ephesians together, what do we learn? We were predestinated, just as we were chosen in Christ from before the foundation of the world by God in love to be placed as sons in the one Son Jesus Christ our Lord. And the proof that this is so is that ultimately we emit the authentic cry of the born-one, 'Abba, Father', God's Spirit witnessing with our spirit that we are the children of God.

This is the proof that we are Christians – that we respond to godly and holy things. There are no slick, mechanical, easy ways of determining who is a Christian. The proof is that we are new creatures, and we show that we are new creatures by being glad to live in a new sphere, a new kingdom, a new world; and of that there is perhaps a two-fold proof. One side of it is that we like to be with God's people, however imperfect they may be; for, for all their faults, we really prefer to be with them than with any others. The other side is this: because we belong to God's people, God puts a care in our hearts for those who are lost. So the Christian fellowship sends us out into the world to seek and find them, as Christ did. And this is all because God's Spirit, by whom we are actually and actively placed in Christ as sons, interlocks with our spirit, and witnesses to us that we are indeed born of God.

You see, a new-born Christian says, 'My, this Bible. When will I ever learn it? When will I ever read it? It's marvellous! Wonderful!

Can this be true, true of me, of you? That fellowship we had together, how different from other friendships and associations, fellowships, clubs and groups. That prayer we had together, I sensed that God was there.' Of course you did, because he was. There is no other subjective, earthly confirmation that it is so than this; we see it in people's lives, and we *know*. It is disturbing if the authentic signs of being a child of God are not manifest. It is best when it is evident early, if not at once, that there has been a deep change, such a deep change that it is unconscious.

When we turn to Galatians, we find the same thing. What is it that Paul says again? 'Because ye are sons God hath sent forth the Spirit of his Son into your hearts crying, Abba, Father.' And the reason why we can emit this authentic cry of the born-one is that we are born of the Son who has been emitting it since before all worlds, lost in the mists and antiquities of eternity. The cry 'Abba, Father,' is the proof that we are born, begotten of God.

Perhaps we may be allowed a word on the rest of the passage in Galatians. Adoption here is something different – not quite the same as in Romans. Adoption here might very well be called 'coming of age'. Doubtless that is in some senses more related to the ancient Roman idea. But you see, Israel (compare Romans 9-11) is but a servant until the coming of Christ. 'But when the fulness of time was come God sent forth his Son, made of a woman, under the law, to redeem them that were under the law, that these might receive adoption as sons.' They were treated as servants until they came of age in Christ. Being adopted as sons, having received the Spirit of the Son we are God's children in Christ, adopted into his family.

At once, we need to say this. God has only one Son, the only begotten (Jn. 1:14,18; 3:16,18; 1 Jn. 4:9). At this point, we need to look into the whole question of the Trinity, briefly. Here is part of the Westminster Confession of Faith's statement about the Trinity: 'In the unity of the Godhead there be three Persons; of one substance, power, and eternity (They are co-equal in substance, in power and in eternity); God the Father, God the Son, and God the Holy Ghost (all God, but one God, not three). The Father is of none, neither begotten nor proceeding; the Son is eternally begotten of the Father (that is to say, he is the Son and not the Father; he is the second

Person of the Trinity. There never was a time when there was the Father without the Son; he is eternally begotten from the Father), the Holy Ghost eternally proceeding from the Father and the Son' (*Confession of Faith*, II. 3). We cannot discuss this here at any length. But here is the Trinity. The Father is of none; neither begotten nor proceeding. The Son is eternally begotten, eternally born of the Father. What does the Confession go on to say about him? It says: the Lord Jesus Christ was 'God's only begotten Son. . . the Mediator. . . the Prophet, Priest, and King; the Head and Saviour of his Church; the heir of all things; and Judge of the world. . . the Son of God, the second Person in the Trinity, being very and eternal God, of one substance, and equal with the Father, did, when the fulness of time was come, take upon him man's nature with all the essential properties and common infirmities thereof (weakness and pain and so on), yet without sin; being conceived by the power of the Holy Ghost in the womb of the Virgin Mary, of her substance. So that two whole, perfect, and distinct natures, the Godhead and the manhood, were inseparably joined together in one person, without conversion (neither nature is converted into the other), composition (a little of the one perhaps being in a sense mixed with the other), or confusion.'

That is the eternal Son – two whole, perfect, and distinct natures. The Godhead and the manhood are joined together for ever. Christ is a man in heaven now and ever will be. It will be a man who will judge the world (Acts 17:31).

These natures then are inseparably joined together in one person without any confusion whatsoever. And so the Confession concludes, 'Which person is very God and very man, yet one Christ, the only Mediator between God and man' (*Confession of Faith*, VIII 1-2).

Now what is the relevance of all this to us?. Christ is the only begotten Son of God. The only way that we can become sons of God is by being placed in him. We are not sons by nature. If you look at Genesis 1:26,27 you will see that God made man in his own image. God indeed made man the crown of creation, above the angels or any beast or created thing. I think the image of God means the image of his Son. That is part of the reason why Christ on earth is called the

Son of man – but that is another story. But in these passages in Genesis chapters 1 and 2 it does not say that Adam is made, in the fullest sense, 'son' of God. (I think it is remarkable that in the first and second chapters of the Bible that word does not occur.) Man, a creature, is first made in the image of God; and then of course, the second thing is that he lost the image of God and became almost unrecognisably defaced through sin. And man, Adam, became a child of the Devil. All those who are not regenerated by the Holy Spirit, who are not chosen in Christ from before the foundation of the world, will go with the Devil at last to his place.

It is interesting that the New Testament makes a play on words that we first find in the prophecy of Hosea. God sends Hosea to take a wife, and she proves unfaithful. He begets a daughter, and God tells him to give her the name, 'Not pitied' because 'I will not have pity on this backsliding people of Israel'; and then he begets a son by Gomer, the unfaithful wife, and God says, Call that son, 'Not my people' for 'you are not my people any longer'. But in Hosea 2:23 God gives this gracious promise to the people: 'Say to the people that I refused to recognise as my people because of their sin, I will say to them in mercy "You are my people".' Now, Paul in Romans takes that up in 9:25,26, although he applies it to a different story. He says, 'As he saith also (as God said in Hosea) I will call them my people which were not my people and her beloved which was not beloved; and it shall come to pass that in that place where it was said to them, "Ye are not my people," there shall they be called "the children of the living God." ' If you look at Romans 9:24 you will see that the apostle is quoting this in application to the Gentiles, while the original reference was to backsliding Israel. God is saying to the Jews that because they have sinned away the day of grace and their opportunity, God has set them aside. This is the theme of Romans 9-11. And now he has said to the Gentiles, 'Come on; you were not my people, the Jews were my people, but they are hopeless; I have set them aside in the meantime; come on you Gentiles'. And that is why we Gentiles can be Christians as well. God has said about Gentiles he brings to faith: 'You are my people; you were not my people but now you are my people.'

There is something very similar in 1 Peter 2:10: 'Which in time past were not a people but are now the people of God; which had not obtained mercy but now have obtained mercy.'

So we are not sons of God, but sons of the Devil by the Fall. Yet God says to us in mercy and grace in Jesus Christ, having predestinated us to it before the world began, in love: 'You are mine; you are my sons, you are my daughters; I place you in Christ and treat you like him.' Chosen before all worlds, predestinated in love; this is love! God's love, having elected us, takes us, chosen in Christ in love.

So, by adoption, we are placed in Christ. We are sons and daughters who were once not sons and daughters. We now become royal, and even in one sense, divine. Now, in what sense can that possibly be true? 2 Peter 1:4 says that we are partakers of the divine nature. We are sons and daughters of God, made sons and daughters of God in Christ who is called the firstborn of many brethren: 'For whom he did foreknow he also did predestinate to be conformed to the image of his Son that he might be the firstborn (that is through the resurrection, I think) among many brethren' (Rom. 8:29).

And then, look at Hebrews 2:10 where the author tells us that *the* Son is to be bringing *many sons* to glory! We are royal, we are divine, we are partakers of the divine nature, we are sons and daughters of God, nothing less in Jesus Christ. God regards us as in Christ, and favours us as he favours Christ himself. We are divine, but of course we never become part of the deity. We are not *Deus*, not God, and we never will be God. We are still creatures, creatures placed as sons, creatures become sons. The distinction between the deity and his sons is perfectly preserved, although his Spirit and our spirits are interlocked so that they will never be broken. We do not become God, and we do not partake of the nature of God in that sense.

Let me prove this to you. Jesus always made a clear distinction between his standing with the Father and ours. When he taught what is called the Lord's Prayer he said, 'You pray "Our Father".' He did not sit among the rest of the congregation of the sons of God and with them say, 'Our Father'. He said in fact, 'My Father and your Father.' That is underlined by what he said to Mary Magdalene after the resurrection: 'Touch me not; for I am not yet ascended unto my Father, but go to my brethren (this is intriguing; this is wonderful!) and say ("I ascend to our Father"? No!), I ascend to my Father and your Father and to my God and your God' (Jn. 20:17).

Thus, we are placed as sons; we are begotten in Christ as sons and daughters of God to receive all his favour and to be chosen and predestinated to this in love. This is to the good pleasure of God.

This is what is offered us in the gospel. Will you be one of those? Will you have him? Will you become one with him? Will you receive him? 'How can I?' you may say. You say, 'Can this be received?' It must be received by faith. Do you think God goes about saying, 'Not you, not you, but you'? However he selects and whomever he selects, they come to him by their own free-will response. True, it is by the grace of God and his drawing, but that is not the point I want to make just now. In fact when God the Holy Spirit comes to our hearts wooing us to himself, and gives us the power to respond to him and to receive Christ, it is the first really free-will act of our lives. Will you have him?

But somebody may say, 'What has this to do with the death and resurrection of Jesus Christ?' Two things. It is only through the death and resurrection of Jesus Christ that we can become sons at all. But the second thing is this. In Romans 8:14-17, Paul says: 'If we are led by the Spirit of God we are sons of God. We have not received the spirit of bondage to fear, but have received the Spirit of adoption whereby we cry, "Abba, Father," the Spirit bearing witness with our spirit that we are the born-ones of God; and if children (if born-ones), then heirs, heirs of God and joint heirs with Christ if so be that we suffer with him so that we may be also glorified together.' You cannot have a resurrection body unless you suffer with him. You have to take up your cross and follow; indeed you have to follow Christ into that death he died for you, at least that part of it that is for you to experience.

Here is another proof that we are Christians. The one I gave at the beginning is that we have a taste for Christian things: the Bible,

Christian fellowship, Christian worship and a care to win the unconverted. Here is another proof. In a sense it is part of the same one, yet it goes deeper. Jesus Christ comes to mean so much to us that we are prepared more and more to stand by him – although we lose our best friends, our own flesh and blood, even our mothers and fathers, if they turn against us. One of the sorest things I have known is the number of apparently very, very nice mothers and fathers – some of them nominal Christians, members of churches and denominations all over the place – who abuse their own adolescent, youthful sons and daughters because they have been converted. It is one of the most hurtful things that can happen to a young man or woman. Yet there may be no escaping it. It may not be in the home, it may be in the college, at work or anywhere. There is no escaping this, because the world does not want Jesus Christ; (the church hardly wants him!) And one of the proofs that we are truly born of God is that we are willing to suffer. I believe that if we are not willing to suffer, there is no hope of being glorified together with Christ, 'For,' says Paul, 'I reckon that the sufferings of this present time are not worthy to be compared with the glory that will be revealed' (Rom. 8:18). Paul says again to Timothy in his very last letter, 'If we suffer, we shall reign' (2 Tim. 2:12), with the obvious implication that if we refuse to suffer we will not reign; and if we are not prepared to suffer ignominy and obloquy for Christ's sake we will never attain to the resurrection of the dead. 'All who will live godly in Christ Jesus shall suffer persecution' Paul says (2 Tim. 3:12)

So there we have it. We are placed as sons and daughters in Christ, as royal children of the divine and eternal Father through the eternal Redeemer. The proof is that we show ourselves to have a taste for God's things, and such a love for the Son that we will be true to him, whatever it cost us, even to death; for death will really be to us 'sudden glory'.

THE CROSS

9: Sanctification

Romans 8:1-17.

Justification has to do with what God does for us, and sanctification with what God does in us. Justification involves forgiveness and the declaration of our righteousness in Christ in heaven; while sanctification involves what God does by his Holy Spirit in us. Sanctification has to do with holiness, with being 'saints'.

Of course we have to ask what that means. Are we to count only particular Christians whom the Roman Church has canonised, as 'saints'? Or are all Christians 'saints'? We must go further back and ask, What is the basic meaning of the word 'holy' in the Old Testament and in the New? It means 'set apart', 'consecrated for God's own use'. When we think of 'holy' and 'holiness', we think of God himself and of his holy Son, and of the third person in the Trinity, the Holy Spirit.

Let me fill out that last statement. It is the Holy Spirit of Jesus Christ, crucified and risen, who comes into the heart of the believer and sanctifies him, who sets him apart for God as 'holy'. It is not a Holy Spirit of God merely. It is not merely the Holy Spirit of the Son of God as he was in heaven before he came to earth. It is the Holy Spirit of Jesus, bearing with him all the fruit of his incarnation, all the fruit of what he was and did on the earth. All that is brought to the believer to set him apart and to sanctify him for God.

'If any man be in Christ Jesus he is a new creation' (2 Cor. 5:17). He is! For he is now 'dead to sin, but alive to God' (Rom. 6:11). He is alive in a new dimension; formerly, as a sinner, as a fallen creature, he was alive to himself, he was alive to others, he was alive to the world. But he was dead to God. Oh yes, dead to God, really dead to God. But by the coming of the Holy Spirit into the believer's life he becomes in Christ, dead indeed to sin, and alive to God.

In 2 Corinthians 5:17 we have these two words that we find so often, 'in Christ'. 'Therefore if any man be in Christ he is a new creation'. In his writings, Paul is constantly speaking about being 'in Christ'.

'In Christ'. What does that mean? To be in Christ is to live in the sphere of his risen life. He is the firstborn of the new creation, of a new world, a new order of men – absolutely new, there has never been the like before. In Christ the Christian dwells in the kingdom of God; and is under the sovereign, all-powerful reign and rule of God; and within that sphere he enjoys in Christ the life of God himself.

But, you may be saying, 'That is what it means to be "in Christ"; that is not what you were speaking about at first, which was Christ in us!' But the two belong together. Christ in us is embraced by our being in Christ. That is the greater reality. We were in Christ before the foundation of the world. And in that sphere, of course, we cannot but be saturated with Christ, as it were, and thus are indwelt by him.

In John's Gospel you find Jesus constantly using the little preposition 'in'. Over and over again in Chapter 15 he speaks about 'I in you,' as he faces the disciples. And again in chapter 17 where he is praying to his Father, over and over again in different forms he speaks of 'I in them', 'I in them' and 'they in us', meaning the Father and the Son. 'In Christ' involves 'Christ in us.'

In the previous study our focus was on adoption. We said that adoption means being placed as sons in the only begotten Son, Christ. God has only one Son, and he is the only begotten, begotten before all worlds. And we who are born his creatures, the crown of his creation, fell away through Satan and the sin of Adam, of which we partake. Although we are still his creatures, we are fallen and are no longer his children; and we have become, in fact, sons of the Devil, the evil one. Yet, before the world began, God, of his great elective, sovereign purpose chose some, not all, but some among men that he might place them in his Son as sons and daughters – to be born of God and partakers of the divine nature (2 Pet. 1:4). Sons and daughters in grace, you might call them.

So although in a sense we become divine, we do not become *Deus*. We do not become God. We are still creatures; yet we are born of God. We become sons and daughters of God and indeed, as we have noted, Jesus speaks of us in various places as brothers, though younger brothers. I do not think that he likes us using the phrase 'O brother Christ' in one of the hymns (I don't care for it!). He may use 'brother' of us, but whether or not we may speak of 'brother Christ' we must understand what Paul means in Romans 8:29, when he speaks of him as the 'firstborn of many brethren'. He is the first Son, the pattern Son, the leader of our salvation, the captain, the first man to go through death and receive a resurrection body.

Let us look at this another way. Read Romans 8:16,17, where Paul says, 'The Spirit himself'. The word 'itself' appears in the Authorised Version because the word 'spirit' in the Greek is the word for 'breath' and is a neuter word, and therefore in Greek an 'it'. But of course that is the best that human language can do to describe the Spirit. He is described as breath, as oil, as fire, as water. All these are inanimate, and are the best that human language can do to describe the indescribable. But he himself is a person, so we should translate 'himself'. 'The Spirit *himself* bears witness with our spirit.' In fact, a literal translation would read: 'The Spirit himself witnesses with the spirit of us.'

How does he witness with the spirit of us that we are the children of God? In our spirit. He comes and touches our spirit. A moment ago I said that we are now, as Christians, alive to God. We were always from our birth alive to ourselves, even before we knew it, and alive to the world. The world knew us and we knew the world and could see it, sense it and perceive it, but we were not alive to God – because our spirit was dead. We were dead in trespasses and sins. An unconverted person can have no living communication with God;

but when the Holy Spirit comes, he enters our dead spirit, alive to ourselves and the world, but dead to God – and quickens it. He pours himself into it. He invades it. He inhabits it. He indwells it and he makes the two one. I have often searched for the best words to describe this. I have sometimes used the word 'interlock'. But even that is less than satisfactory, since this is a union that cannot be broken. Death cannot break it. The bodies of believers are still united to Christ in the grave – that is what the *Westminster Confession* says, drawing it from the Scriptures. The Holy Spirit of the divine, eternal Christ comes and touches our spirit, and makes his home in our spirit which was dead. What a home for the King of glory! And he is there to live; and these two spirits are one for ever; and yet the Spirit of the Son of God never becomes our spirit and our spirit never becomes the Spirit of the divine, Son of God; yet they are one for ever (1 Cor. 6:17)!

Now, when we speak of the Holy Spirit of Jesus Christ coming into our hearts, we must not allow our thinking to be determined by only the impersonal metaphors used in Scripture – water, air, fire and oil, because he is a person. Certainly there are degrees and measures of the outpouring of the Spirit. In that sense we might speak of having more or less of the Spirit. Sometimes we have more liberty in praying in the Spirit than at other times, in preaching in the Spirit than other times; but you cannot have more or less of the person of the Spirit. He is there or he is not there; and if he is there, he is all there. But if he is not there, he is not there at all.

Yet the Spirit does dwell in us, if we belong to Christ (Rom. 8:9), and we must come to grips with ourselves and take ourselves to task here and say, 'Really, what kind of a creature am I in Christ? Think what kind of Spirit dwells within me!'

So, this Christ who dwells in us, and has brought us to the birth, who has planted the holy, divine seed partaking of the divine nature in us, is holy and makes us holy. You say, 'Does this happen automatically?' Well, let me ask you this question: Did you become a Christian automatically? Nobody becomes a Christian automatically. Well, when you became a Christian, if you are a Christian, you received the holy life of God; and the rest of your life must be spent realising that, pondering it, until you say, 'I really begin to believe that this is true.' If you do, you will find that it will make such a difference to your life that you will be transformed.

Of course there is so much here! If we think of our new life in Christ as a seed, it has got to grow. If we think of it as an embryo life, it has got to grow, it has got to be nourished, it has got to be fed. We will come to that later.

The holy life of God is in my soul, not as a foreign body, not stuck on, not merely grafted (although that might do as an illustration), but the Holy Spirit enters our spirit and becomes inseparably joined with it (says the *Westminster Confession of Faith*).

Yet you might say 'Yes; but what has all this to do with the death and resurrection of Jesus Christ?'

Well, it is the Holy Spirit of Christ crucified and risen that brings us to the birth in God. We are not brought to the birth in the Son as he was in heaven before his birth and before his earthly life, death and resurrection. The Holy Spirit that you have, who has made himself one with you, is the Spirit who helped Jesus to die and to be raised on the third day.

This is the answer to everything, what you have in your heart, and who you now are. If you are a Christian, you are a saint. You have got the holy seed, the holy life of God in your soul. The apostle Paul, in this sense, is no more a saint than you, for even he cannot have more than one Holy Spirit in his heart! You too have received the whole of him. Of course, what we do with him is another story.

Now, I would like to sense a difference in our fellowship as a result of what we have just seen in the Word of God – a new dignity, a new simplicity, a new humility, a new warmth, a new atmosphere of the sacred, the holy. Do not let Satan snatch this from us like the seed on the pathway, for surely our hearts are not stony. Satan is not running backwards and forwards across your heart making it a hard, stony paved path. Not a bit. Do not let him snatch it away from you!

Ponder this: I am a saint of God. And if this does not make a difference to our lives, brothers and sisters, nothing else in heaven or earth will. Nothing!

THE CROSS

10. Growth – the life of God in regenerate man

1 John 3:1-10; 1 John 4:13; 1 John 5:4,11,12,18,19.

We have now examined the divine and eternal miracle. The Spirit of the Lord Jesus Christ crucified, risen, ascended to the right hand of the Father – that Spirit of God bearing with him the Christ, in all the excellencies of his redeeming work – comes to bring us to the birth and to quicken our dead spirits and interlock (but not interfuse) with them. And so the life of God in the soul of man can and does grow.

We are now going to look at the possibilities of the divine growth in the soul of man, according to two horticultural principles. First we shall consider how the 'seed of God' (1 John 3:9) in the souls of men needs room to grow, and then we shall consider its nourishment.

Consider Jesus' great parable of the Sower, and especially the third and fourth categories of soil in which the seed of God is placed. Our Lord gives four descriptions of what happens when the sower sows his seed. The first is seed that is cast upon the hard trodden pathway; and the second was cast upon ground that had a thin layer of soil on top of solid seams of rock; the third was seed that was cast in ground that had already within it the seeds of thorns and thistles, weeds; and the last was the good ground prepared of God, cleansed by God and prepared for fruitfulness – thirty, and sixty and one hundredfold. The difference between the third category of soil (in which the weeds grow up and choke the divine life), and the fourth (in which the soil was good) is that it was prepared; it was cleansed by God so that those who received it might have 'hearing ears'.

Does it not strike you as awful that the Word of God can be preached and taught over and over again, and people can sit and listen in some kind of fashion for umpteen years, and nothing ever penetrates the soul, and the mind, or the spirit, to make any transformation or change?

God needs to cleanse the soil. God must take possession of us so that all our life is his. Although the flesh is still there – there is no doubt about that – yet it is the new nature, the life of God, the life of Christ that is upon the throne of our lives. He takes none other than the central place. He takes the place of command and direction in our lives. He will have no other; and so it is the principle of his divine life that calls the tune.

Thus, as we learn the truth (particularly in Romans 6) about the death and resurrection of Jesus Christ and how the Holy Spirit has brought that potency to bear on our lives, so we take our stand upon it and dare to tramp our way round Jericho until the walls crash down and our lives are delivered from their bondage to self, in order to serve and love Christ.

Now, as far as cleansing the life from the seeds of weeds, thorns and thistles are concerned one devout scholar has this helpful comment: 'The characteristic of this class of hearers, those of the soil which has the seeds of thorns, is prepossession (possession beforehand) of the soil, by alien things (things that do not belong to Christ) which have not been weeded out.' Could it be that the hopelessness of any progress in sanctification and any growth in grace and knowledge of Jesus Christ, and any growth of holiness of personal life, is due to the fact that there are still many seeds, and seedlings of carnal, selfish and sinful things that have not been removed? Could this be true of you too, that 'The characteristic of that class of hearer is prepossession of the soil by alien things which have not been weeded out'?

So, in the interest of the growth of the life of God in the soul of man, the first thing we need to do is to have a clearing out. Think for a moment of the labour, the toil, the sweat (almost tears sometimes!) required to cleanse a plot of ground, or a garden which has been left to the weeds! You could hardly believe that so many seeds of so many different kinds of growth could be in that soil, that you perhaps dug, and raked, and sought to cleanse. Alas, the strength of them takes all the nourishment out of the soil.

Only God can cleanse our hearts, yet he does so by means of our obedience. We have to obey his commands when he shows us what has got to go if we are to enter into Canaan and enjoy that pleasant land. He shows us what has to be removed from our lives, what has to be hacked off, what has to be pulled up by the roots before the life of Christ can grow in our souls.

I have not the slightest doubt that if we consult the Lord in all sincerity, in an exclusive consultation that permits no one else to be near, that he will tell us what next must be removed from our lives to give room for the seed and life of God to grow in our souls. As far as human things are concerned we live in the liberty of the Spirit and not in the bondage of the law. Yet, in one sense, our lives need to become narrower and narrower. This is possible only by facing and accepting this fact that Christ can grow within us and possess us more and more, and consume us with holy desire to be like him and serve him.

This must be. Why? The end of this is a life that is delivered from all carnality, all this-worldliness, delivered from yielding any ground to Satan and his demons in our lives at all, absolutely delivered from all evil; yet not delivered from humanity, for the Christ who changes us to be like himself is a man forever. Humanity does not go, but the sinfulness of it must go. And so, since the end is that we are to become perfect, spiritual men and women, with perfect spiritual bodies, we should work toward that end by letting our life on the horizontal level grow less important to us, and that of the spiritual more.

Will this not make us more narrow-minded? No! Except in the best and necessary sense. It will make us more broad and deep minded. We shall become more human; and yet our minds will become so set on the one thing, the life of Christ in the soul and his purposes for coming to us, redeeming us and sanctifying us, that there will be literally no time for anything else. We will do our duty in the world and do it faithfully, and do it well, better than we have ever done it before; but we will have a new preoccupation. You have seen people who are completely preoccupied and possessed by an idea, or by a friendship, or an association, or a love affair. They go to work, they eat their food, they do all the things that other people do; but you can see in their faces, you can sense about their lives that there is one dominant thing – the one I love. This is it.

Now, our Lord Jesus Christ is jealous; he wants us for himself, and he will have us for himself. And all I am trying to emphasise here is the necessity of working upon that principle, accepting the fact of it, and acting upon it, day by day. We need room to grow, not merely room to exist. A plant must grow. A life must grow.

Then, secondly, we require nourishment. If you push any figure too far, it breaks down, we know that; but we can perhaps push this a little bit further, and do so in the words of this same, godly scholar. He says about the third and fourth categories of soil: 'The land contains in itself the elements needed for the nourishment and growth of the plant; and hence, the great thing for man to do is to bring together those mutually adapted things. God has made the seed for the soil, and the soil for the seed, and they are made to fit one another . . . in the spiritual realm there is the same adaptation of the truth (the truth of God, his holy Word) to the spirit of man. The mind of man is related to the truth, as the soil to the seed.' Do you understand this? The mind of man is related to the truth! God has made man so that when his Holy Spirit comes upon him, the bodily and spiritual life of man is a fitting place in which to set the seed of the word and truth of God. There is no point in putting it in a pig, or in a tree! There is no point, in a sense (although this is a different story), in putting it in an angel; but in a man. The mind of man is related to the truth as the soil to the seed. I think we need to know this, because too often we take wisps of the Word of God, and we weave our own fancies with them until we really begin to think that the life of God in our souls is an alien, foreign, uncomfortable, embarrassing thing. But it certainly is not!

All the trust of man in the greatness and prevalence of the truth is warranted by this fact alone, that the mind of man is related to the truth as the soil to the seed. The mind is adapted to truth as the eye to the light. This single fact creates the confidence shown by Jesus in

the ultimate establishment of his kingdom, even through us thrawn
sinners, in spite of the obstacles which obstruct its progress.

And so to continue the figure – the seed is made to germinate and
put forth its shoots and grow, as it gets room and is nourished. But,
careful here! For certain kinds of nourishment, it may be by tears and
prayers, it may be by holy enough desire, may nourish weeds that
still remain in the soil; thus we find that we are nourishing weeds, as
well as nourishing the soil.

What do I mean by that? There are some people who are
apparently so incurably worldly, who will, and can see things only
from a worldly, material, earthly point of view. If they come under the
sound of the Word, and they often do, they try to channel all the
promises of divine blessing into carnal ways, the fulfilling of their
earthly desires. 'God's blessing', they say, and some are quite bold
about this, 'God's blessing is seen in my earthly prosperity, and my
health, and the loveliness of my children, and how well they do at
school, and how well they do at college' and all that kind of thing.
You may say, 'Weeds? Do you call that weeds?' Some of them may
be. You remember what Jesus said to those that would follow him,
'If any come after me and hate not father, and mother, brother, or
sister, he cannot be my disciple' (Lk. 14:26).

There must be room for the seed of God to grow, and nothing else
must be allowed to rival it. Here is what James says: 'You ask, and
receive not because you ask amiss' (not in a sense that you ask for
the wrong things, but you ask them for the wrong reasons). 'You
ask that ye may consume it upon your lusts' (Jas. 4:3).

One of the most penetrating things in the Word of God is in
Hebrews 4:11,12, where the writer speaks about the Word of God
penetrating between our religious soulishness – our sanctimonious
piousness which simply sanctifies our carnality and our worldliness
– penetrating between that and the spirit, between the soul and the
spirit. James' words do precisely that: 'You ask amiss that ye may
consume it on your desires.' No, the life of God in the soul of man is
a new creation; and it is a new creation that is to take up our lives
more and more, until the whole shall be consumed, and shines with
resurrection glory when Christ comes. It therefore needs room and

nourishment in order to grow. It needs – and here we break away from this figure – it needs bread. But what sort of bread can feed the life of God in the soul of man? Would you feed him with husks? Oh, no! The only feeding adequate for the life of God in the soul of man is his own precious Word that he gave, the Word incarnate, Jesus Christ. The Word that comes to birth in our lives can be fed only by his own precious Word made soluble by the tears and prayers of his people, so that it is able to be absorbed into the whole life of the soul as the bread of God.

A word or two should be said about that. In 1 Timothy 4:6 Paul speaks about Timothy being nourished up in the words of the faith, meaning the body of teaching. In fact he goes on to say this, 'Being nourished up in the words of the faith and the good teaching whereunto thou hast attained or followed.' This alone – once we have given the life of God in our souls room to grow by progressively removing all that would hinder – this is the great essential for true growth and nourishment, the Word of God made acceptable by the prayers of God's people.

Peter also speaks about this at the end of his second epistle. After talking about the day of the coming of God, he says: 'Nevertheless, we, according to his promise, look for new heavens and a new earth wherein dwelleth righteousness; wherefore, beloved, seeing that you look for such things, be diligent that you may be found of him in peace, without spot, blameless. And account that the long suffering of our Lord is salvation, even as our beloved brother Paul also, according to the wisdom given unto him by the word, hath written to you, as also in all his epistles speaking in them of these things, in which are some things hard to be understood which they that are unlearned in the word (of unstable moral or spiritual character) wrest (or tear) as they do also the other Scriptures unto their own destruction. You, therefore beloved, seeing you know these things before, beware lest you also, being led away with the error of the wicked, fall from your own steadfastness. (Keep your eye on Christ. He is your life, which is hid with Christ in God.) But grow in the grace and knowledge of our Lord and Saviour Jesus Christ' (2 Peter 3:13-18).

Now, let me ask a question. What is the essence of this food, this bread of the Word? We call the Word of God the bread of God; we seek to feed and nourish our own and one another's souls on the bread of God. What is the essence of it? What is the essence of the Word of God? What is the essence of the Bible? You know what is coming! It is all the blessed potencies of the death and resurrection of Jesus Christ ministered to us. It is the outworking together in one, blessed, dual, composite operation that is continuous and progressive – the outworking of the fruits of the death and resurrection of Jesus Christ in our souls. The life of God in the soul of man is the death and resurrection of Jesus Christ in the soul of man, nothing less. What is its effect? It is what Paul speaks of objectively in Romans 8:4, 'walking in the Spirit and not in the flesh.'

Look at what this meant for Paul, sitting but not languishing in prison in Rome. In Philippians 1:20 he talks about the possibility of his being arraigned before Nero and being condemned to death and martyred. That possibility apparently hung over him every day. 'According to my earnest expectation and my hope that in nothing I shall be ashamed; but that with all boldness as always, so now also Christ shall be magnified in my body, whether it be by life, or by death; for to me, to live is Christ and to die is gain.' Have you got that angle on life yet? You will never be a Christian until you get it. You must live there. 'For me to live is Christ and to die is gain. But if I live in the body,' he says, 'it will be in order that I can be fruitful.' So he says, 'I am torn between two. I want to go and be with Christ. I would far rather go and be with Christ; but if, for me, to live in this body is Christ, then I can be of use to others, even to you, Philippians. Therefore', he says, 'I am in a dilemma. I don't know which to choose. I have a desire to depart and be with Christ, which is far better; nevertheless, to abide in the flesh is more needful for you.'

That is what it meant to him. You say, 'But he was in extreme circumstances'. If we are Christians, we are all in extreme circumstances. We are living to God, having to give account for our every moment once the breath of God has entered into our lives. If we do not know this it is because our eyes are too blind to the heavenly realm. There is not such a damnable sin amongst Christians as such complacency. Our hearts should be burning. Look at the need in our land! Yet we Christians are sitting fat and sleek. It is all wrong.

Is what Paul says in 1 Corinthians 3:1 true of us? 'I could not speak to you brethren, as to spiritual, but as to carnal, even as to babes in Christ.' Now, let me translate what he means by that. 'I could not speak to you as grown-up Christians, spiritual men, but only as babes'; because you were only newly converted – babes in Christ. Newborn Christians cannot be grown up at once! He goes on: 'Indeed I have fed you with milk and not with meat' (v. 2) – and that is fair enough for babies. You do not give babies solid food. The problem is that now, when you are grown old in years and experience, having been Christians one year, or five, or fifteen, or perhaps thirty, or more, you still are not able to bear it. You are still babies, grown-up babies!

The writer to the Hebrews says the same thing (Heb. 5:12 - 6:1): 'Considering the time that you became Christians, you ought to be teachers but you have need that one teach you again the very first principles of the oracles of God; and are become such as have need of milk and not of strong meat; for every one that uses milk is unskilful in the word of righteousness, for he is a babe; but strong meat belongs to them that are of full age, even those who by reason of use, have their senses exercised to discern both good and evil. Therefore leaving the first principles of the doctrine of Christ, let us go on to full growth.'

And where will that growth be most clearly and publicly manifest? In the quality of our service to our fellows, so that our love of Christ will be seen. For the quality of that love is a death and resurrection love. It is a love in, and for Christ, utterly different from any merely carnal love, however noble and sacrificial.

May God help us to begin, and more and more to be brave enough to live like this; for if we love, it will cost. It is going to hurt some of us, to make room for the seed to grow. But we must nourish it with prayers so we may grow up to the glory of God and our fruitfulness in the world.

THE HOLY SPIRIT

1: The Holy Trinity

Our subject is the third Person of the Trinity: the Holy Spirit. The three Persons of the blessed eternal Trinity are God the Father, God the Son and God the Holy Spirit.

But then God, meaning the Godhead, the three in one God is Spirit. Jesus says so, speaking to the woman at the well in John 4:24: 'God is a Spirit.'

Now what does this mean? Are all three Persons Spirit, and if so, how is the third Person different? Listen to what the *Westminster Confession of Faith* says, 'There is but one only living and true God who is infinite in being and perfection, a most pure Spirit, invisible, without body, parts, or passions.' The first article of the Thirty-Nine Articles of the Church of England uses the same words, when it says that there is 'one only living and true God who is infinite in being and perfection, a most pure Spirit, invisible, without body, parts or passions'.

Similarly, the *Westminster Larger Catechism* says, 'God is a Spirit, in and of Himself infinite in being.'

But, if God is a Spirit, in what distinctive sense do we say that there is the Father, and the Son, and the Holy Spirit? Listen to what a godly Professor in the United States says about this: 'Since God is said to be Spirit (John 4:24) the whole Trinity has been thought of by some in terms of spirit. This has tended to cloud the distinction between the Spirit, the Father and the Son. Moreover to speak, as some do, of the Spirit as the relation of love between the Father and the Son, or further to define the Spirit as the living action of God in the world, while emphasising a valuable yet partial truth nevertheless tends to depersonalise the Spirit and to reduce him to an influence or force.'

Now, the word for 'Spirit', which of course is simply the word for 'breath' in the Greek of the New Testament, is neuter. In a sense it is unfortunate that this is so. And of course the symbols that the Scripture uses for the Holy Spirit like fire, water, breath, oil, are all sub-human and inanimate things. But the Spirit himself cannot be neuter, even though in the Authorised Version if you were to look at Romans and other places you would see the Spirit spoken of as 'it'. That is a great mistake. Spirit in symbols of breath and water, fire and oil and so on may be neuter, he himself is not neuter for he is the third Person of the Godhead.

If God, meaning the Godhead, Father, Son and Spirit, is Spirit, as Jesus says – in what sense do you distinguish between the Father Spirit and the Holy Spirit? It is important to think about this. I want to delve as deeply into this as I can as an introduction to very practical matters. But I want our application of biblical truth to practical matters to be on the grounds of a really profound study of the whole subject. We may have greater light on this later on and it is just possible we may need it, and surely if we do God will give it.

Perhaps a partial answer to the distinction there must be between Father, Son and Holy Spirit is this. If there are three Persons in the Trinity and the Godhead is Spirit, there must be a distinction between the Father Spirit and Son Spirit (if you like) and the one who is called the Holy Spirit. There would seem to be a necessity for one to be the head of what I like to call the heavenly domestic family of the Trinity. Every house needs to have a head. We learn that from the Scriptures and also from experience of human life. The eternal God who has been forever was a family before the world was created. For that reason the theologians say that God is sufficient in himself, and has no need of any of his creatures. He is sufficient in himself because the Godhead is a family in which the members are always communicating with one another. So in John 17 our Lord tells us about the love that there was between the Father and the Son in eternity before the world began. The world of the Godhead was a world of inter-communication, a divine eternal world before anything was thought of. The three Persons were communicating with one another in love, whether we think of the Holy Spirit as the love between the Father and Son or not.

Did there need to be a 'head' of that 'family'? If we think of that simply from human analogy, we may be misled. Let me give you one or two wisps of Scripture that suggest this is so, that the Father must be the Father and there can be no violation, nor was there any danger of any violation, of the Father's headship by the Son or the Holy Spirit; because they were in perfect agreement and accepted their place, their status and their functions. The Son was glad to be the Son and did not want to be the Father; the Holy Spirit was glad to be the Holy Spirit and did not want to be either the Father or the Son. How different from us! It is part of the sickness of human nature that we want to be other than we are. And in doing so you see we insult God who says, 'I want you to be yourself, if you please! I do not want you to be anybody else. You be your best self and that will please me.' And there is nobody higher to please or better. In the Trinity, then, all three Persons were perfectly satisfied with their role and station.

Listen to this from 1 Corinthians 3:23: 'Christ is God's.' He is God's Christ. Does that suggest possession? Just as if you were sitting next to your son or your daughter, and could put your arm round them and say, 'John is mine. Mary is mine.' Just like that, Christ is God's. Similarly, Paul says in 1 Corinthians 11:3, 'The head of Christ is God.' The head is God. Or take the resurrection chapter, 1 Corinthians 15:24. Paul here has been talking about 'each in his own order: Christ the first fruits, then at his coming those who belong to Christ, then comes the end (after the great day of our resurrection and the outshining of Christ) when he (Christ) delivers the kingdom to God the Father.' I often think about this. You read very little about it, even in the book of Revelation. Yet this is one of the ultimate truths in the whole Bible. 'Then comes the end when he delivers the kingdom to God the Father after destroying every rule and every authority and power. For he must reign until he has put all his enemies under his feet. But when it says (in the quotation from Ps. 8:6) "all things are put in subjection under him" it is plain that he, God, is excepted who put all things under him. When all things are subjected to him, then the Son himself will also be subjected to him who put all things under him that God may be all in all.'

Notice one thing more here. Here is what the *Westminster Confession of Faith* says, 'In the unity of the Godhead there be three Persons of one substance, power and eternity: God the Father, God the Son and God the Holy Ghost. The Father is from none (he is the first), neither begotten nor proceeding.' Here is a hint about the Son and a hint about the Spirit: 'The Son is eternally begotten of the Father.' There was no time when there was the Father without the Son. He is eternally begotten, he is always the Son. He is eternally born of the Father. That is the nearest you can get to sense in discussing something so transcendent as that. Then we read of 'the Holy Spirit eternally proceeding from the Father and from the Son'.

And this is what Article Five of the Thirty-Nine Articles says about the Holy Spirit, 'The Holy Ghost proceeding from the Father and the Son is of one substance, majesty and glory with the Father and the Son, being very and eternal God.'

There is another aspect of this great mystery we must explore. The Creeds and Confessions of the Church use the word 'invisible' when speaking about God. And of course 'spirit' (*pneuma*, wind or spirit) is invisible; no one has ever seen the wind. Jesus discusses that with Nicodemus. But why should God be invisible? Is it something superior to the visible and the tangible, the substantial and the material? Is there something inherently and intrinsically superior to being invisible than being visible? Or must the visible, the tangible, the palpable be less enduring or durable than the invisible? Is it not exasperating that the eternal God is so invisible to us?

The writer to the Hebrews says that from the invisible God made the visible (Heb. 11:3). Is the invisible then intrinsically superior to the visible? Or is the nature of ultimate reality more mysterious than we would have thought? Or has the Fall blinded us? Is God visible to the angels and not to the fallen men? You see what I am asking. Is it the Fall that has blinded us? God and man were apparently in happy fellowship in the Garden of Eden before the Fall. But after the first sin Adam did not want to see God and hid from him.

This is the most we can say about it. For fallen creatures it is hard to believe in an invisible spirit, either good or evil. Most people actually find it harder to believe in an evil invisible spirit than in a good invisible spirit. Far more people in the world, it seems to me, believe in God than believe in the Devil – I mean believe that he exists. If it is partly something to do with our fallenness that spirit is so invisible to us, is this to teach us dependence and faith? Doubtless it is. Because you see thereafter, right through the pages from Genesis chapter 3:15 onwards we have a progressive revelation of God in which God reveals himself to man.

Turn for a moment to another area. Think of some of the names that God uses to reveal himself. The first name we have is in the very first verse of the Bible where it says, 'In the beginning God created the heavens and the earth.' The word for God there is Elohim, which expresses the notion of absolute power, and some people think there is a suggestion of the Trinity here, because the word has a plural form (indicated by its ending *im*), the manifoldness as well as the absoluteness of the power of the Almighty.

Later on in Exodus 3:14 God reveals himself to man as Jehovah, or Yahweh. And God himself gives a definition of what that means. He says it means 'I am that I am', although some people say it should be in the future, 'I shall be what I shall be'. 'I am that I am.' That is the next revelation. First, that he is absolute power, manifoldness if you accept that the plural form *elohim* is really significant; secondly 'I am that I am', that is to say Jehovah, the God of the Jews, not merely Elohim, the general word for God in use in other religions. God says 'I am your God.'

Then we also have God called 'the Lord' – Adonai. This of course is sprinkled all over the Old Testament, from Genesis on. It refers to the Lord in relation to other persons, in personal relationship.

Let us run on, although in a sense it is back. In Genesis 17:1 God reveals himself to Abraham as El Shaddai – God Almighty, God All-sufficient. He reveals himself in the encounter with Melchizedek as

El Elyon – the Most High God. In Genesis 21:33, he is the Everlasting God – El Olam. This is at the time of the covenant between Abraham and Abimelech at Beersheba. In Genesis 16:13, God revealed himself to the poor Egyptian, Hagar, thrown out from Abraham's household: 'Thou God seest me.' What a wonderful revelation of God to that poor bedraggled thrown-out lassie that was!

Then in Genesis 22:14 he is Jehovah-jireh – the Lord will provide (remember the ram at Mount Moriah). He is Jehovah-rapha, the Lord that healed, at the waters of Marah (Exodus 15:26); or, Jehovah-nissi, the Lord my Banner – where Moses' hands were held up in the battle with Amalek. He is also Jehovah-shalom, the Lord as Peace, or the Lord sending Peace as Gideon named the altar he built after seeing the angel (Judges 6:24). Jehovah-tsidkenu (Jeremiah 23:6) – the Lord our Righteousness, the robe of our righteousness in which we will stand before God the Father and be accepted in heaven's glory. Lastly, Jehovah-shammah, (Ezekiel 48:35) – Ezekiel's vision of the New Jerusalem: the Lord is there.

So, you see, in all these names God is progressively revealing himself, from the invisible to the perceptible to those minds and hearts that are open to see the invisible. This is why God is invisible, so that he may be seen and known only by those whose eyes of faith have been opened.

Before we go on to speak more specifically of the Holy Spirit, here are some further words from this most wonderful passage in the *Confession of Faith*. It says, of God and the Holy Trinity, 'There is but one only living and true God who is infinite in being and perfection, a most pure Spirit, invisible, without body, parts or passions, immutable (unchangeable), immense, eternal, incomprehensible (he cannot be fully explored), Almighty, most wise, most holy, most free, most absolute, working all things according to the counsel of his own immutable and most righteous will for his own glory, (here see the progression of his revelation) most loving, gracious, merciful, long suffering, abundant in goodness and truth, forgiving iniquity, transgression and sin (these are simply different definitions of sin), the rewarder of them that diligently seek him and withal most just and terrible in his judgments, hating all sin and who will by no means clear the guilty. God hath all life, glory, goodness, blessedness, in and of himself and is alone in and unto himself all sufficient, not standing in need of any creatures which he has made, nor deriving any glory from them but only manifesting his own glory in them, by them, to them, and upon them. He is the alone (that is the sole) Fountain of all being from whom, through whom, and to whom are all things, and hath most sovereign dominion over them to do by them, for them or upon them whatsoever himself pleases. In his sight all things are open and manifest. His knowledge is infinite, infallible and independent upon the creature so as nothing is to him contingent or uncertain. He is most holy in all his counsels, in all his works and in all his commands. To him is due from angels and men and every other creature whatsoever worship, service or obedience he is pleased to require of them.'

That grand statement is completed by the following, 'In the unity of the Godhead there be three Persons of one substance, power and eternity: God the Father, God the Son and God the Holy Spirit. The Father is from none, neither begotten nor proceeding, the Son is eternally begotten from the Father and the Holy Spirit eternally proceeding from the Father and from the Son.'

Now let us turn to the fact of the equality of the three Persons of the Trinity. The Fifth article of the Thirty-Nine Articles of the Church of England speaks in terms similar to the *Westminster Confession* of 'The Holy Ghost proceeding from the Father and the Son' as 'of one substance, majesty and glory with the Father and the Son, very and eternal God'. Similarly, the *Larger Catechism* says, 'There be three Persons in the Godhead, the Father, the Son and the Holy Spirit and these three are one true, eternal God, the same in substance, equal in power and glory although distinguished by their personal properties.'

In the light of these things, there is a fascinating statement in John 10:29,30. Jesus says, 'My Father who has given them (that is his sheep) to me is greater than all and no one is able to snatch them out of the Father's hand.' Now, here Christ is owning the Headship, the greatness of his Father, but he also says in the next sentence, 'I and the Father are one.' He is greater, yet, 'I and the Father are one.' What does it mean? That and many other scriptures I could give to you indicate to us that the Son is equally God in power, glory, majesty and eternity with the Father and with the Spirit. You see there is nothing in the wide world that is as practical for a Christian as that, because the Holy Spirit not only brings God the Father and brings God the Son, but *is* himself God the Holy Spirit in your breast if you are a believer. That is the first thing, the equality of the Holy Spirit with the Son and the Father.

Does this not make the line from the hymn, 'Think what Spirit dwells within thee' take on fresh meaning? There is nothing so edifying for a Christian as to think on who the Holy Spirit is within him. It is the most edifying and elevating thing you can think of. You can think about it until it almost frightens you with the majesty and the glory of it.

But there is something further to notice. The Holy Spirit is not an influence. He is not a breath, even though he is spoken of in human language in that way. You can have more wind or less wind. You can have more water or less, more oil or less. All these symbols of the Holy Spirit can be spoken of quantitatively. But, of course, we must realise that these are only symbols. They should not be understood in a flat, literalistic fashion.

If the Holy Spirit is a person, as a person he is absolutely indivisible. You must never, never talk of the Holy Spirit in terms of measure and quantity. We have to be exceedingly cautious, for he is a person and he is either all present, as to his person, or he is not present at all.

Mind you, that can be difficult when we think of God's complete self-giving of himself to his creatures. Yet we must preserve the clear distinction that the Holy Spirit is a person. And what a person! I have said that he is equal with the Son and with the Father, and while you could mistakenly imagine the successive Persons of the Trinity each being regarded as less than the former, yet think of the onus that is upon the Holy Spirit. If he is to bring God the Father and God the Son into our lives. What a burden! He needs equality with the Father to bear it.

I think we can put it like this: think of the burden that was Christ's. It was first given to Christ to represent God in man. It was first given to him to be seed in the woman's womb, and then the infant in the manger, the child and the boy. Think of his wisdom at the age of twelve, his 'grown-upness', his penetrating understanding of who his Father was and his filial duty and love to him, right on to thirty – what progress Christ must have made! That was a long apprenticeship: thirty years for three. And then in his three years of public ministry, and his dying, to bear the full responsibility of showing the immortal, the eternal, and invisible God to men. God was in Christ reconciling the world – what it must have cost, the strain of it! And if I may say so, think of the double strain to the Holy Spirit. You see this great strain to the Holy Spirit scarcely began until Pentecost, because it was then that he came to indwell believers with the very life of God the Father and to bring to bear upon man's life the whole work of Christ the Son.

Writing to the Galatians, Paul says, 'Because you are sons God has sent the Spirit of his Son into your hearts crying, Abba, Father.' Look at Romans 8:26. 'Likewise the Spirit helps us in our weakness . . . we do not know how to pray as we ought but the Spirit himself intercedes for us with sighs too deep for words and he (undoubtedly God from the context) who searches the hearts of men knows what is the mind of the Spirit because the Spirit intercedes for the saints according to the will of God' – in perfect agreement with him and full understanding of the Father.

Now proceed from that to 1 Corinthians 2:10-11, which says that 'the Spirit searches everything, even the depths of God. So also no one comprehends the thoughts of God except the Spirit of God.' This must be the most practical thing in the world for Christians!

Perhaps you have been converted for only a week or two, a month or two. Dear one, God Almighty who made the heavens and the earth, and his Son who became man and died on the cross and spilt his human blood for our salvation and was raised on the third day by the Father and ascended to heaven to sit at his right hand and rule over all worlds and put down all evil spirits and powers – he is within you. You have him in your breast. He has come to dwell in you and join with your spirit which he quickens into life. You have received eternal life, and become a partaker of the divine nature. You do not become God, but God gives himself completely to his believing chosen creatures.

The New Testament never confuses our relationship with the Father and the unique relationship his Son has with him. When Jesus gives us the Lord's Prayer he does not stand and say with us, 'Our Father'. If Jesus were personally, corporeally present with us and we all began, 'Our Father', he would have to say, 'My Father and their Father', because he is God the Son, and we are the sons of God by adoption. Yet he pours himself out and gives us the fulness of his being so that we might be partakers of his divine nature. And that is the glory of the Christian faith and life, and always will be, even if you live to be a hundred, 'Think what Spirit dwells within you', says Henry Francis Lyte (in his hymn 'Jesus, I my cross have taken'). Think that, and it will change you. Never forget that the Spirit is a person; he does not come and go. He is grieved when we sin, but he does not run away. He stays, personally stays, and lives. You will never be able to have more of him than you had at the beginning, (although his gifts are another story – to which we will return in due course). He himself is the seal of our salvation, and he stands guard over our lives and keeps the enemy at bay. If you are regenerate, he is present. He is present in person to stay forever, and after you are dead he will guard your dust and bring you a resurrection body when Christ comes. 'Think what Spirit dwells within you.' And worship him! Worship him and think of your value to God.

I sometimes see the look of infinite love and care and concern in the eyes of a young husband for his dear one with child and I can imagine what he is thinking: 'Ours', he is saying, 'our child. She's carrying our child.' Think of it, you are carrying God's Spirit. Oh, worship him!

THE HOLY SPIRIT

2: New Birth

We have already pointed out that the Holy Spirit must be equal with the Father and the Son, because it was he who had to bear the communication between God and man.

There lay a heavy burden on Christ to reveal the Godhead perfectly and fully to men. How much greater, in a sense, was the responsibility of the Holy Spirit, to do all that and in addition to reveal to men fully the life and the work of the Redeemer! His task was to communicate to men not only a true revelation of God the Father but of God the Son, to communicate to them all the fruit of the Son's work in redemption.

We think too often of the Holy Spirit as if he were some quantitative essence of which we can have more or less. That is one of the biggest mistakes that is made in the Christian church. One or two verses in John's Gospel are very illuminating in this connection. In John 14:18, Jesus is speaking about the coming of the Holy Spirit. Perhaps his appearance after the resurrection is also in view, but surely it is more probable that he is pointing forward to the coming of the Holy Spirit. Certainly he is in v. 23.

'I will not leave you desolate (orphans). I will come to you.' You say, 'That is the Holy Spirit?' Yes, but it is the Holy Spirit of Christ himself. It is *his other self*. He explains this further in John 14:23. Oh, this is rich. Jesus is answering their questions, 'Lord, how is it that you will manifest yourself to us and not to the world? And Jesus answered . . . . If a man loves me he will keep my word and my

Father will love him and we will come to him and make our home with him.' You see? Not only will Jesus' other self come, but the Father as well! In a sense the entire Trinity is in view here, but we are looking at Christ's other self, and thinking about the Holy Spirit as a person.

Later, in John 14:28, Jesus says, 'You heard me say to you, I go away and I will come to you . . . I go to the Father, for the Father is greater than I . . . Believe . . .'. Here again, he is speaking about the Holy Spirit coming to the church.

The Holy Spirit is Christ's other self. He is a person and indivisible, and he comes in his personality to the individual believer. We receive the whole Spirit. We do not have all his gifts. Jesus is the only one who has a monopoly of the gifts of the Holy Spirit. They are only given without measure to the Son, but we have, if we have him at all, the whole of the Holy Spirit.

It is in this glorious context that we come to consider the question of the new birth, birth by the Holy Spirit. Christians are born of God, born of the Spirit of Jesus. Think of that for a moment, born of God, becoming sons and daughters of God! Let me put this before you. How can God give himself to his creatures, yet retain his deity inviolate ? We do not become God by being born of God, born from above of the Holy Spirit of Jesus Christ. We remain creatures, and yet we *are* born of God and *do* become sons of God. How can it be that God gives himself by Christ and the Holy Spirit *personally*? It is not something passing from him to us, but he comes himself and says 'Here, I have come to stay.' The Father and the Son and the Holy Spirit come, as it were, in a trio, a Trinity, and say, 'We have come to stay' (Jn. 14:23). Yet God retains his deity, and we do not become God.

Peter tries to express it by saying that we become partakers of the divine nature (2 Pet. 1:4). Paul expresses the same thing like this, 'Now, we have received, not the spirit of the world but the Spirit (capital S) which is from God, that we might understand the gift bestowed on us by God' (1 Cor. 2:12). You see? When we become partakers of the divine nature it means that we can understand godly things. We can understand what the Father and the Son and the Holy Spirit were discussing in eternity before the world began – not it all, but we can understand it and when it is revealed in his Word it makes sense as far as we understand it. We begin to understand his language. Our minds are not blinded. The Holy Spirit opens our eyes to understand what God is talking about. And the only way to understand is to be a Christian.

In John 20:17, where Jesus, speaking to Mary Magdalene after his resurrection, says, 'I go to my Father and to your Father,' he did not say to Mary Magdalene, 'I go to our Father.' He calls God, 'Father.' She calls God, 'Father'. But there is a difference. They are not standing on the same platform, because he is God and she is not and never shall be.

It would appear that in coming to man and becoming incarnate in human flesh, God created what we can only call, in our weak, frail way, a tension within himself. Some people think there are strains of tension between judgment and mercy within God, and it would seem so, although God is so great that he is able to contain all that. But we may still think in our human terms of a tension between God as Judge and God as merciful Saviour. Well, I am suggesting a tension within the Godhead as to how far he is to go in creating and redeeming men to be a bride for his Son. True man is made in the image of God – and I believe that is the image of his eternal Son, the prototype of man. But to make of man a bride for his Son is one thing; to dignify her with his own nature is another. So he can speak of himself as our elder brother! I do not like to use these terms too frequently lest they seem too casual and familiar, yet they are there in Hebrews 2 and hinted at in other places. That God should send his eternal Son to earth as a man, and speak of him as our elder brother – that is the modesty, the humility of the eternal Son. He comes and sits among us as one of us. It is one thing to make man, redeemed man, the bride of his Son, but it is another thing, it is almost unbelievable, that God should dignify him with his own nature.

Or take another problem. If you look at 1 Corinthians 6:17 you will see there that Paul says, 'He that is joined to the Lord is one spirit with him.' This is one of the most extraordinary statements in the New Testament. One spirit? Our spirit joined with his Spirit? I suppose there are bound to be certain limits to that, because we remain creatures and God is God. I am sure it is possible to exaggerate it. But I am simply pointing out and trying to grasp what the Scriptures are saying. How can a Creator-spirit be joined to a creature spirit and be called 'one spirit'? How can God so accommodate himself in his Spirit – that Spirit who carries the Father and the Son and all his work? How can the Spirit of God come and inhabit my spirit and quicken it into life? How can he accommodate himself to my poor, humble home?

Some thoughts such as these ought to give weight to our consideration of the new birth and give a greater dignity to our conception of being born of God, to deepen our understanding and give it weight. Is it not C.S. Lewis who says that 'Spirit is heavier than matter'? Paul speaks about a 'weight of glory'. What we are trying to do is to weigh something of the heaviness of this idea of the new birth.

Now, let us be simple, if it is really simple to turn to John's Gospel. (It is simple in a rather deceptive way!) In John 3 we are told how Nicodemus came to Jesus by night and said to him, 'Rabbi (teacher) we know that you are a teacher come from God; for no one can do these signs that you do, unless God is with him.' We should remember at this point of course that the other fellow (Satan) can do signs, very wonderful and miraculous signs too, so Jesus Christ does not set much store by signs and miracles and wonders. Anyway this is what Nicodemus said and Jesus almost contradicts him. He certainly confronts him. You see the man began very graciously. He had crept through the night, stealing round the corners, hoping he would not meet any of the rest of the Sanhedrin. 'Sh . . . ', he whispered, 'Rabbi, we know. . . . ' That is to say, 'See how much I am conceding to you, Jesus. I respect you and regard you as a wonderful teacher sent from God.' And Jesus graciously but faithfully brushed the whole thing aside and said, 'You must be born from above, Nicodemus.' That is to say, he did not answer the implied question. Instead he answered the need of Nicodemus' heart. He said, 'What your little mind needs to know, Nicodemus, is that you need to be born again.' That is how Jesus, you see, flies to the point, with an unerring rapier thrust. This is why people do not like him, because he speaks the truth. But if it is a cutting, thrusting, painful truth it is a healing and saving one too. 'Oh,' he says, 'Nicodemus, leave all that out. Let us save hours of argument. Come to the point. Let us begin at the end, Nicodemus. You must be born from above or you cannot see the kingdom of God.'

'How?', he asks. Jesus says, 'Keep to the point. You must be born from above. You are not going to confuse the two, Nicodemus. You are not so silly as to be puzzled about being born again and going into your mother's womb a second time. You have more sense than that Nicodemus. You are not a fool. And you are not trying to be funny. You are not a comic. You are not trying to trip me up either. You are asking quite sincerely, but can you not think a little more deeply than that? Don't be at all surprised, Nicodemus. Come on, use your head. Isn't the Spirit of God dealing with you at all Nicodemus? Don't you know that you wouldn't have come to see me tonight if it hadn't been for the Spirit of God drawing you? You must be born from above. It is like the wind'. And he goes on, 'Are you a teacher in Israel and you don't know these things? We are talking about what we *know*, and bear witness to what we have *seen.*'

But what had he seen? He tells us in John 17:22. 'The glory which thou hast given me (says Jesus to his Father in prayer) I have given to them, that they may be one even as we are one. I in them and thou in me . . . .' We find here the same thing as in the 14th chapter, the personal-ness of the coming of Jesus and the blessed communion of Father, Son and Holy Spirit in the believer. And all this comes by the new birth. By the new birth comes the homely Jesus to dwell in our hearts.

Let us move on to the fact of his indwelling Spirit. Paul says in Romans 8:9, 'But you are not in the flesh, you are in the Spirit if the Spirit of God really dwells in you.' Now, this does not mean that we cease to be human, it means that the old self has been done away, as Paul says in chapter 6:6. You are not merely a fallen, fleshly creature; you are in the Spirit – if the Spirit of God really dwells in you; and the Spirit of God will give life to your mortal flesh. If Christ is in you, although the body is dead, the Spirit is alive because of righteousness (Rom. 8:10-11). Christ by his Spirit comes to dwell in our hearts. The new birth involves the homeliness of the coming of Jesus Christ, by his Spirit, into our hearts.

Paul talks about both the fact of the indwelling Spirit, and then its result. He says in Romans 8:14-16: 'For all who are led by the Spirit of God are sons of God,' (this is the proof) 'for you did not receive the spirit of slavery to fall back into fear but you have received the spirit of sonship which makes you cry "Abba, Father",' like a new-born babe. So 'the Spirit himself bears witness with our spirit that we are the children of God.' That is to say, 'He that is joined to the Lord is one spirit.' His Spirit comes in and quickens my spirit, and they interlock. They interlock eternally. Now there must be a distinction because there is a created spirit and there is Creator Spirit, but they are one and they are inseparable, even in death.

Galatians 4:6 has something to say about that. 'But when the time was fully come, God sent forth his Son, born of a woman, born under the law, to redeem those who were under the law so that we might receive adoption as sons, and because you are sons God has sent the Spirit of his Son' (his only-begotten Son) 'into our hearts crying, "Abba! Father!".' As Paul said before, 'It is the Spirit that bears witness within us.' Can I put it like this, very chastely? The babe in our womb leaps and responds. Isn't that what happened to Elizabeth? He cries from within us.

This leads us instantly to Romans 8:23. Not only is the creation groaning, waiting for its redemption, but we ourselves who have the firstfruits of the Spirit groan inwardly as we wait for adoption as sons, the redemption of our bodies. That is to say, the Holy Spirit of Jesus Christ within us is groaning within and he is saying, 'Oh this mortal body, this prison that I am in, this frail house of clay, this tent that is to be taken down when Jesus comes, this poor frail house, this earthen vessel! Oh God, give me a body that I can depend upon.' And Jesus within us, his Spirit working within our spirit, moving our spirit to the depths and making us speak out, says, 'Oh God, when, *when* shall I have my immortal body?'

That leads us in turn to Romans 8:26,27, 'Likewise the Spirit also helps us in our weakness', for he *understands* all about this. How does he understand? Because, you see, the Spirit of God in Jesus Christ must have groaned like this at his human limitations, although he gladly accepted them and played fair and lived within them! So the

Spirit groans within us, for we do not know how to pray as we ought but we depend upon the Spirit.

One of the things we often say when we gather together for prayer is this: 'Oh God, give us the spirit of prayer. Unless you give us the spirit of prayer we will only blether.' At such times we have this wonderful promise, 'The Spirit himself intercedes for us with sighs too deep for words' (although he helps us to find words nonetheless). 'He who searches the hearts of men knows what is the mind of the Spirit because the Spirit intercedes for the saints according to the will of God.' Paul is speaking of course about the agreement between the Spirit and the Father.

Here are two things, two results of the new birth of the Holy Spirit of Jesus Christ in our hearts. First, he instantly cries for the Father. For he is the Spirit of the Son, you see. It is the same as Jesus running away before the break of dawn, up that gentle slope on the Mount of the Beatitudes, before it was light, almost stumbling his way up that hill. 'Father, I have a lot to do today. Father, Father, Father.' It is like that; that is the first thing.

Secondly, there is the longing for immortality, the longing for lastingness. Do you know how God called me to the ministry? He spoke to me sitting at the organ stool in the Methodist church where I was organist. I said, 'Oh God, I want to do something with my life that will have lasting significance.'
He said to me, 'I have got the very thing.'
And I said, 'Oh God, not that', because I remembered when I passed some Bible examinations in my schooldays, and my father said to me, 'I see nothing for it, boy, but you'll have to be a minister.'
And I said, 'Oh no, I could never wear one of those collars.'
But it had to be, because I had confessed to the Lord that I wanted him to use me, and it was he who put that desire in my heart. I had confessed to the Lord that I wanted to do something with my life that would go on and on and would last and have ultimate and eternal significance. And this is it. You see the longing for eternity and immortality.

Lastly, in 1 Corinthians 2:6, Paul says to the Corinthians, 'among the mature we do impart wisdom' (although it is not a wisdom of this age or of the rulers, the big-wigs of this age who are doomed to pass away) '. . . secret hidden wisdom of God which God decreed before the ages for our glorification . . . as it is written' (in Isaiah 64:4,65:17) '"What no eye hath seen or ear heard . . . God has prepared for those who love him", God has revealed to us through the Spirit, for the Spirit searches everything, even the depths of God . . . no one comprehends the thoughts of God except the Spirit of God. Now, we have received, not the spirit of the world, but the Spirit which is from God that we might understand the gifts bestowed on us by God and we impart this in words, not taught by human wisdom but taught by the Spirit interpreting spiritual truths to those who possess the Spirit. The unspiritual man does not receive the gifts of the Spirit of God, for they are folly to him and he is not able to understand them because they are spiritually discerned. The spiritual man judges all things but is judged himself by no one. For who has known the mind of the Lord so as to instruct him?' (Is there anybody to put him right?) Then we come to another of the most fabulous statements in the New Testament. 'We have . . . (Can you take it in? Are you ready for a shock?) *We have the mind of Christ.'*

Now, there is more there than I can deal with. This is how deeply the Spirit of God interpenetrates our spirit and our humanity: we have the mind of Christ! This is what lies behind Paul's words in Romans 12:2, 'We are transformed by the renewing of our minds.'

When the Spirit of Jesus Christ, the eternal Son of God, comes to dwell in our lives he enables us to have an affinity with God. He establishes a bond, a kinship. We belong to a new lineage and enjoy an 'at-homeness' with God. The life he comes to bring us (which is his own life) we contain within a creature spirit. It is a life that is congruent, belongs to and grows from his. We belong to the new Adam, the last Adam, who is Christ. The wonder is – I come back to what I said at the beginning – God comes down, and accommodates himself to our humanity and our frailty so that he loves above all things to live in our lives. Do you know that there is nothing you could do for God beyond that? If you had a power beyond God's, let us imagine, to say to God, 'What is the greatest I could do for you?', he would say, 'To let me live in human beings.'

I am reading *The Screwtape Letters* again. It is so long since I read C.S. Lewis' wonderful book about a junior and a senior demon corresponding with one another about how to get at the saints. Here Screwtape is speaking to Wormwood: 'To decide what is the best use of the dryness and the dullness which comes upon your patient (a Christian whom this demon spirit Wormwood is trying to seduce from Christ) when he is in a trough you must ask what use the enemy (of course the whole thing is turned round, and the enemy here is God; it is a satire) wants to make of the man's dullness or dryness and then do the opposite. Now, it may surprise you to learn (says Screwtape) that in his efforts to get permanent possession of a soul our enemy (God) relies on the troughs even more than on the peaks. Some of his special favourites have gone through longer and deeper troughs than anyone else. The reason is this; to us a human is primarily food; our aim is the absorption of its will into ours, the increase of our own area of selfhood at its expense. But the obedience which the enemy demands of men is quite different. One must face the fact that all the talk about his love for men and his service being perfect freedom is not, as one would gladly believe, mere propaganda, but it is an appalling truth.'

Then he says this, 'He does really want to fill the universe with a lot of loathsome little replicas of himself, creatures whose life on its miniature scale will be qualitatively like his own, not because he has absorbed them (this is very penetrating) but because their wills freely conform to his. We want cattle which can finally become food, (says Screwtape) he wants servants who can finally become sons. (Isn't that magnificent?) We want to suck in; he wants to give out. We are empty and would be filled; he is full and flows over. Our war aim is a world in which our father below (the Devil) has drawn other beings into himself. The enemy wants a world full of beings united to him but still distinct.' But more than that he wants to do this in such natural and human terms that he comes to us in Jesus Christ and says, 'Come here to me. Come to me – all you that are full of strain, and who are heavy-laden and burdened, come to me and I will give you rest, relief, refreshment tingling with life. Take my yoke upon you and learn from me, because I am meek and lowly in heart and you shall find rest to your souls, for my yoke. . . (You don't like the word yoke? You say, 'Yoke? – hard labour?' Listen!) my yoke is easy and my burden is light.' 'Come to me and let me come in to you and let me come down and sit at your kitchen table and let us have bread together, and let's wash the dishes together, and let's go to work together and come home together and do everything together' (see Revelation 3:20). That God should come in to us at all is beyond our imagining, but that he should want to live our ordinary lives with us and go to work with us tomorrow morning, I do not begin to understand it, but I just know it is true. This is what the new birth means. Hallelujah!

THE HOLY SPIRIT

3: The Seal of God

Somebody said this to me recently about my preaching, 'The thing that I find most satisfying about all this teaching is that you are constantly dealing with the Trinity.' Now, here is a tip to preachers! If you are dealing with the three Persons of the Trinity you are not only covering the whole range of God's revelation, but you are doing so in a way that is satisfying to the mind as well as comforting and sustaining to the heart.

We are turning now to a further aspect of the work of the triune God in us through his Holy Spirit. Part of the blessing of the indwelling Spirit in the heart of a believer is his eternal security, the assurance of heaven, the confidence that he is really and truly and fully and finally saved. This is ours because the Holy Spirit is the seal of God. Now, sometimes in the New Testament the word 'seal' is used along with the word 'guarantee'. There are many words we could use for that. But one of the best translations of it is the Scots word 'arles'. 'Arles' is a word that was used by those who were involved with the Scottish fisher lassies who used to go down to Lowestoft and Yarmouth for the herring season in the late autumn. As soon as they arrived they made their contract with their employer, and were given 'arles' before they began to gut the fish at all. That was a guarantee, a pledge, a deposit, an instalment of their full wages for the whole season which would last about eight weeks. The Holy Spirit is not merely a seal but a guarantee (or Guarantor, thinking of him personally, as we must). He is the pledge, the deposit, the instalment, the warranty, the promise. The Holy Spirit is the down-payment, the first instalment of the full redemption of God at the resurrection of our bodies.

Let me give you the four scriptural references that deal with this. Here is our first text: 2 Corinthians 1:21,22, 'But it is God who establishes us with you in Christ and has commissioned us. He has put his seal upon us and given us his Spirit in our hearts as a guarantee.' The guarantee is of course ultimately of resurrection bodies, nothing less. Indeed it possibly covers even more than that here.

Next look at 2 Corinthians 5:5: 'He who has prepared us (or wrought in us), this very thing (that is the hope of the resurrection), is God who has given us the Spirit as a guarantee (of our full salvation, which as Paul tells us in Romans 8:23 *is* our resurrection body).'

Ephesians 1:13,14, is a beautiful reference. 'In him you were sealed with the promised Holy Spirit who is the guarantee of our inheritance (and again the inheritance is our heavenly body) until we acquire possession of it, to the praise of his glory.'

The fourth reference is in the same letter, Ephesians 4:30, where Paul says, 'And do not grieve the Holy Spirit of God in whom you were sealed for the day of redemption.' The 'day of redemption' again is the day when we receive our resurrection bodies.

Four times, then, we have this same statement, that the Holy Spirit is given to us as the insurance, the guarantee of that blessing to come of our resurrection bodies. Since he is the Holy Spirit of Jesus Christ, the Holy Spirit brings to us the seed of Christ's resurrection body (1 Jn. 3:9). The Holy Spirit who comes to us comes with all the efficacy of Christ's redemptive work. He brings to bear upon us all the fruit of Christ's death and resurrection. And of course that *must* be, if this is the Holy Spirit of Jesus Christ, the Redeemer, who comes to us. He must bring to us the seed of the resurrection bodies we are to have. Not only are they modelled on his, but they are from the very seed of Christ's own resurrection body. So, this is why we can be so sure that, being laid in the grave, buried in the sea, or cremated, or whatever, nothing at all can prevent our resurrection bodies being given to us on that day. We have the guarantee with us now, the first instalment of our inheritance.

I want to link with that something we have dealt with before which is very important. We must keep tenaciously in our minds the fact that the Holy Spirit is a *person*. If you slump into notions of the Holy Spirit as a mere force or power you will dishonour God and at the same time become a different sort of Christian. You will not be nearly so confident and poised if you lose your grip on this: the Holy Spirit is a person and is in all his coming to us a person. But, you may say, there are some references to the Holy Spirit in the New Testament that might suggest otherwise. There are four some have regarded as rather embarrassing. We will look at them now.

Acts 2:17. On the day of Pentecost, Peter is quoting Joel. He says, What you see before you (the outpouring of the Holy Spirit on the day of Pentecost) is what Joel spoke of and prophesied so long ago. 'And in the last days it shall be, God declares, that I shall pour out my Spirit upon all flesh, and your sons and your daughters shall prophesy, your young men shall see visions and your old men shall dream dreams. . . . ' Peter is describing Pentecost in terms of that great event. It applies in one dimension to the coming of the Holy Spirit on the day of Pentecost; and that is past. It will one day apply more fully of course. Actually, the RSV does not bring out the words in the original which should really read like this, 'pour out *from* my Spirit'. Similarly later on, in the 18th verse. You see the point? Does that suggest that despite all we have said about the personality of the Spirit, these are influences, emanations, gracious benefits or gifts from the Holy Spirit that God is going to pour out – but not the Holy Spirit himself?

Look at another reference, Romans 8:23. This is more difficult. Paul is talking about the whole creation groaning under the weight of the Fall. 'We know that the whole creation has been groaning in travail together until now, and not only the creation but we ourselves who have the firstfruits of the Spirit groan inwardly as we wait for adoption as sons (that is *full* adoption), even the redemption of our bodies' (resurrection bodies).

Professor John Murray has a good deal to say about this phrase, 'firstfruits of the Spirit', or 'firstfruit of the Spirit' (singular). He asks the question, 'Should this be expressed in terms of a genitive of apposition?' That is to say, should we speak here of the Spirit as firstfruits in the way that we speak of the Spirit as an earnest? Not an earnest of the Spirit, something from the Spirit but not himself; a *part* of the Spirit or a *gift from* the Spirit and not himself; or should we speak of *the Spirit himself* as firstfruits?

Listen to what Murray says. 'The firstfruits of the Spirit in accordance with the analogy of Scripture (he goes over all the references to firstfruits in the New Testament and shows that they are all related to the full fruits) should preferably be taken as the token gift of the Spirit given to believers now, as the pledge of the plenitude of the Spirit to be bestowed at the resurrection.'

Now, what does that mean? John Murray is saying that the Holy Spirit we have now, the firstfruits of the Spirit, is a token gift given to believers now as a pledge of a fulness of the Spirit to be bestowed at the resurrection. What is exceedingly important is that however much we speak of the firstfruits and the fulness of the Holy Spirit we must hold on to this that as a person he is either present or absent. And if he is present then his whole person must be there.

Having accepted that, we can then go on to speak of increasing fulness and outpourings and blessings of the Spirit and his gifts. But first of all we must hold on to this. This will be the secret. If the whole pentecostal movement is to be contained within the Christian church and not go to seed and die, as some groups have done already and some are doing now, then it will be because they hold on to this.

Now, we must hold on to the fact that the Holy Spirit is personally there, not only to bring us to birth but to stand guard over our lives and seal us for God with absolute eternal security. Indeed, do we not often say that when we receive the Spirit of Jesus Christ into our hearts some of us seem to show him into a little room? It may be in the cellar, it may be in the garret, it may be a little more respectable, saying, 'Will you please occupy this room?' And we go out and we shut the door saying, 'You can use that room, but you can't use this one and you can't go here because I have other lives to live.' It is only in the fulness of time when, by the grace of God, the Spirit inclines us to increasingly yield ourselves to him that we unlock all the doors and open all the caverns, the cavities and all the dark places under the stairs and that kind of thing. Then we say, 'Here Lord, have the run of my house.' Then the fulness of the Spirit comes from within-out, not from without-in. We do not say, 'Give me the Holy Spirit in conversion and give me a fuller Holy Spirit after that – from without.' That is bad doctrine, and it is also bad psychology. If you are looking for a further blessing of the Holy Spirit from within you will have an entirely different attitude to the Christian life than if you are looking for something from without. Psychologically they are as different as could be.

The next of these references is Philippians 1:19. Paul writes here of the 'help of the Spirit of Jesus Christ.' Here is another place where I wish they would translate what is there. The word is 'supply'. If you have the AV you will see that. And indeed the word has the prefix *epi*. It is an intense word and should be read, 'full supply'. 'The full supply of the Spirit of Jesus Christ.' Here again there is the suggestion of quantity – quantitativeness, measure, more or less. Again the danger is that we think of the Holy Spirit as so much essence, a measure of this, a quantity of that. That is a danger. So, we have to take these difficult texts and wrestle with them.

Here is what Bishop Moule says about it, this 'full supply' of the Spirit. 'This refers to a developed presence in me of the Holy Spirit, coming from the exalted Saviour and revealing him and applying him.'

Here is what J.A. Motyer, says in his wonderful commentary on the Letter to the Philippians. 'Of these words "full supply of the Spirit", "of the Spirit" means either that the Spirit is the bearer of the full supply to us in his great office of making real in our experience all the blessings and benefits of faith in God, or else it means that the Spirit himself is the full supply as he indwells the believer.'

I think Motyer expresses it perfectly: 'He is called the Spirit of Jesus Christ because his presence in us and his gracious work for us have been purchased by the saving work of Christ. Thus, God not only rules our lives from the throne but he also sustains our lives from within.'

The last difficult reference is 1 John 4:13, where we have these words, 'He has given to us of his own Spirit.' The difficulty is here again that God has given to us 'of' or 'from' his Spirit, but not his Spirit as a person.

These four references taken together might easily lead some to think that the Spirit is quantitative and can be measured; you have so much of him. You see, talking of the Spirit as a first instalment easily could lead you to think of a second instalment of the Spirit, and then possibly a third. But *the instalment is the Spirit himself*, as we learn from Ephesians.

This is what Dean Alford says about 1 John 4:13: 'It is obvious that all references to the expression 'of his Spirit' which speak against the personality of the Spirit are quite beside the purpose. We each have the indwelling of one and the same personal Spirit, but each according to our measure. Only one had the Spirit without measure in all fulness, even Christ (John 3:34), and the presence of the Holy Spirit is most aptly adduced here where love is in question, his firstfruit being love and his presence being tested by his fruit.'

So I am satisfied that these difficult references to the Spirit, that might suggest supplies and quantities of a Spirit that is less than personal, can be satisfyingly integrated into the general teaching of the New Testament. It is the Spirit himself who is our guard and our seal.

The use of a seal, especially by kings, emperors and people in high authority, is surely as ancient as history itself. There are various references to it in the Old Testament. The references in Revelation chapter 7 are taken from Ezekiel 9, and even in the New Testament our Lord himself tells us in John 6:27 that he was sealed for his own task by the Father. Herod tried to destroy him. The Devil tried to destroy him. But the Son is sealed for his task on earth. He is secure. Nothing can happen. The Father seals the Son.

The principle part of what I want to say, and the most comforting part, comes now. I want you to look at certain references in the Scriptures that show the passion, the vehemence, almost the ferocity of God's assertions about our security in him.

We start with the Song of Solomon 8:6. Here the bride is speaking about her security in her lover, the Lord. One of the things that we say to some of the young couples we marry is this: God calls a man to take a woman that he might be her protector and give her security, and it is part of the nature and constitution of a woman that she seeks such protection. This is what is being spoken of here. 'Set me as a seal upon your heart, as a seal upon your arm, for love is strong as death. Jealousy (and jealousy here is used in a good sense. God is jealous. He won't let anyone snatch his chosen ones from him) is cruel as the grave. Its flashes are flashes of fire, a most vehement flame; many waters cannot quench love . . . .'

Now, that is poetical, but the message is very clear, especially the line 'Love is strong as death; jealousy cruel as the grave.'

Look now at Luke 22:28 where Jesus says: 'You are those who have continued with me in my trials' (he is speaking to his disciples)' . . . so do I appoint for you that you may eat and drink at my table in my kingdom and sit on thrones judging the twelve tribes of Israel. Simon, Simon, behold Satan demanded to have you that he might sift you like wheat (and sift him like wheat he did, but he could not have him) but I have prayed for you that your faith may not fail, and when you have turned again strengthen your brethren.' That is to say, Peter in his sifting, in his ordeal and his shame was safe, for his Lord had prayed for him; his prayers are always heard, and always effective.

Turn now to something that is not so much a seal and guarantee as a promise and an oath. Although this is different terminology, it is still germane to our theme. Hebrews 6:13: 'For when God made the promise to Abraham, since he had no one greater by whom to swear he swore by himself saying, Surely I will bless you and multiply you . . . . When God desired to show more convincingly to the heirs of the promise the unchangeable character of his purpose, he interposed with an oath so that through two unchangeable things (his promise and his oath) in which it is impossible that God should prove false, we who have fled for refuge might have strong encouragement to seize the hope set before us. We have this as a sure and steadfast anchor of the soul, a hope that enters into the inner shrine behind the curtain, where Jesus has gone as a forerunner on our behalf, having become a high priest for ever after the order of Melchizedek.' These words form the motto of the Boys' Brigade. You often see a ship casting an anchor into the sea; here is an anchor that is cast into heaven.

Turn back now to John 10:27. Dear doubting ones, grip these texts; live by these words. Jesus says, 'My sheep hear my voice and I know them and they follow me, and I give them eternal life, and they shall never perish, and no one shall snatch them out of my hand. My Father who has given them to me is greater than all, and no one is able to snatch them out of my Father's hand.'

But how do we know that we have the Holy Spirit? If we do not have the Holy Spirit we do not have this guarantee, and none of these blessed words are for us. The witness is within. Here is 1 John 4:13-18, 'By this we know that we abide in him and he in us, because he has given us of his own Spirit and we have seen and testify that the Father has sent his Son as the Saviour of the world. Whoever confesses that Jesus is the Son of God, God abides in him and he in God. So we know and believe the love God has for us. God is love and he who abides in love abides in God and God abides in him. In this is love perfected (or completed) with us that we may have confidence for the day of judgment and look towards the day of judgment because as he is, so are we in this world. As he is so are we in this world (as secure as if we were sitting in heaven with him!) There is no fear in love, but perfect love casts out fear. For fear has to do with punishment and he who fears is not completed and perfected in love.' And then John adds, 'He who believes in the Son of God has the testimony in himself' (1 Jn. 5:10).

So, you see, all subsequent fears and feelings have to be dealt with. When the Devil reminds us of our sin and we are tempted to doubt our salvation, we must go back to the point when we know there was a clear sky right up to heaven and we saw the face of God and heard him, as it were, saying to us and witnessing in our souls, 'You are mine. You are mine, and I will never let you go.'

Our security thereafter depends on confronting the Devil and all his agents with that assurance grounded upon God's Holy Word, bringing him to that point and saying, 'Go.'

You see when we begin to doubt and fear and yield to Satan he comes in like an express train with a thousand demons and absolutely overwhelms us. Then we feel completely lost, and we need help to emerge from that heavy demonic blanket that blots out all hope and the blue sky and the sun shining above. We must get back to the place where we knew by the witness of the Holy Spirit in our own hearts that we belonged to Christ. We must put our finger on the place in God's Holy Word, brandishing the Bible before the Devil and defying him and making him go. The old enemy comes over with such power and such darkness, and with such conviction. We must resist him absolutely. If he can spoil a Christian, turn his head and confuse his emotions and rob him of his peace, he likes nothing better.

Remember when Jesus was asleep in the boat? What a picture! Now, the boat was in a storm, and they were afraid the boat would founder. Could it have foundered? If that boat, with Jesus lying asleep on it, that little barque on the midst of storm-tossed Galilee, had foundered, do you know what would have happened? The universe would have disintegrated. For Jesus is the One who 'upholds all things by the word of his power' (Heb. 1:3). He holds all things together. So, I love this picture. Jesus lying sweetly sleeping because he was tired; he had worked hard all day. They were as safe as if they were in heaven, because they were with him!

You see, what we need when Satan comes at us is to reassert our sanctified reason and think our way through to certainty and assurance and confidence. The Devil knows that we are susceptible to our emotions, and he loves to make our emotions work overtime. We have got to resist him and stop feeling so much, and start thinking more. Jesus could not sink, so the disciples could not either.

Trust him. Pin your faith to his Book, to his Word, and learn to defy and defeat the enemy.

Do you know that William Booth on his death bed was enveloped with a sense that he was lost, until God came to him. He said, 'The waters are rising. The waters are rising.' He meant the waters of death. And then, 'But I am rising with them.' That is assurance! Paul speaks of wearing the armour of God and having our 'feet shod with the preparedness of the Gospel of peace' (Eph. 6:15). I like to think of a soul with these shoes on, these great strong boots that can grip the rock of God's Holy Word. You put on these great tackety boots and you get a footing on the rock which is Christ Jesus, and you almost dare to say to the Devil, 'Come on. Come on. Move me if you can.' And you stand there, and you keep standing. In Ephesians 6:11-14 there are four 'stands'. 'Stand, with-stand, stand, stand.' And that is what we are committed to: resisting the enemy, gaining absolute victory over him. For some it will cost unspeakably, but it is the only way to come through to that peace and that poise, that fruitfulness that we all need. We have the guarantee of God, the Holy Spirit in our lives. God help us to prove victorious in these things.

THE HOLY SPIRIT

4: God's Love

In Romans 5:3-5 Paul says that 'we rejoice in our sufferings, knowing that suffering produces endurance, and endurance produces character, and character produces hope, and hope is not disappointed (it is not the kind of hope that will fail to materialise) because (and this is the assurance that our hope is not misplaced) God's love has been poured into our hearts through the Holy Spirit . . .'. When you are seeking assurance about salvation and a platform on which to stand for your life, you can go out into the world and stand firm for Christ with words like this. The apostle states the reason here so categorically, 'because God's love has been poured out into our hearts.'

Before we get involved in the whole passage just think clearly and simply about this. You are a Christian? God's love, the love of the eternal God has been poured out into our hearts. He has given us his love, which is tantamount to his giving his all. He has given himself in the love which embraces the totality of what he is. This is the truest word about God, the richest way of describing him: he is love, and he has poured out his love into our hearts. So we are going to think about the Holy Spirit as the communicator of God's love.

This affords encouragement to our hope for that which is ultimate. Paul sees the encouragement of our hope as the climax of this process he describes here, after peace and access and the hope of glory. He says 'More than that, we rejoice in our sufferings because suffering produces endurance, and endurance produces character, and character produces hope,' and it is at the climax of this he adds that

---

we know that our hope will never be frustrated – all because of something that God has given. And what God has given is himself in his love by the Holy Spirit. This self-giving of God (as we learn from verses 6-11) has an astonishing, sovereign ground. You might want to argue and say, 'On what ground have I any assurance that God's love has been poured out into my heart?' You may say, 'How am I to *know* that this is so? I believe that I am a Christian – I have been a Christian perhaps for years – I really believe I *am* a Christian, but I don't *feel* this.' Well, look first at this question. How am I to be sure that it is God who has poured out his love into my heart? How does Paul prove this? The proof is in verses 6-11. There never was a God like this. There never were ideas like those we have in these verses'

Paul begins with our hopelessness and helplessness. He describes this as radically as he can, 'While we were yet helpless at the right time, Christ died for the ungodly.' Christ died for those who had turned their backs upon God. Do you want to have some assurance that God really loves you, although you do not feel his love? Well, look at this: he sent Christ to die for those who had turned their backs upon him. What kind of love is this? What kind of sovereign, masterful, world-transforming, life-changing, man-turning-about God is this? He sends his Son Jesus Christ to die for man, and in doing so says to man, whose back is to him, 'Turn round and see what I am doing for you!' Man might say, 'I don't want you to do this. I don't want anything to do with you at all.' But God, who is sovereign and all-powerful, says to man, 'I will not be diverted from loving you simply because you do not want to have anything to do with me; I am sending my Son to die for you. Turn round and face it. You cannot escape him.'

You see, it is a love that is fearless in its activity; absolutely masterful, authoritative and commanding. In Romans, Paul goes on to use a marvellous illustration with its distinction between cold righteousness and warm goodness. What a difference there is!

Let me ask a question here in passing: I wonder what it is about poring over reformed theological writing that makes so many Christians so horribly cold? I do not understand it, because I think it is wonderful literature. The grace of a truly biblical Calvinist or Puritan is wonderful, because it is so biblically and theologically informed by the truth of God. But may God deliver us from the coldness! It is something like this Paul has in mind. He was a cold Pharisee once, a cold fish himself.

So, notice what Paul says: 'Why, one will hardly die for a righteous man, though perhaps for a good man (what a distinction; do not miss it. And please do not miss its application to life. Occasionally take these two words, righteous and good, and look in the mirror with them, and ask which you are) one will dare even to die.' Then comes the contrast. Paul's 'buts' are sometimes highly significant! '*But* God shows his love for us in that while we were (neither good nor righteous but guilty) sinners, Christ died for us.' So this is the nature of God's astonishing sovereign love for man, that when he was ungodly and unrighteous and a guilty sinner, Christ died for him. That is the ground upon which Paul may declare that God has poured out his own love into the believer's heart. Notice, it is into his heart, not into his head. It goes through his head, it goes on into his heart! It is by intelligent understanding of the word of God that the truth comes home to us, but it goes right down into the heart, into the spring of our whole being. It is there that conscience and will and mind and emotion meet, for it is the heart that moves us. Our heads may be stuffed full of knowledge but that does not have any effect upon our life – our moral life, spiritual life, and all our actions. But God pours his love into the heart. He says, 'I will pour it right into the spring of your being.'

That is the ground upon which we may have assurance: he has given us his love. Now we must look further at what Paul says about the gifts of this love. Following our justification by faith – itself a gift – the first gift is *peace with God*. Now, some people are converted very undemonstratively; Christ just steals into their hearts and at the time they do not know that something as elemental as a transformation has taken place – from the kingdom of darkness into the kingdom of light. They simply see the light of Jesus Christ and respond to him, and say, 'I ought to become a Christian.' They really, actively believe in Jesus Christ, but they do not have the faintest idea of the dimensions of what has happened: they may not know that something has happened in heaven, that news has gone round every angel.

I want you to take this seriously. God proclaims the news with a trumpet voice in heaven. 'Have you heard I am at peace with John Smith? Tell the whole creation. Angels, tune your harps. Come on, orchestra leader, choir leader, organist, get on your toes. Let's have a hallelujah chorus. Shout and sing. I am at peace with John Smith. He has come to terms with me. We are friends. *I* say we are friends, not he. I will tell him about that later on. But I am saying it to you in heaven. I am declaring it. I am writing it down. I am promulgating it. I am at peace. I am friends with John Smith (you must put in your own name).' And of course all *subjective* feelings of peace flow from that, when you know it.

In his great commentary on Romans, John Murray discusses whether 'access' (Rom. 5:2) means introduction or access. Does it mean (as we might put it) being in the vestibule or in the living room? Murray is quite sure, as I am quite sure too, that it is the living room. 'Access' – this word is also used in Ephesians, 'For through him (that is, Christ on his cross) we (Jews and Gentiles) both have *access* in one Spirit to the Father.' We can walk right in to the Father's presence and say, 'Father, listen to me, your child' (Eph. 2:18). Again Paul says, 'In whom we have boldness and confidence of *access*' (Eph. 3:12). You see, we do not just creep in through the vestibule and go through the hall to be ushered by some flunkey into the presence of the Lord; only to creep round the side of the door and take the lowliest place and hide behind all the people who are there. We walk right through the crowd – not proudly, not arrogantly, but self-confidently, assured that we are children of God and that he is there on the throne to speak with us as much as to speak with anyone else there. And we say, 'Father, I have something to say to you about my life which I believe interests you.' We walk right up (if necessary, we push our way through!) and say, 'Father' – humbly but assuredly. We are not nervous, our knees are not knocking. We say, 'Father.' That is access. That is what he is talking about when he speaks about our 'access into this grace in which we stand.'

The hope of sharing the glory of God is connected with the fact that God is going to display his eternal glory, the eternal glory of his Person and his work in Jesus Christ at a particular point in time – the climactic point when he decides to return and glorify his whole church. That is the moment, the split second when the whole universe, including the holy angels, are going to see the glory of God unleashed in creation. So the hope of sharing the glory of God is not only that we are going to be glorified, but that our glorification is a participation in the glorification of God – that manifestation of his glory which, if it were unleashed before the time, would consume the universe.

So we possess a hope for the future. There is peace for the past. And in the present, in his presence, go right up to his throne, and say 'Father'. We are able to enter. In the future his eternal glory is going to be released and unleashed on the universe. Yet we rejoice not only in what is to be, we rejoice also in the manufacturing process. Some people have no interest whatsoever in knowing how their motor car or their fridge was made; but Paul is interested in how saints are made. The more he knows about this, the more he is able to endure the trials by which saints are made – the chisel and the hammer and all that – the more he can rejoice. After every blow with the hammer and every cut with the chisel he says, 'Hurrah!' Paul said, 'I want to know this because if I am to endure trials and pressures, I want to know not only what it is going to produce but I want to rejoice beforehand at the prospect of the production.' So he says, 'More than that we rejoice in sufferings.' Similarly in Hebrews 12:2, we read about Jesus, 'Who for the joy that was set before him (and the joy that was set before *him* was the conversion of sinners and the glorification of saints. The reason why he died was for us) endured the cross, despising the shame.' It was as though he said, It is nothing, Father. I can stand it. I can stand the spitting and the shame. I can stand it all Father. It is nothing – to get these saints.

How are you able to hope? How is it that the hope of glory which is produced through suffering, endurance and character can be so sure? How is it that you can have such serenity about God whom you have never seen, that you know you are safe in his hands and can put your head on the pillow and lie down and die and not be afraid? It is because God is here with you already. He has come into your heart by the Spirit. He has poured out his love into your heart – the love of God himself.

In Philippians 2:1-11, Paul speaks about Christ emptying himself. He writes about the mind of Christ, who was willing to leave heaven and lay aside the outward insignia of his glory and 'empty himself'. What does that mean? Did he empty himself of the content of his being? How could that be? Jesus was God. Jesus, as a man, Jesus incarnate was no less God than he was in heaven with his Father. He did not empty himself of any essential aspect of his being or his nature; not a bit. I think this is what it really means, 'He poured himself out'. There came a day in heaven when the Father said to the Son, 'Make ready, gather all together. Take off these Sonly robes; you will not need them, although you remain my eternal Son. Take that off. Now, roll up your sleeves. Have you everything ready? Then pour yourself down, the whole of you, into the earth, the whole of you into the womb of the Virgin Mary.' 'He emptied himself.' So he devoted himself utterly, and poured himself out into man.

The meaning of that is this: the words, 'God loves you', have become something warm, and palpitating, inward, intimate and personal, an intellectual conviction that is an overmastering compulsion within your being. *God loves you* has become *God in you*, knocking at your door from within. He plants the seed of Christ, the Spirit of Christ in the core of our being. I like this metaphor. It is as though there were a little sacrosanct chamber at the very heart of the building of your life, the hub, the central office if you like, and God plants the seed of Christ there at the centre of your being, the source of all action, and he says, 'I place myself there.' 'God loves you' is a reality that has come into your office, into your engine room. Now, flood the building, open the doors, through into the hall, up the stairs, down the stairs, into every room. Shout it, spray it, pervade the whole atmosphere, permeate the whole building. God loves you. God loves you – from the roof to the basement, from side to side and corner to corner, God loves you! This is what Paul calls 'his *great* love' (Eph. 2:4). In the incarnation God has come down himself to say, 'I love you'. He is saying it inside you. 'Ah now,' you say *'why don't I feel it*? Why don't I feel it more?' Well, there are barriers.

Why do we not feel God's love more, when God is there shouting it loud to us in our breasts? There are barriers. What are the barriers? I think we can answer that question by looking at what Peter says in 2 Peter 1:3. He begins with indicatives, statements of fact. Imperatives by contrast, have to do with action which is commanded. The passage begins with indicatives. It tells us what God has given to us, and then goes on to say what we are to do about it (imperatives). Perhaps we have done nothing about it. This may be the difficulty.

Look at 2 Peter 1:3-11. 'His divine power' has 'granted' us promises; and not promises merely, for he means the implementation or the fulfilment of these promises. That is the indicative part, that is what God has given. That is what you have as a Christian. Now, the challenge. 'For this very reason make every effort to supplement your faith (this is the first thing on the list) with virtue, and virtue with knowledge (that is personal knowledge of God, knowing Jesus Christ in your heart), and knowledge with self-control, and self-control with steadfastness, and steadfastness with godliness and godliness with brotherly affection, and brotherly affection with love (in the richest sense), for if these things are yours and overflow they keep you from being ineffective (or unfruitful) in the knowledge of our Lord Jesus Christ' (and knowledge of course of his love). For whoever lacks these things is blind and short-sighted and has forgotten that he was cleansed from his old sins (the past is blotted out). 'Therefore, brethren, be more zealous to confirm your call and election, for if you do this you will never fall; so there will be richly provided for you an entrance into the eternal kingdom of our Lord and Saviour Jesus Christ.'

The point is this: first of all, by faith, God gives us all these indicatives (vv. 3,4), then he says, 'Now, that is what you have got, what are you going to do about it? I have poured my love into your heart; act upon it, develop it, enjoy it.'

That will deal with the barriers to feeling the love of God. The first barrier may be guilt. You may feel so guilty, so unworthy. You may feel 'God ought not to love me'. What an awful thing! God is standing in the hall of your life, standing there at the foot of the stairs shouting to the whole house, 'I love you, I love you, I love you', and you are calling down the stairs, 'You shouldn't, you shouldn't.' But he can shout louder than we can. 'While we were yet sinners, Christ died for us'. Do not be paralysed by guilty feelings and guilt complexes. Hold on to the truth. Reach up to heaven and pull heaven down and say, 'He loves me'.

The second barrier is often our own feelings. To say to somebody that you have to live in the luxury of God's love seems idealistic, a luxury too extravagant to entertain in such a troubled, aching, disaster-ridden world as this is. But Peter tells us that we are to escape the corruption that is in the world through lust. He is saying to you in the midst of this rotten world, 'Look, I love you. There is nothing so important for you to know in the whole wide world but that I love you, and I have given my love to you. It is in your breast. It is in your bones. It is in this body you carry about with you. My love for you will go home with you tonight and go to bed with you and rise with you in the morning.'

The third barrier may be competing loves, false loves, idolatrous loves, love of something that allows us to set ourselves on the throne and says to the Lord, 'Excuse me, I have something rather important to do, something better to do than chat with you. You know, I like you all right and I want to do my duty by you, but there's someone that I think I can perhaps get to worship *me*.' So God gets the go-by. You have to look at all these things, the guilt and the feelings and the competitors for love in our hearts. We have to put God first and stand him over against anything that objects or competes, and let him say loudly and clearly and constantly, with increasing crescendo, 'I love you, I love you: love me back, I love you; love me back.' Let the truth of that break through, that God's love *has been* poured out into your heart. It is a *perfect* tense!

I want to say a dangerous thing here. Seek the Lord in your own heart, but do not seek him apart from the Book. Seek the Lord in your heart with the Book in your hand. Let the Book tell you who and what is there for you. Realise by faith what the Book is saying to you, and accept what the Book says. But seek the Lord in your heart. Seek him as you surrender to him. Give yourself to him. He has poured out his love into your heart, so seek him there. Commune with him. You don't feel like it? You are cold? God seems like a million miles away? He is just as there on Monday morning as truly he is on Sunday night. You may not feel the same; that is beside the point. Never mind what you feel, the way to deal with feelings is to deal with facts. Faith rests upon facts!

THE HOLY SPIRIT

5: Fruit of the Spirit: Love and Joy

Speaking about love, the first fruit of the Spirit in Galatians 5:22, Martin Luther says:

> It had been enough to have said love and no more, for love extends itself unto all the fruits of the Spirit. And in 1 Corinthians 13 Paul attributes to love all the fruits which are done in the Spirit when he says, love is patient, courteous *etc.* Notwithstanding he would set it here by itself among the rest of the fruits of the Spirit and in the first place, thereby to admonish or warn or challenge the Christians that before all things they should love one another, giving honour to one another through love and every man esteeming better of another than of himself because they have Christ and the Holy Spirit dwelling in them and because of the word, baptism and other gifts of God which Christians have.

You see that Luther regards love as the fruit of the Spirit in relation to other people, although most scholars today think Paul means it in relation to God first of all.

Here is what Luther goes on to say about joy.

> This is the voice of the bride-groom and the bride. That is to say, sweet cogitations of Christ, wholesome exhortation, pleasant songs or psalms, praises and thanksgiving whereby the godly do instruct, stir up and refresh one another. Therefore God loveth not heaviness and doubtfulness of spirit.

There are some people would give you the impression that Christians should be not only exceedingly sad, but pompous. It is a great danger. We must learn to read deep theology without becoming too heavy and thinking that heaviness and solemnity and lugubriousness have to do with holiness. Holiness has a lightness of touch. Holiness dances – did you know that? – it dances with joy because it has to do with wholeness. More than that it has to do with being set apart to God, and you know when we are set apart to God, when we give ourselves utterly to God, the freedom that we have is such that we could dance our whole lives through. It is so wonderful to belong to God and to be set free from all that is evil and harmful and injurious. Here is Luther again:

> Therefore God loveth not heaviness and doubtfulness of spirit. He hateth doctrine, heavy and sorrowful cogitations and loveth cheerful hearts (and some people think God only loves us weeping. What a mistake! He has to make us weep sometimes because we will not behave ourselves and be good as he wants us to be, but he does not want us to be sad) for therefore hath he sent his Son, not to oppress us with heaviness and sorrow but to cheer up our souls in him. (I notice that the Latin here 'to cheer up our souls in him' means to exhilarate ourselves!) For this cause the prophets, the apostles and Christ himself do exhort us; yea they command us to rejoice and be glad.

Zechariah 9:9 says 'Rejoice, thou daughter of Zion. Be joyful, thou daughter of Jerusalem, for behold thy King cometh to thee.' And in the psalms it is often said, 'Be joyful in the Lord.' Paul says, 'Rejoice in the Lord always' (that is to say, find your joy in the Lord). Christ says, 'Rejoice because your names are written in heaven.'

> Where this joy of the Spirit is there the heart inwardly rejoices through faith in Christ with full assurance that he is our Saviour and our Bishop, and outwardly expresses this joy with words and gestures.

Now, notice these two things. I am going to take Luther's words as a kind of a structure for what I am going to say in a moment. 'Where this joy of the Spirit is there the heart inwardly rejoices through faith in Christ with full assurance that he is our Saviour and our Bishop and outwardly it expresses this joy with words and gestures.' Do not tell me that if you are filled with the joy of the Lord it may not be seen! 'Also the faithful rejoice when they see that the Gospel spreadeth abroad, that many be won to the faith and that the kingdom of Christ is enlarged.'

That is what Luther says then about love and joy. Here is what another, much later, scholar has to say about the importance of the distinction in Paul's mind between the fruit of the Spirit and the *charismata*, the gifts of the Spirit, otherwise spoken of as the manifestations of the Spirit. In his commentary on Galatians in the New International Critical Commentary series, E. de Witt Burton considers the two lists, the fruit of the Spirit in Galatians 5:22-3 and the gifts of the Spirit in 1 Corinthians 12. He writes:

> The apostle includes in the gifts of the Spirit and the manifestations of the Spirit, those extraordinary experiences and powers which were not necessarily evidential of moral character in those in whom they appeared, but because of their extraordinary character and of their association with the acceptance of the Gospel message, the Word of God, they were regarded as the effects and evidences of the presence and activity of the Spirit of God. These are all external and easily recognisable. On the other hand, under the term of the fruit of the Spirit are included those ethical qualities and spiritual experiences which were not popularly thought of as evidences of the Spirit's presence but which to the mind of Paul were of far greater value than the so-called charismata or gifts. See 1 Cor. chapters 12-14, especially 12:31,13, 14:1. Thus, while retaining the evidently current view which found in the gifts of tongues and prophecy and power to heal disease evidence of the Spirit's presence, he transferred the emphasis of his thought, and he sought to transfer the thought of his disciples from these things, the external to the internal and ethical qualities which issue in and control conduct.

In the Tyndale Commentary on Galatians, R.A. Cole writes about the term 'fruit of the Spirit' being in the singular:

> The use of *arpos*, as mentioned above, suggests that all these spiritual qualities and many more are the spontaneous product of the presence of the Spirit of Christ within the heart of the Christian.

Then he goes on to discuss the word 'fruit'.

> The metaphor is a very old one with its roots deep in the soil of the Old Testament. Perhaps we might add that it is a metaphor natural to an agricultural people like Israel. While the word means any kind of fruit, it is most frequently employed of the product of the fruit tree or vine. John uses it in the latter sense in chapter 15 of his Gospel which we have referred to already. It was a principle referred to by the Lord himself that a tree could be recognised by the fruit it bore – Matthew 7:16. So, by the presence of these 'fruits' the presence of the Spirit is proved.

The fruit of the Spirit is love, and then joy, in the list – love, joy, peace. Now, there is a sense in which were I to abstract these three words I could be less than satisfied with their sequence. If I set them in an expanding or amplifying sequence, or an ascending scale, it would be undoubtedly 'peace, love, joy', and the fourth one would be 'glory'. You have a different order in Romans 5:1-5. You have peace first, and then joy, and then you have love. Here it is 'love, joy, peace', and in Romans 5 you have 'peace, joy, love'. But the order that I would like if I were to abstract the three words from the series is 'peace, love, joy' – and, ultimately, glory. But that is the unfolding sequence of experience. It is interesting, you see, that joy comes *after* love. If we were to discuss this with the apostle Paul he would surely say, 'Yes, peace, love and joy.' But you see, as Luther said, 'love embraces them all.' It embraces them all, for it is the greatest of them all – because it expresses the glory of the character of God. There is no other word in the Bible describing him like that. Love therefore embraces joy. But in experience, you know, joy is an intensification of love, as glory will be hereafter. So, after love is joy

– of the most vibrant, most heavenly, most glorious, most expansive kind. The Holy Spirit comes to give us joy.

Now, what is the cause of this experience of joy in our hearts? We can answer that question by looking at a number of occurrences of the word 'joy' in the Scriptures.

What is the cause of the joy? It is, if you like, quoting from Isaiah 7:14, Immanuel – God immanent, God remaining, God abiding, God coming down to live with us. That is the cause of the joy. The joy is Christ. 'So the angel said to the shepherds, "Don't be afraid, for behold I bring you good news of a great joy which will come to all the people, for to you is born this day in the city of David a Saviour, who is Christ the Lord" ' (Lk 2:10). And if we know that 'great joy', the cause is Jesus in our hearts, Jesus living, moving, burning in our hearts. Let us be plain. The question is: have you Jesus in your heart? I could not live without Jesus in my heart every moment of the day and night. I have nothing else. I have no one else. Oh, to have Jesus in your heart!

Look what he himself says about being in our hearts. John 15:7: 'If you abide in me and my words abide in you . . .'. That is to say: Branch, cling to the stem of the vine, hold on to it. And you have to abandon the metaphor here because branches do not actively cling to anything. But you see, 'Abide in me', is a very active word. Shall I tell you why it is active? Because there is somebody trying to pull you away all the time – the Devil. You will only abide in Christ and cling close to him if you also resist the Devil. That is what abide means – saying 'No, I am not going. I am staying here.' So that 'my joy may be in you, and that your joy may be full' (Jn. 15:11).

In the marriage service of the Church of Scotland this is the last of the Scripture readings, and it gives me the greatest relish and joy to come to the climax of the Scripture reading with these wonderful words, and to devour them, as if to say, 'Oh God, let us taste the succulent last morsel of them': 'These things have I spoken unto you that my joy may be in you and that your joy may be full.'

There are some people who have been brought up with the idea that God is a policeman and Jesus is a tyrant, and although they are very pious and all that, they are really rather frightened of Jesus. If you are one of them, you have got it all wrong. If only you knew how he understood you, how utterly sympathetic he is with you in your struggles, your fears, your doubts and your questionings. He stands by you and looks into your eyes as he looked into the eyes of the rich young ruler, and 'beholding him, loved him.' He is saying, 'I want you to have my joy, and when my joy becomes your joy I want you, dear son or daughter, to be *full*. I want you to be filled up to the brim with my joy.'

But what is the nature of this joy? The answer is found in Psalm 16, one of the choicest of the psalms, and also in a sense one of the most poignant. I believe that this is a Messianic psalm, in which the psalmist, by the Holy Spirit, is speaking deeper than he knows. He is speaking the private, inner, secret thoughts of the Christ, hundreds of years before he was incarnate. After all, the Psalter is the autobiography of Jesus Christ. You learn the inner thoughts and feelings, the mind and heart of Jesus almost as much by the Psalter as you do by the Gospels.

So, here the Holy Spirit is putting into the mind of the psalmist some of the thoughts of Christ. 'The Lord is my chosen portion and my cup. . . . Yea, I have a goodly heritage (v. 5. He is speaking about the church); because he is at my right hand (even in Gethsemane and even on that hideous cross) I shall not be moved. Therefore my heart is glad (Oh Jesus, hanging there with the blood streaming down your face and down your body – glad?) and my soul rejoices; my flesh also shall dwell secure (his body did not undergo corruption v. 8). Thou dost show me the path of life (resurrection!): in thy presence there is fulness of joy, in thy right hand are pleasures for evermore' (v. 11).

I ask what is the *nature* of his joy? It is a joy that comes out of pain. It is a joy that comes out of death. We cannot get away from that. The heart of the Christian faith is the Cross. If your joy is not a joy that embraces and grasps the Cross of Jesus, then is it not a Christian joy. The nature of this joy is a joy that goes through blood, fire and water.

Hebrews 12:2 is a classic statement on joy. Is there anything so wonderful in the New Testament as these words? 'Who for the joy that was set before him (that is, having you and me set before him in heaven. Oh yes, it is. I am not saying it. He says it. That is his joy) endured the cross, thinking little of the shame (minimising it, saying It's nothing. It's nothing. I can stand it. I can bear it. Gladly I'll bear it. I don't like suffering, I don't enjoy agony. I don't enjoy pain, but I am willing to go through that to the very utmost to gain them, to have that John and that William and that Mary sitting beside me in heaven. That's Christ's greatest joy) and is seated at the right hand of the throne of God.'

We must talk a little more about the cost of this joy. It is a joy that costs. It cost Christ and his Father a great deal. It is a joy that will cost us. We will have to endure the hatred and scorn of Satan if we are intent on letting the Holy Spirit, whose fruit is joy, fill and flood our soul with God's holy joy.

Satan is constantly seeking to trip us up and lead us astray, until there is absolutely no joy in our lives. Think well about it, and make up your mind and count the cost if you are to follow him utterly – in blood and sweat and toil and tears – because if you become a Christian and then slip back, you will be far unhappier than you ever were as an unbeliever. There are no souls so unhappy in the world as Christian backsliders.

So, the psalmist cries out in 51:12, 'Restore to me the joy of thy salvation.' And of course really to enjoy the joy of our Lord's salvation involves us in dying to self and to sin and to Satan. You know what that means? It means drawing upon the various dimensions of the grace of God in Jesus Christ to say 'No' to our flesh and 'No' to the remnants of our fallen nature and 'No' to Satan trying to stir them up. It means breaking our hearts before the Lord and saying, 'I cannot do that. No, I had rather die than do that.' You see it was when David died – it was a bit late mind you, because the nation had been potentially ruined by his sin – when David had died to what he had done to Uriah the Hittite, as both adulterer and murderer (David, who is called in the Scriptures a man after God's own heart!), he cried to God, '*Restore* unto me the *joy* of thy salvation.'

There is another wonderful statement about joy in Isaiah 12:3, 'With joy you will draw water from the wells of salvation.' The joy is a different dimension from mere salvation from hell or deliverance from evil. When we renounce sin and turn our back upon evil and die to all that is sinful and perverse in God's sight, by the grace of God we receive a dimension of salvation that fills our whole beings with joy.

Moreover, because death is involved, this joy is often sober, and it can be solemn. There is something about the joy of the Lord that is wonderfully controlled, that never loses its head. Yes, it is happy and it can be carried into transports of delight, and can sing, dance and rise to ecstasies of joy, 'joy unspeakable' says Peter, 'and full of glory' – as if the glory of God had come down and flooded our soul. And yet it is always under control. Not only so. It is not seeking its heaven here, because it knows it has to be careful – because there is a Devil.

Joy is also for sharing. This is what John says, 'No greater joy can I have than this, to hear that my children follow the truth' (3 Jn. 4). In Philippians 4:1 see how Paul was able to contain his joy. 'Therefore my brethren, whom I love and long for, my joy and crown, stand firm thus in the Lord, my beloved.' In 1 Thessalonians 2:19 he writes, 'What is our hope, or joy or crown of boasting before our Lord at his coming?' What are we going to dance about with delight before the Lord? First at seeing him of course – this is not mentioned here but it is obvious. Think how marvellous it will be on that day; you'll look at him and say, 'Oh it is *you* who were in my heart when I was down there. It is *You*. That must explain why sometimes I felt as if my heart would burst, and it burned and glowed and often rebuked me too. It's You.' So, we will dance before him with joy at the sight of him; we will join hands and dance round him in a holy circle like children at a Sunday School picnic!

But then there will be something else. We will run for this one and for that one and say, 'Lord, look at him. Look at her. Look at these friends I have brought to you.' 'What is our hope or our joy or our crown of boasting before our Lord at his coming, *is it not you*? For you are our glory and joy.'

Here are three things we must learn. Firstly, if the Lord is going to pour out his joy into your heart and through your heart and overflow from you to others, you must learn that his joy is related to his death and his sufferings and the resistance of evil. Christ by the power of his death will help you in that.

Secondly, the more you delve into the meaning of the death of Christ the more you will love Jesus and the more you will find your joy in him. You will be overcome with delight at the very thought of Jesus. Does he ever move you to tears? Does the thought of him sometimes come up and choke you?

Thirdly, you will develop a love for people. Oh, this is the thing: the joy of fellowship, the joy of caring for people and going out searching for them – like Paul. 'For you are our glory and our joy.' Oh men and women, boys and girls, this is what to live for. There is nothing else. You are not living for money, or position are you? Surely you are not devoting yourself to advancement in some profession or other? That is all very well; God can do that for you. But you are not going to live for that; you live for him and for others and you will know joy, the joy of the Lord.

THE HOLY SPIRIT

6: The Fruit of the Spirit: Peace

'Love, joy and peace' (Galatians 5:22): this triad describes the effect of the presence of the Spirit on the inward character of the believer. The inward character of course includes our own personal subjective experience, what we feel and experience in our bodily and mental and spiritual life, these three together. We know love, for inasmuch as Paul is speaking about the fruit of the Spirit he is speaking about something that is expressed – not love objectively so much as subjectively, love expressed and experienced. This is not the kind of love we might have in our hearts and never show until we are driven to some crisis. There are people like that. You would never know that they loved another until something terrible happened to them, and then they show it all, a bit late. But this is love that must show itself.

Love, joy, peace. I want you to take these three and consider them in relation to one another. How would you put them in order? We could give them in an ascending scale of peace, love and joy, but that is not the order here. Love is first because love is the sum of them all. But then joy suggests something fuller or yet more expressive. Joy comes next, and then peace.

We might think that peace after love and joy is a kind of anti-climax. Sometimes I do not fully understand the Scripture, but it will never be the Scripture that is wrong; so I have to try and find out why it is that way. In fact, some of the deepest, richest truth in the Scripture yields its essence, its juice, its sweetness just at the point where there is a difficulty. If you go on chewing and chewing, seeking what help you can and just like a terrier refuse to let it go, while you may not find out all about it, you will find out something satisfying to the intellect and to the emotions too.

Love, joy, peace – in that order! I wonder if joy and peace are set after love to suggest the *range* of God's love – love in the expansion of joy, and peace in the depths of settlement and satisfaction. When we think of peace as a fundamental blessing we think of it in relation to the past. The past is blotted out. There are other people no doubt who could accuse us of former sins, but God will never do that. It is almost as if God cannot recall the sins he has blotted out. We can. But he has turned his back upon them. This is the fundamental blessing of the gospel, and it is the ground of all subjective peace in the Christian life.

The fundamental blessing of peace is set on a sure objective basis, as we see so clearly in Romans 5:1.

After Paul has expounded the core of the gospel in the second half of Romans chapter three, he goes on in chapter four to illustrate the gospel by reference to Abraham and David. Having done that, the whole of chapter five is a kind of summing up. It is a chapter that points two ways. It speaks about justification, which is what God *has done* for us, and points the way to speak of sanctification, which is what God *seeks to do* in us. That is really quite simple. These two belong together. God has done something objectively for us that we could never do for ourselves; he has blotted out our sins. Having done that in a composite action he also comes to us by the Holy Spirit to work out the fruit of that justification in what we call sanctification, cleansing us by his Holy Spirit.

'Therefore (he says, looking back through chapters three and four) since we are justified by faith, we have peace with God through our Lord Jesus Christ.' What I am stressing here is that 'we have peace with God' means that God is at peace with us. In the first instance, peace is not something that God gives to us. We are not in the realm of God *giving* anything yet; we are in the realm of God *doing* something. He is doing something, as it were, in his own heart. This is how we may express it in time. He is doing something in his own heart by the death of Jesus Christ, and by our faith in that death. And when we say 'he died for me' from the heart, which is the beginning of a new life, God says, 'All right then, that's settled and finished for ever. I now see you in Christ, and you now have his righteousness, and I declare and regard you to be righteous in Christ in my sight. There is a long way to go yet, I know, but this is what I do to begin with.' God begins at the end in a sense. He says, 'I am now at peace.' See how objective it is! It has to do with God before it ever has to do with you. God is at peace with me about my sins; that is the first thing.

Read on in Romans 5. 'Therefore since we are justified by faith, we have peace with God through our Lord Jesus Christ. Through him we have obtained access to this grace in which we stand.' It is as though God were saying: 'Come into my home, come on; into my palace, into my kingdom. Come away. Come into the realm of grace, where everything is favoured, everything is lavish in its grace. Come on, the best is here for you.' 'And we rejoice in our hope of sharing the glory of God' – of one day shining like God, because shining with the glory of Christ. But more than that (though this is a kind of step backwards) – 'More than that, we find our joy (we aren't in heaven yet; back a bit, retrace your steps and pick something up that you have missed. It seems painful at first but it is not really, that is why he uses the word 'joy') in sufferings.' In *sufferings*? Ah, for a reason – there is nothing slick here. 'We find our joy in sufferings knowing that suffering produces endurance (stability), and endurance produces character, and character produces hope.' Such hope is not a vain hope, it does not disappoint us; it is not a fraud or an idle dream. Why? Because of this guarantee, the Holy Spirit is in us, and the Holy Spirit stands guarantor until we receive our resurrection bodies. He has come to pour himself out and to pour God's love into our hearts. 'God's love has been poured out into our hearts through the Holy Spirit who has been given to us.'

Thus, it seems, the apostle says: how can I explain this further? How can I show the lavishness of God's love in giving me not only peace as to the past, access to grace in the present, and the hope of the glory of God in the future – and joy even in painful experiences, because they are working something good and lasting, in God's purposes? 'While we were yet helpless (as if to say, let me explain another way) at the right time Christ died for the ungodly.' See how gracious he is. 'Why, one will hardly die for a righteous man (one who is correct, meticulous in his ways. He could be quite a cold man, but he is correct) though perhaps for a good man (a man whose righteousness is warm with humanity and love and compassion and care) one will dare even to die.' But that is not like God's love. 'God shows his love for us in that while we were (neither righteous nor good but miserable) sinners Christ died for us.' You see, he has overtaken us and presented us with an accomplished fact. He has died for us and said, 'Look, you are a sinner but I have already died for you.'

'Since, therefore (you see the conclusion of it), we are now justified (declared by God to be righteous by Christ's death) much more shall we be saved by him (not merely by his death, but saved by him as a person saying, 'Here, I want to live with you. I want to live in your heart') from the wrath of God. For if while we were enemies we were reconciled to God by the death of his Son (God came and put his arms round us and said, 'Come on; I want you. I won't let you go.' That is more than justified), much more, now that we are reconciled, shall we be saved by his life.' It is all done so that he can come and dwell within us. 'Not only so, but we also (oh, more joy! How am I going to contain it all?) find our joy in God through our Lord Jesus Christ, through whom we have now received our reconciliation.' We have friendship with God, who puts his arms round us saying, 'Come on, I want to love you, to possess you and give you delight and pleasure to all eternity. That is what I made the world for – that I might save you for myself to belong to my Son.' That is something of what is involved in this fundamental objective peace that God has with us when we believe in what his Son has done for us to save us.

We are now going to take that just a step further. Pick up the words at the end of the passage: 'we have now received our reconciliation.' Let me express this in terms of Jesus' words in John 15:27: 'My peace I give to you.' It is one thing for God to be satisfied in heaven that our sins are blotted out, but that is only the first half of the story, the transcendent half. But what is to be done *in* us? Ah, he says, I put my peace *in* him. 'My peace I give to you.' My peace. Now, Jesus was a man. He knew human pain. You never had nails through your hands or your feet, did you? You were never as hungry as he was in the wilderness of temptation, were you? He has known the worst, and his peace has stood the test. He is saying, I am giving my peace, which is absolutely full of human experience, which has been tested to the hilt until the devil lay in the corner crumpled up and hopeless before Jesus died. I'm giving you that perfect shining thing that kept me in Gethsemane and kept me on the cross all these hours until I had gained the final victory over the devil and he was finished and I said, 'Now, Lord, we have got him absolutely beaten, I give myself back to you.' And with kingly dignity he bowed his head and said, 'Lord, I give my spirit back to you.' Do you not see the dignity of that? Some people think that he just expired, that he had come to the end of himself. Not a bit of it. How long could he have gone on after that? He *chose* the moment to die, and I don't believe at all that it was his last moment. If you think I am exaggerating, consider the poise, the dignity, the perfect assurance with which he did all this. His peace was not shaken by an iota, not by a thousandth of an inch. No. And he is asking: 'Do you realise what I am saying to you?' We are so accustomed to prosaic factual things in our lives, things that are not a bit surprising. It takes an awful lot to surprise us. But when you delve into this Bible you find all these wonderful things; vast things like the distance of the stars just fade into insignificance against what it says here. We do not take it in, because we are not really versed in the realities of the blessed Trinity. This is why he made the sun and the moon and the stars, because he wanted a sphere in which to work out our redemption perfectly. When you begin to think about that it thrills your soul! Somebody was saying to me, 'You musn't be too emotional. Don't be too emotional and don't shout.' Well, you'll need to take the Bible away from me!

'My peace' – Jesus' peace. Think again. Sometimes you are disturbed, whenever a crisis comes in your life – you get a letter tomorrow or something happens and you are tempted to panic. Just say to yourself as a Christian, 'I have got inside me what kept Jesus up on the cross.' Oh God, can this be true? Have I got inside me what kept Jesus on the cross? You see? It takes my breath away. Do you not think that will help?

Picture Jerusalem, set there on its hills. Look at a relief map that shows the ridge of Judea. The geography of the Holy Land is one of the wonders of the world. Did you know that? Take four strips from the Mediterranean to the Jordan: the coastal strip, the foothills, the backbone of Judea which is a great big ridge that rises to nearly three thousand feet above sea level, then a great, almost sudden drop through the wilderness of Judea where Christ was tempted, down to Jordan and down to the Dead Sea which is 1,200 feet below the level of the sea, so that the Dead Sea is 4,000 feet below Jerusalem. In a sense, from all directions except perhaps a little bit to the north, the way to Jerusalem is up. But once you are in, you are safe. 'Thou dost keep him in perfect peace, whose mind is stayed on thee, because he trusts in thee.' In you go, in through the gates and shelter behind these walls, the walls of salvation and trust in the Lord forever, for the Lord God is an everlasting rock and no one can break in to this impregnable fortress.

You see, this is peace in a different dimension from the peace that God has in heaven in respect of us. Once you are within Jerusalem, once you are sheltered and protected by the peace of God that is heaven on earth.

Let me draw to a conclusion. 'Find your joy in the Lord always,' says Paul in his love letter to the Philippians. 'Again I will say it, Find your joy in the Lord. Let all men know your forbearance (even if they count it weakness). The Lord is at hand.' (Find your joy in the Lord and let men do what they will to you. 'The Lord is at hand. Have no anxiety about anything.' You say, 'Yes, I can take that in every particular except this one thing.'
'What is this one thing?'
'I'm not telling you,' you say, 'but it is something personal and special to me.'
But what Paul says about God's peace must include that – the thing that worries you to death. Because it says here, Have no anxiety about *anything*.
'Oh,' you say, 'I can't attain to that'. No, you cannot attain to that because you have not got the wherewithal, have you? Jesus left that bit out when he gave it to you, didn't he? He said, 'Now, see what I have given you. I have given you my peace, and it can deal with everything except that.' Is that what he said to you? Come on, 'Have no anxiety about *anything* but in *everything* (this is the secret. Your anxiety about that is because you dwell on it, you have

become obsessed with it. Take your mind off it positively) by prayer and supplication with thanksgiving let your requests be made known to God (say, 'Oh God, I thank you for having given me Jesus Christ's peace with all the fruit of his terrible experience in Gethsemane and on the cross. I thank you for giving me all that. I haven't made it work in this, but you are going to help me to make it work even here.' Can you get as far as that? If you can, sitting in that chair, a peace has come upon you. That is what he has promised) and the peace of God, which passes all understanding will keep your hearts and your minds in Christ Jesus' (Phil. 4:6-7).

THE HOLY SPIRIT

7: The Fruit of the Spirit:
Patience and Gentleness

One of the things that is astonishing about the nine-fold fruit of the Spirit is that they are so little demonstrative and active. For instance, there is nothing like courage there; that always surprises me. Most of them are, if not exactly passive, at least inward, or perhaps it would be better to say they are gentle and self-effacing. Look at them again: love, joy, peace, patience, kindness, goodness, faithfulness, gentleness, self-control. In a sense, apart from the last one, you might think that they are qualities that describe soft people, too – gentle people, people who are not particularly manly or womanly. You could not ascribe weakness to any of them but you wonder if some of them are getting a bit near it. You see what I mean? – patience, kindness, goodness, and so on.

We come to the fourth fruit of the Spirit, which is longsuffering. Now, all sorts of translations are tried for this word in modern versions of the New Testament. It is exciting to see what each new translation offers. Yet the wonderful thing about it is this – this compound word is fully explanatory to the simplest soul. Longsuffering, that is exactly what the word says – *long-suffering*. It refers of course to the ability by the grace of God through the gift of the Spirit to put up with difficult and bad people for a long, long time. That is what it means. It is as clear as could be.

We find this word quite frequently in the New Testament. The noun is found fourteen times and the verb ten times, and the adverb at least once. Let us look at some of the references in the New Testament.

We will start with him who is the author of longsuffering, he who has longsuffered the longest, our God and Saviour. Peter has a good deal to say about that. 1 Peter 3:17-20: 'It is better to suffer for doing right, if that should be God's will.' For example (a lot of Peter's theology is given as examples) 'Christ also died for sins once for all, the righteous for the unrighteous (suffering long and sore for us) that he might bring us to God, being put to death in the flesh but (as soon as the breath went out of his mortal body) his Spirit was quickened and he went and preached to the spirits in prison (we cannot go into all that now. While his body is lying dead in the tomb Jesus is busy preaching, proclaiming, not evangelising notice, but proclaiming to the spirits. I believe that they were fallen angelic spirits, but other people believe otherwise), who formerly did not obey when God's patience waited in the days of Noah (if you want to compare that with Genesis 6:1ff. that is interesting, and there are some good authorities for linking these two together, but don't let's miss the point!) who formerly did not obey.' For a hundred and twenty years Noah preached a gospel by building the ark, declaring God's righteousness, that God was going to send a flood that would sweep them all away, and they laughed at him. God gave patience to Noah and he hammered away and hammered away and they laughed and jeered at that silly old man building a great big ship-like thing in the middle of the country. But they laughed on the other side of their faces when the water started to come down. Yet, for one hundred and twenty years God's patience waited.

2 Peter 3:13: 'We wait for new heavens and a new earth. . . . Beloved . . . count the forbearance (longsuffering) of our Lord (the apparent slowness of his coming in judgment and glory) as salvation.' He waits a long, long time before he comes in final judgment.

So, you see, the longsuffering we are speaking about – which is a gift of the Holy Spirit – is given by God to us.

In 2 Corinthians 6:6 Paul is trying to answer and if possible win over his critics in Corinth. He is saying that he has tried from the beginning to remove all obstacles in himself to the preaching of the gospel, so that the ministry may not be blamed. 'We put no obstacle in anyone's way so that no fault may be found with our ministry . . . by purity, knowledge, forbearance (longsuffering again), kindness (what a beautiful word), the Holy Spirit, genuine love.'

Ephesians 4:2: 'I therefore beg you to lead a life worthy of the calling to which you have been called . . . and meekness, with patience (that is, with longsuffering) forbearing (that is enduring) one another'.

Colossians 1:11. Here Paul prays that the Colossians may be strengthened with all power according to his glorious might, for all endurance and longsuffering with joy. 'Longsuffering with joy!' How can we encompass and experience longsuffering with joy? Only when we know what we are doing – or when we know what God is doing in respect of someone else. That is maybe the way to win somebody for Christ, when they expect you to fly into a temper and you do not. At first it exasperates them, but later it makes them think. Longsuffering: how far are we from this? That is the question.

Colossians 3:12. 'Put on then, as God's chosen ones, holy and beloved, compassion (feeling for people in the depth of your heart, with a feeling that touches the innermost part of your body), kindness, lowliness of mind (and here it comes again), longsuffering, forbearing one another.' One more text and then we are finished and can gather all these texts together. In James 5:10,11 Job is set before us: 'As an example of suffering and longsuffering take the prophets who spoke in the name of the Lord. Behold, we call those happy who were steadfast. You have heard of the steadfastness of Job (we talk about the patience of Job, but here is a stronger word) and you have seen the purpose of the Lord . . . .' That is it! This is the secret of longsuffering with joy; it is because you see God's purpose, just as our Lord saw that purpose when he went to his death: for the joy that was set before him he endured the cross, thinking nothing of the shame. It needs penetration. It needs insight and foresight to understand what is going on, why God is allowing what he does in our lives. He is working towards something. Jesus penetrated the gloom and darkness of death and saw why he was dying. He did not want to die. He did not like his body being hurt. He did not like his mind being tortured. We know from his experience in Gethsemane that he did not want to bear the sins of the world on his back. Who in the world would? He did it only because he loved us and wanted us to be rid of them. It was for us. That was the *purpose* you see. And here we read of the *purpose*: '. . .and you have seen the purpose of the Lord (have you? Have you read Job to see God's plan for him?) how the Lord is compassionate and merciful.'

Now, what can that mean? It can mean that you do not understand Job unless you read chapter 42, when the Lord turned his captivity and gave him more than all he had before and blessed him and healed his body – and I suppose reconciled him with his girning wife! But that is another subject.

Now let me tell you what not to do. Do not let anybody here beat their breast and say, 'Oh, I am so far from this. I am so far from this.' We all are! Look, the only one who can suffer long in the face of all that is hellish and sore is Jesus. You need *his* long-suffering. But then, if you are his you have already got it. You have got it if you have got him. We are not talking about the *gifts* of the Spirit that are distributed: one to you, maybe two to you or three to you. We are talking about the *fruit*, these nine fruit (and the word 'fruit' here is singular. They say it is used in a collective sense. There may be more in that than meets the eye). They are all the fruit of the person of the Holy Spirit in our lives. That is to say, this person of the Holy Spirit in our heart can provide us with all these graces and gifts. Every Christian can have all these: love, joy, peace, goodness, gentleness and all the rest. They are all for us, every one of them, and we are to seek them all.

We may stumble many times. We may make up our minds that we are going to be very, very patient with that impossible person (who maybe thinks the same about us!) and within half an hour in the office or workshop or wherever we have blotted our copybook and things are worse than ever. What are we going to do about that? Well, has Jesus in us failed? You would hardly dare to say that! *We* have failed. Why have we failed? Oh, because we have not allowed the gift of God, the Spirit within us, to be driven deep enough into our lives. We are not saturated enough with the purposes of God. We would never have been saved at all if God had not been patient. You see, he could have wiped us all out. We might think he should have wiped Adam and Eve out as soon as they had sinned. And he could have begun before that, he might have wiped the Devil out when he first sinned. But you see he had more sense. That was not the way. Look at the harm that is done by intolerance and impatience and anger. Something bitter comes out in the sudden burst of anger that may mar a friendship and a fellowship for ages. It may never be quite the same again, or it may take a great deal of humility in coming together to put it right before mutual trust and regard and affection are restored. It is just not good sense. But of course sudden passion, with the Devil behind it, never thinks of that – never!

We could put it another way. I said that the virtue of long-suffering has not been driven deeply enough into our character. We have not been saturated enough with it. That could be described in other terms: we have not been dipped deeply enough in the death of Jesus. Think of it like that. He died for us to give us the virtue, the fruit of his death, including long-suffering. On the cross, he prayed, 'Father, forgive them; they know not what they do.' That was penetration. He was speaking the truth; that is why he was patient and long-suffering. They actually did not know what they were doing. You see the example? Longsuffering is a kind of higher intelligence, spiritual understanding and wisdom.

Now, look at meekness. It is translated here as gentleness. Meekness is really the word. Look at meekness in prayer; it is far removed from weakness. It is as far removed from weakness as heaven is from hell! Meekness never abrogates manliness, it never renounces character. Meekness does not by being meek unman itself, although people may think that the meek man looks silly, as doubtless they thought that Jesus looked silly. Nor does it abandon its character, its qualities and its gifts. What meekness does (I love this thought and hope you will too) is to defer and appeal to One that is greater. That is why meekness can be so meek, because it is not a matter of grovelling in the ground and letting somebody trample on you, but rather recognising how you stand before someone who is greater than you are.

Look at Moses. Moses was not perfect any more than any other man but look what we read about Moses in Numbers 12. Miriam,

Moses' sister, and Aaron, his brother, had spoken against him because he had married an African woman. They had found fault with Moses. These two apparently were running round looking for some faults in Moses. Why? Because they were jealous of his leadership, of his power and authority. They did not dare to say that. You do not say that kind of thing! Instead, we find some way to dig at them, as they did. So, he had married a Cushite woman; but notice what their complaint is: 'Has the Lord indeed spoken only through Moses? Has he not spoken through us also? And the Lord heard it. (Yes, he heard it, he always does. He is not deaf and he is never asleep.) Now, the man Moses was very meek, more than all men that were on the face of the earth. And suddenly the Lord said to Moses and to Aaron and Miriam, "Come out to the tent of meeting." And the three of them came out. And the Lord came down in a pillar of cloud and stood at the door of the tent, and called Aaron and Miriam . . . . And he said, "Hear my words . . . . With (Moses) I speak mouth to mouth, clearly, and not in dark speech; and he beholds the form of the Lord. Why then were you not afraid to speak against my servant Moses?"' That is what God said to them. 'And Miriam was leprous, as white as snow.' And Aaron changed his tune! And Moses cried to the Lord (Oh, dear old Moses) 'Heal her, O God, I beseech thee' (Num. 12:13).

Look at 2 Corinthians 10:1. 'I, Paul, myself entreat you, by the meekness and gentleness of Christ.' He sees that, of himself, in the remnants of the old nature he is not really all that meek. He was one of a crowd of Pharisees, wasn't he? Then, of course the Devil was goading him. So he says to the Corinthians: look, I am entreating you as Christ would entreat you, and as he said, 'I am meek.' Is there any man on earth who could say that without conceit? In the saying of it he would be denying it. Yet, Jesus says, 'I am meek.' So Paul is saying, 'Look, I am appealing to you on the basis of meekness of Christ', that is to say I know that Christ is meek and lowly in heart and easy to be entreated, his yoke is easy and his burden is light And do you know, dear Corinthians, I could wither you with scathing searing words, but I have gone down into the depths of my being and I have looked around and said, 'Holy Spirit, Holy Spirit, (reverently he would say this) where's Jesus' meekness? Let it come up.' And he says, it has come up. 'I feel it. It is rising in my heart.' He was like Moses, when Israel criticised him another time and he fell flat on his face before God. That was his meekness, as if to say, 'Your controversy is not with me. I am nothing. I am flat on my face. I am simply a bundle of dirt. Your controversy is with God.'

You see, that was Jesus' meekness. Jesus, the eternal Son of God, was able to efface himself completely. That is meekness. That is what I said earlier. Meekness does not unman itself, nor abdicate its responsibility, nor abandon its character, quality and gifts – but defers and even appeals to one who is greater.

Now Paul, you are delving for meekness. If you have got God's common sense, it is the easiest thing in the world because common sense says, 'You are just a blob of grease anyway. God is all and Christ is all and so it is not difficult to be meek, although no-one would profess to be meek. It is not difficult to be meek when you see God as all in your life.' But you see the Devil will not let us live like that. He wants us to think we are great, and that is our undoing. Better to live the other way.

I will tell you what this does – when we see God as all and ourselves as nothing, we begin to love Jesus with a real affectionate love, not with a cold kind of respect that has no feeling to it. Could you comfort the bereaved without putting your hand on their shoulder or gripping a hand, or getting down on your knees beside the weeping one and touching them? Love *feels*, and you never really love Jesus properly until you feel love. I'll tell you something else, that is the only way to love people. That is the only way to love people for Jesus' sake!

THE HOLY SPIRIT

8: The Fruit of the Spirit:
Goodness, Faithfulness and Self-Control

Someone recently handed me this about the fruit of the Spirit: 'Joy is love singing. Peace is love resting. Long-suffering is love enduring. Kindness is love remaining with patience. Goodness is love's character. Faithfulness is love's habit. Meekness is love's true touch. Self-control is love holding the reins. But the greatest of these is love.'

It is to the subject of self-control that we now turn, and then to the more outgoing ones, kindness and, of course, faithfulness, loyalty or fidelity.

The fruit of the Spirit is self-control. 2 Peter 1:6 is interesting in this connection. You will notice from the end of verse 4 that various virtues, qualities and graces (including self-control) spring from the fact that by God's grace we are made 'partakers of the divine nature'. Not only have we an equal standing before God in the righteousness of Jesus Christ, so that we might know God and his Son, but we become 'partakers of the divine nature' – and of course the divine nature effects self-control, control of our persons and our lives.

1 Corinthians 9:24. 'Do you not know that in a race all the runners compete, but only one receives the prize? So run that you may obtain it. Every athlete exercises self-control in all things.' We know that this is true. 'They do it to receive a perishable wreath, but we are imperishable.' Then Paul makes this comment: 'I do not run

aimlessly (in the race of life, as a Christian athlete) I do not box as one (and here the figure changes) beating the air, but I pommel my body and subdue it.' That word could be put even stronger. You could read it: 'I beat it black and blue and subdue it.'

These are pretty harsh things that he is saying, and we would need to find a balance in them. I am sure he could have put it more gently. We are not to be morbid. What he is really saying in perhaps more acceptable terms is this: 'I give my body and the whole of my bodily life to the death of Jesus Christ, because of course there is no death of Jesus Christ without a resurrection.' All death in Jesus Christ is with a view to resurrection. Death is not an end in itself, so if he is beating or pommelling his body black and blue to subdue it and keep it under, it is for a good purpose. It is not because he enjoys beating his body – he is no masochist; not at all, there is nothing morbid, nothing unhealthy here, but he knows the propensities of his human body – not merely to indulge itself; he is thinking of something far more sinister than that.

You may say that a little self-indulgence by itself will not do a lot of harm. But it is the beginning of an enslavement by the enemy, and the enemy intends it so to be, and that is another thing altogether. Paul will not let the enemy into his life, so rather than give way and give in he says, 'I pommel my body and subdue it, lest after preaching to others I myself should be disqualified.' (You might say to me: this seems far too extreme for a Christian. Yes, but you are maybe not as concerned for souls as he was; that is the difference. You say, I would not go as far as that. No, you would not, and very likely you would not go as far as him in winning souls.)

Paul is speaking not only of his ministry to others, but also of that place that would be accorded to him in heaven by his faithful service. He is thinking about the whole subject of reward and loss. Or you could put it another way. 'Disqualified' here could mean disqualified from further service. There are many servants of God who have been one way or another disqualified from further service because they have rendered themselves unfit to be of service to God. They have fallen away, been led astray by something or another, popularity, or possessions, or whatever.

The subtlest temptation of the enemy to those who are called upon to minister to others is this. You will find it in Romans 2:17. After one has ministered to others, one tends to count oneself in a privileged position, up in the box, up on the rostrum, as if to say, 'Of course it doesn't apply to me, it applies to my pupils, to my members, to my flock but not to me.' Now, that is exactly what is happening to the Jewish teachers that Paul is dealing with here. 'But if you call yourself a Jew and rely upon the law . . . and if you are sure that you are a guide to the blind, a light to those who are in darkness (I think Paul is using phrases that preachers or teachers might use, Jewish teachers as well as others, though with just a little touch of contempt) you then who teach others, will you not teach yourself? . . . The name of God is blasphemed among the Gentiles because of you.'

1 Corinthians 7:8,9. This takes us into a subject that naturally arises in this context, the whole realm of sex. Admittedly Paul here is setting the whole subject of Christian marriage on the lowest level. I am not using the word 'lowest' in any disparaging sense, but this is not the highest level of Christian marriage by any manner of means. Yet he is dealing with a specific problem. 'To the unmarried and the widows I say that it is well for them to remain single as I do. But if they cannot exercise self-control, they should marry. For it is better to marry than to be aflame with passion.'

Acts 24:24,25. Here, Paul has been speaking to Felix. 'After some days Felix came with his wife Drusilla, who was a Jewess; and he sent for Paul and heard him speak upon faith in Christ Jesus (because Felix wanted to know why Paul had appealed to Caesar in Rome). And as Paul argued about justice and self-control (and some of the things about Felix and Drusilla in that connection would not be very pleasant to hear), and future judgment, Felix was alarmed . . . . Paul knew what was going on in that wicked man's soul.

2 Corinthians 5:13. Here Paul is dealing with critics who have come to the church in Corinth, which he founded under God. Since they have stirred up some people against him, Paul is speaking to defend himself. 'For if we are beside ourselves (I think he means private ecstasy. There is no doubt that Paul enjoyed wonderful seasons of worship and prayer with God that nobody knew anything

about, but he occasionally betrays a little of it to us) it is for God; if (on the other hand before men) we are in our right mind it is for you (to commend ourselves as sane, rational and spiritual to you). For (notice the connection) the love of Christ controls us.' When the AV and some other versions use the word 'constrain' people get the idea it means to goad or impel or drive on. But the real meaning is: 'The love of Christ holds us in!' You see the point? In respect of others he holds in. And of course that is exactly what is required of someone who is set in authority over other people: 'For a bishop (overseer, shepherd) as God's steward, must be blameless; he must not be arrogant or quick-tempered or a drunkard . . . but hospitable, a lover of goodness, master of himself, upright, holy and self-controlled' (Tit. 1:7-8).

So you see something of what the New Testament says about self-control. Remember that it was through becoming partakers of the divine nature that we were given the power to control ourselves and our bodily life by the Spirit of Jesus Christ within us. He is in you and it is a matter of appealing to him within you. You see the point? You do not cry to God as if he were a million miles away, and say, 'Help me, help me wracked with passion', but 'Lord, you have given me your power. You died for this.' And he will, won't he?

Kindness is fruit number five. Although Bishop Lightfoot says we are to think of this word 'kindness' as referring to disposition yet perhaps we can also think of it as an outgoing fruit of the Spirit.

There are various references in the New Testament to God's kindness. We are going to look at them first, because if God requires of us to be kind then we must look to him who is a kind God to give us the power to be kind. Paul speaks of God's kindness in Ephesians 2:4. 'God, who is rich in mercy, out of the great love with which he loved us . . . . made us alive ... and raised us up ... and made us sit ... that in the coming ages he might show the immeasurable riches of his grace, in kindness toward us in Christ Jesus.' Perhaps there is a deliberate play on words here, for in the Greek language there is only one letter different between *chrestos* (kindness) and *Christos* (Christ). Well, that is the kindness of God. It is manifested in Christ, as Paul says in Titus 3:4: 'But when the goodness and loving kindness of God appeared, he saved us, not because of deeds done by us . . . .'

Then we find it also in Luke 6:35. Jesus says, 'Love your enemies, and do good, and lend, expecting nothing in return, and your reward will be great, and you will be sons of the Most High.' This is the proof that we are sons, that we do what the Father does. We imitate the Father. The true child imitates his father – he can't help it. 'For he is kind to the ungrateful and the selfish.'

This, then, is the kindness of God. But, what does it come from? It comes from his love: 'Love is patient and kind' (1 Cor. 13:4). That is its nature, to be kind. Remember what Jesus says in the famous 'comfortable words?' 'My yoke is easy and my burden is light.' The word 'easy' is perhaps not the best translation, it is this word *chrestos* again. 'My yoke is kindly.' Jesus says, 'My yoke, the discipline I impose upon you, is kindly.'

In the light of this, what is said in Colossians 3:12-13 takes on a new light. Paul says to us: 'Come on, put on Christ like a garment. Put on that gown, wear that robe. Put on the Christian garment (the overall righteousness of Christ) as God's chosen ones (there are beautiful words in this verse; look at them!) holy and beloved, compassion, kindness, (cover yourself in kindness, enshroud yourself in the robe of Jesus' kindness, say to God, 'Oh God cover me, envelop me, swamp me, saturate me, soak me in your kindness until from the depths of my heart all bitterness, all the acid of hostility and inferiority complex and all that comes from that is done away and my soul is bathed with such a spirit of love towards God and man that I just will be overwhelmed with kindness) lowliness of mind, meekness and patience which is longsuffering, forbearing one another and, if one has a complaint against another, forgiving each other; as the Lord has forgiven you, so you must also forgive (and *want* to forgive; even before people are sorry, you must have the desire to forgive).'

Then consider Ephesians 4:30-32. What a lovely passage this is! I think of an anthem we used to sing with this in it. It is marvellous, to sing the very words of Scripture. This is why we are so glad that young people learn these choruses the words of which are pure

Scripture (though sometimes the tunes are dreadful!). If you can drive the words of Scripture into your minds and your hearts you will retain them and be able to say them over to the end of your days. 'And do not grieve the Holy Spirit of God, in whom you were sealed . . . . Let all bitterness and wrath and anger . . . and slander (O, the dangers of this, how Christian churches are wrecked by this kind of thing!) be put away from you with all malice, and be kind to one another, tenderhearted (we are tenderhearted enough towards ourselves and those who are dear to us. O that we would extend this and not regard others as second class in relation to God and ourselves. If you are very tenderhearted with yourself and those you love, whoever they may be, you ought to be very tenderhearted with others – for they are of the same value to God as you and yours) forgiving one another, as God in Christ forgave you.' You are to do to others as God has done to you. And if God has not been hard on you, why in the world do you want to be so hard on other people? Where does that come from? It comes from the pit. 'Therefore be imitators of God . . . and walk in love, as Christ loved us and gave himself up for us, a fragrant offering and sacrifice to God.' Be kind!

Goodness is fruit number six. Bishop Lightfoot suggests this is something more active than kindness; it is kindly activity. Various scholars, ancient and modern, argue about the precise meaning of this word. In his Greek Lexicon, Alexander Souter (a very devout man and a very able scholar) says that 'with regard to this word "goodness" in the original the emphasis is on the word kindness rather than on righteousness'. Now, what is the difference between kindness and righteousness? Well, I think everybody would agree that the word righteousness at first suggests something more stern, or at least firm, and perhaps a little cooler, even cold. You see the difference brought out in Romans 5:7,8. Paul is talking here about Christ dying for the ungodly and the unrighteous, and he wants to illustrate the marvel of the perfect God in heaven through his Son coming down to die for rebellious sinners. He makes this comparison. 'Why, one will hardly die for a righteous man – though perhaps for a good man one will dare even to die.' You see the difference? The suggestion is that there is something warmer, more gracious and kindly about the good than the merely righteous.

On the other side Jerome, the ancient scholar, and Archbishop Trench more recently, say that goodness refers to the sterner qualities. Another scholar claims it refers to something like Christ cleansing the temple or, in Matthew 23, withering the Scribes and the Pharisees with godly and holy scorn. Here are three references to the word goodness in the New Testament; you can see for yourself. The first one is Ephesians 5:9. Paul has been speaking in verse 8 about walking in the light. 'The fruit of light (the fruit of walking in the light with God) is goodness, righteousness and truth.' When you associate goodness there with righteousness and truth there is something with a certain sternness about it; goodness perhaps related to moral rectitude.

In 2 Thessalonians 1:11, Paul writes of God fulfilling 'every good resolve (every resolve of goodness) within you', 'every good will'. It is the same word in the announcement of the angels of peace and goodwill to men. The point is that if you are challenged about your lack of self-control and kindness and say, 'Oh dear, dear, these standards are far too high for me, I'll never attain to them'; if you are a Christian you have already got them inside. What are you doing about what you have got inside? You see there is nothing the devil is so keen on as to keep from Christians what God has given us in our hearts. If you are sure that you are a Christian you have these resources in your heart by his Spirit. What are you doing with it then? You say, 'Oh yes, but it is difficult to work out'. But it is not impossible. You begin by getting into your thick skull, as I try hard to get into my doubly thick skull, that I have got all that there – and God is commanding me, as Paul said to the Philippians, to *work out* what he has *wrought in* (Phil. 2:13). He says, 'I have put it in. Will you please do something about it. Open the doors and let it out!'

Consider further what is said in Romans 15:13,14. 'May the God of hope fill you with all joy and peace in believing . . . . I myself am satisfied about you, my brethren, that you yourselves are full of goodness, filled with all knowledge . . . .' Can I say of you whom I know, and can you say of me whom you know that we find one another full of goodness?

Now we must look at *faithfulness*, fruit number seven. The fruit of the Spirit is faithfulness. Now, this also is from God. We read of 'the faithfulness of God' (Rom. 3:3). This word in the Old Testament is a word that speaks of firmness, security, fidelity, personal stability and truth. And the fruit of the Spirit is faithfulness, that is to say God gives us by the Holy Spirit of Jesus Christ a faithful and a loyal spirit from himself.

Look at Psalm 36:5. 'Thy steadfast love, O Lord, extends to the heavens. Thy faithfulness reaches to the clouds. Thy righteousness is like the mountains of God.' I love how the psalmist looks at the vastness and the glory of nature and expands his soul as he thinks of the greatness of God who made it all and the greatness of the attributes of God. He says, 'Thy steadfast love extends to the heavens.' I do love the psalmist's love of nature and his linking it so often with the God who made it all!

Then look at Psalm 89 with all its references to God's faithfulness. 'I will sing of thy steadfast love, O Lord, forever; with my mouth I will proclaim thy faithfulness to all generations. For thy steadfast love was established for ever, thy faithfulness is firm as the heavens.' And so also in verses 5,8,24,33.

Now, Psalm 119, at verses 89,90. 'For ever, O Lord, thy word is firmly fixed in the heavens. Thy faithfulness endures to all generations.' Again, Psalm 143:1: 'Hear my prayer, Oh Lord; in thy faithfulness, answer me.' You are trustworthy. You are true to your word. We can depend on you absolutely. Your very word is absolute truth. Look also at Hosea 2:19,20: 'I will betroth you to me in righteousness and in justice, in steadfast love, and in mercy and you shall know the Lord.' And this is what he has done to us. He has married us. He has united us to himself with all these qualities. He has given them to us that we might work them out in our daily lives. That is the whole point of the Holy Spirit.

Now, some Christians are very excited about all the wonderful experiences you can have from the Holy Spirit. We are coming to that in the fulness of time and we will seek to deal with it as faithfully and with as much balance as we can. *But the fruit comes before gifts*, because character comes before service. Too many young Christians want extraordinary experiences of the Holy Spirit to enjoy them and even boast about them to others. But that is not what they are *for*; they are *for* serving God. Before service, before we are fit to serve, we have got to learn and receive, and our characters have at least to be begun to be formed.

Look now at Titus 2:9,10. Paul is writing about slaves. 'Bid slaves to be submissive to their masters . . . to show entire and true fidelity, so that in everything they may adorn the doctrine of God our Saviour.' C.K. Barrett says that 'adorn the doctrine' means 'add lustre to the doctrine.' Of course, you cannot add lustre to what has perfect glory already. No man can add anything to God. You can only bring out what is there. Paul says he wants even the slaves to be real, faithful Christians to their masters, even masters who may not be very kind to them. He wants them 'to show entire and true fidelity' in order that in every experience of life, however humiliating, they may 'adorn the doctrine' of God our Saviour. The word 'adorn' is the verb *kosmeo* related to *kosmos*, the word for the world or the universe. It has to do with arranging. It is sometimes used for an arrangement of jewels. You see you do not just take everything out of the jewel box and stick it on. You arrange them to show them off. You see the idea? You set them off to their best advantage. 'I would that even the slaves show entire and true fidelity', being so loyal and faithful and true to their word to their masters and to their servants that they set forth, or set off, and show to best advantage, the doctrine of God the Saviour. We are called upon as Christians with the fruit of the Spirit in our lives to show forth Jesus, and that includes love and joy and peace and longsuffering and meekness, and self-control and kindness and goodness and faithfulness. How gentle and meek these graces are! As I have already said, courage is not even here, nor is daring. These fruits are all so gentle and meek. And that is like Jesus. Sometimes they scorn the hymn 'Gentle Jesus, meek and mild.' It is true, he was lots of other things. He had a courage that no man who ever lived on the face of the earth ever had, to go to that cross knowing what it would cost. But, never, never take the lines out of the hymn, for they are true of him and they need to be true of you and me before we get into heaven: 'Gentle Jesus, meek and mild.' John and Mary and William and Helen – gentle and meek and mild. God help us!

THE HOLY SPIRIT

9: Christian Character and Christian Service

Let me begin with a question. How far are the distinctions valid between the fruit of the Spirit and the gifts of the Spirit? You will see lists of the gifts in 1 Corinthians 12, Ephesians 4, Romans 12: apostles, prophets and teachers, preachers, evangelists, helps, government and so on. How far is there a valid distinction between Christian character and Christian service? That is, how far may we make a valid distinction between personal, Christian qualities and super-added or supernatural power in the exercise of gifts in the service of Christ?

I want to establish a tradition from the one, the fruit of the Spirit producing Christian character to the other which concerns Christian service. To do that, we are going to compare the Beatitudes (Matt. 5:1-16) with the fruit of the Spirit (Gal. 5:23).

The Beatitudes provide a progressive picture of the Christian's life and character. Professor Tasker says this: 'The Beatitudes are not statutory definitions as with the Mosaic Code, but indications of direction and action.' Here is what Calvin says. 'The Beatitudes are a brief summary of the doctrine of Christ placed before our eyes out of his many and varied discourses.' Dr Martyn Lloyd-Jones preached a tremendous series of sermons at Westminster Chapel on the Sermon on the Mount (now in book form) years ago. He says most emphatically that the Beatitudes are both a summary of the Sermon on the Mount, and also a description of Christ's character and of the character that Christians have to bear in his image.

What are the correspondences between the Beatitudes and the fruit of the Spirit? We have meekness in both lists. We have peace in both lists. We have mercy (Matt. 5:7), and in the fruit of the Spirit you would surely include that in love, longsuffering and kindness? We have purity in Matthew 5:8, whether you think of it as moral (sexual) purity or more widely, singleness of mind and heart. Self-control (Gal. 5:23) is related to that. Then in Matthew 5:10-12 the Beatitudes go further than the fruit of the Spirit in explicit terms, and speak of rejoicing in persecution. But can we not relate patience and faithfulness (Gal 5:22) to that?

But notice this particularly: there is no correspondence between the first three Beatitudes and the fruit of the Spirit. Poverty of spirit, mourning for sin, hungering for righteousness, all seem to be foundational, part of the *root* of God's working in us rather than its fruit.

Now, our text is Matthew 5:16: 'Let your light so shine before men, that they may see your good works and glorify your Father which is in heaven.' It is all very well to let your light shine. You draw back the curtains to take away all that would hinder and hide, so you do not conceal Jesus Christ who is in your life and whom you love. But is that all that has to be done to show men and women Jesus Christ? – 'that they may see your good works and glorify your Father which is in heaven.' That is what the text says, and it is a pretty complete statement. But there is something involved here that is not expressed. If Jesus is in you and you are not hiding him you have got to *believe* that he is showing himself through you; that is very important. You could be living the Christian life and not concealing your Christian witness at all, and yet it is not having much impact. It may be because you are ignorant of the Scriptures and what they say; you do not *believe* that your life is telling. But you have *got to* believe that Christ is telling in your life. You have got to *believe* it – because you cannot see it. You cannot see the impact that your friendship with the ungodly and the unconverted is having. If you are trying to see it, you will perform, you will act. You will engage in all sorts of antics, hoping that you are showing Jesus Christ; but instead you become a clown. You have to be absolutely un-self-conscious about this, and yet behind it there has to be a quiet, firm assurance that when you go out into the world just being what you are in Jesus Christ (with all your imperfections, warts and all), Jesus Christ is being seen. It takes a very, very, dirty window not to show when there is a light in it – very dirty indeed. You have got to believe that the light is showing.

Notice what is said about believing in Mark 11:24. 'Therefore I tell you, whatever you ask in prayer, believe that you receive it, and you will.' Many years ago Billy Graham said that he never preached the gospel but he expected people to be converted – and they always were, many or few. You see the point? Now, shouldn't we all have that kind of humble confidence in the Holy Spirit using us? I like to think that the Word is never taught in big meetings or small without there being fruit. I would like to think that I never walk into a hospital ward but Christ enters that ward (even though I am not as like Christ as I long to be – and I know that better than you!). It is a conviction that has to grow because that is what you are made for. I wonder if young people feel this as strongly as they should. I am sure that my life must tell every day one way or another. I think you can believe the same.

Here is another text. 1 John 5:13-15. 'I write this to you who believe in the name of the Son of God . . . . This is the confidence that we have in him . . . . If we know that he hears us in whatever we ask, we know that we have obtained the requests made of him.' There is absolutely nothing passive or automatic about this. It is something you have got to *do*: you have to *believe* that your life is telling. Now, I am sure there are some people who would never dare to do that, because they do not think they are good enough. You have got it all wrong. This is a factual business. Is Jesus Christ in your life, by the Holy Spirit, or is he not? That is the first thing.

The next thing is this. Are you hiding him or not? If you are not deliberately hiding him – you don't need to flaunt him – then believe that somebody is seeing him. Some will not like it, and that is the sore bit. But even that is encouraging, although we are not glad that people do not like him. But that is still encouraging because Jesus Christ is showing himself to others through your life. And it may be some time before we know that Jesus Christ is showing. It will be a good thing if not too many people tell us that he is showing, because we will get conceited and become self-conscious and begin to act like clowns.

I remember the first time that my Salvation Army officer spoke about this when I was quite a young man. It came to me with an intellectual shock that I still recall. He was a mighty preacher of the gospel, and there was a real revival down at the Citadel when he was there. I remember him talking that night, and he suddenly stopped and began to speak about what he called unconscious influence. I thought: My word, that speaks volumes about Christian character – unconscious influence; no self-consciousness, just being what we are in Christ with all our faults and believing that Jesus Christ is being seen.

Here is what Paul has to say about this in Colossians 4:5-6: 'Conduct yourselves wisely toward outsiders, making the most of the time. Let your speech always be gracious, seasoned with salt, (our speech should have a certain 'tang' to it! Being gracious does not mean that you trim your speech so as to avoid any suggestion of challenge to people at all. Think of the challenges Paul was writing into his second letter to the Corinthians saying, 'Have you heard how generous the people are in the north?' That was a bit of salt, wasn't it? You Corinthians in your great, sprawling, wealthy, wicked city in the south, you think you are great but there are very, very generous people in the north!) so that you may know how you ought to answer (speak to people).'

You see, salt has these two qualities – a tang in respect of taste, although that is not the more important thing here, and a preservative quality. I recall in the two or three months that I was a fish worker in my father's business, that when the fish had been beheaded and filleted and packed with the ice that was put in the boxes for travelling down to the south of England there was always a sprinkling of salt added. Why? To preserve the fish, to prevent corruption. Do you see the point?

It is remarkable that in the Beatitudes Jesus suggests that when Christians lose their tang or their preservative quality their challenge becomes useless in both worlds. They are no use to the world outside, and no use to the Christian world either. So it is a real challenge to consider going out into the world with the Christian character we have acquired, and letting that tell.

That brings us to what Jesus says about our being light (Matt. 5:16). I love this verse; I think it contains so much that I want to ponder it, and I want you to do so too. 'Let your light so shine.' We have all got to learn to draw upon the resources of the Spirit, the nine fruit of the Spirit, to work out our salvation in our daily lives – for God's pleasure and for the sake of the world. First of all, let the light so shine and the heavenly character of Christ's beautiful human life be seen in you. Don't flash it. That is to say, let them shine out – the inherent properties and qualities and excellencies that are in Jesus Christ who lived on the earth these thirty-three years, and died and was raised and is sitting at the right hand of the Father.

C.S. Lewis was so right in writing to Christians, 'Let's pretend.' Let's pretend that we are kind and be kind, because if you are a Christian the kindness is already there. It is given. It is not a pretence at all. Lewis was only using a figure of speech to bring out the fact. Let's pretend that we are kind and patient, and long-suffering, and do it. You will find when you try to be like Jesus that he helps you. We say, 'Oh, I can't do that. I can't.' Is that the faith that saves? 'I can't. I can't. I can't.' And the Lord in heaven is saying, 'Oh bless you, what wonderful faith! I have given you faith and all you can say is, I can't. I can't. I can't.' God help us. You can and you must.

Do you know the story about old Mary Slessor (who was born in the parish of Gilcomston, Aberdeen, incidentally, though she became a factory girl in Dundee). When she was a great missionary out there in Nigeria, a young missionary came out and at first she was embarrassed because everybody seemed so busy. She saw people running around doing things, and she could not see anything she could do. She went to Mary Slessor and she said, 'What will I do?' And Mary said to her so roundly, but so kindly too, 'Lassie, ye're no here to do, ye're here to be.' Because to be is to do, if Jesus is in you. Isn't that right?

It is often in someone's face, it is often in the most casual remark that Christ is seen in us. Think back to how you first saw him. I think of some of the people who have been won to Jesus Christ by their fellows. I make a point sometimes of asking them, 'Can you tell me the first time that it struck you there was something different about that person?' And sometimes they say, simply, 'It was just something about him that I saw before he ever uttered a word.' You see?, We must learn just to *be*. It is not so exciting at first as doing, and some Christians will not like being as much as they enjoy doing. But you have to *be* – that is, once you have Jesus Christ in your heart. Do you have him there?

THE HOLY SPIRIT

10: The Baptism of the Spirit

In the last study we build to set a bridge between the fruit of the Spirit and the gifts of the Spirit. The fruit of the Spirit is character; the gifts of the Spirit are for service. Having established that bridge, we now turn to the question of the baptism of the Spirit.

A great many people profess to have had what they believe many other Christians have not had, a baptism, what they call a baptism of the Spirit.

Let me say quite clearly that no one is questioning that Christians can have a second experience of God's grace, or a third one, or a fourth. That is not in question. Many would agree that there can be a second critical experience of God's grace. Many who hold that might call it a new consecration, or something like that. There is no difficulty about that. The difficulty lies in what in one sense is a quibble about words, and on that level is not of supreme importance. But sometimes it is much more than a quibble about words because fundamental Christian doctrine is involved, and people are led astray and confused. Something goes seriously wrong in their lives. It is a misuse of terms to speak about a subsequent blessing of God or experience of God's grace as a 'baptism'; for the very term 'baptism' implies an initiation. A baptism has to do with beginnings. Sometimes people use the term, the baptism of the Spirit, for a second experience of grace, and we let it go because one doesn't want to be finicky; but where wrong doctrine is involved we must not let it go because that is going to mislead them.

Let me put it as simply as this: you will not find any evidence in the New Testament for holding that a second experience of God's grace, whatever else it is, is to be called a baptism of the Spirit. It is just the wrong term.

I want to link this with our earlier emphasis on the unity of the Godhead and the inviolability of the Person of the Holy Spirit. There are three persons in the unity of the Godhead, and the Holy Spirit is a person. He is not an influence, he is not measurable or divisible. He himself is the very person of God. God the Father, God the Son, God the Holy Spirit; not three Gods but one.

Let me run over a sentence or two from the *Confession of Faith.*

> There is one only living and true God, who is infinite in being and perfections, a most pure spirit, invisible without body, parts or passions, immutable, immense, eternal, incomprehensible, almighty, most wise, most holy, most free, most absolute.

Then in another statement the *Confession* says: 'God hath all life, glory, goodness, blessedness in and of himself.' Then take the third paragraph of chapter three of the *Confession*:

> In the unity of the Godhead there be three Persons, of one substance, power and eternity, God the Father, God the Son and God the Holy Ghost. The Father is from none, neither begotten nor proceeding, the Son is eternally begotten of the Father, the Holy Ghost eternally proceeding from the Father and the Son.

Now, you need to know that. There is nothing so absolutely necessary for the practical things of your Christian life as sound teaching on the Trinity. Some people, as soon as you begin to use some of these biblical or theological terms or seem to be the slightest bit abstruse, just switch off. But that is very, very foolish of them for this is the most practical thing in the world. Some people who are called upon to conduct worship just cannot find anything to say to God in prayer at all except a few gracious and sweet platitudes. There is nothing wrong with them; they mean them every bit from their hearts. But if you want to speak pleasurably and satisfyingly to God in prayer, speak about him, who he is and what he has done. And there is no end to that. You can pray forever about that. That is what we will be doing in heaven, praying forever and praising too, all in one. The more we know about the God who has revealed himself to us in the Word and in Jesus Christ, we will be better worshippers of God and the better livers of the Christian life outside in the world. So this is the most important thing for you to know for your practical life, that the Godhead is a unity, that there is no division nor ever can be, any disagreement between God the Father, and God the Son, and God the Holy Spirit; they agree perfectly. They are absolutely at one.

But let me take this statement also, a categorical statement of John the Baptist which we find, interestingly enough, in all four Gospels. He says, 'I baptise you with water but he (Christ) will baptise you with the Holy Spirit.' Some of the Gospels say, 'with fire' (Matt. 3:11, Mark 1:8, Luke 3:16, John 1:26,33). The whole implication of this is that it is an operation of God, a once-for-all operation of God himself, not only something that he does but *someone* that he gives. You could almost say that the baptism of the Holy Spirit is not something that God does so much as God himself coming to live in us. It is as simple and radical as that.

Sometimes people try to drive a wedge between baptism and the first experience of Christ which we call conversion, on the one hand, and, on the other, the coming of the Holy Ghost to a person in grace and power. They instance Acts 19:1, 'While Apollos was at Corinth . . . he said to them, "Did you receive the Holy Spirit when you believed?" They said, "No, we have never even heard that there is a Holy Spirit." (Some people think this means that they had never heard the Holy Spirit had come, because they would have heard of some Holy Spirit if they knew anything of the Old Testament at all.) And he said, "Into what then were you baptised?" They said, "Into John the Baptist's baptism." Paul said, "John baptised with the baptism of repentance, telling the people to believe in the one who was to come after him, that is Jesus." On hearing this they were baptised into the name of the Lord Jesus. And when Paul had laid his hands on them the Holy Spirit came on them.'

The truth is that they were not really converted! The Holy Spirit had not come upon them. They had heard the gospel and they believed what they had heard but it was an incomplete gospel. John spoke to them about Jesus who was coming, but he could not point to his death and resurrection (which is the heart of the saving matter) because John the Baptist was dead before Jesus died and rose. And although I think they believed in what they knew, it was only when they accepted the whole gospel, the full gospel, that they could really and properly be said to be saved and the Holy Spirit came upon them. There was no question of a wedge of division there at all; absolutely none.

So that is where I want to start. The controversial instances of the coming of the Holy Spirit in the Acts of the Apostles show no evidence of a division into first and second works of grace. There is no invariable rule of baptism by water before the coming of the Holy Spirit, or the coming of the Holy Spirit before baptism. This can be domonstrated quite clearly. Take these four instances of conversion and the coming of the Holy Spirit: Acts 8, Acts 9, Acts 10, and the one we have read about in chapter 19. In Acts 8, when the apostles are in Samaria, baptism comes before the coming of the Holy Spirit. In Acts 9 the Holy Spirit comes upon Saul of Tarsus before he was baptised. In Acts 10 once more the Holy Spirit comes down upon them before they were baptised. And in Acts 19 it is the other way round. They are baptised first and then the Holy Spirit comes upon them. You see the first and the fourth instances here go together (Baptism – Spirit) and two and three are the other way round (Spirit – Baptism). So you cannot propound any rules about this. You cannot confine the Holy Spirit. He will come down and fill and bless and charge and thrill anybody he likes at any time he likes, irrespective of what is going on in any place in the world! He is sovereign, you see.

Look over these passages and see what happened. Here is Acts 8:4-17:

Now those who were scattered went about preaching the word. Philip went down to a city of Samaria, and proclaimed to them the Christ. And the multitudes with one accord gave heed to what was said by Philip, when they heard him and saw the signs which he did. For unclean spirits came out of many who were possessed, crying with a loud voice; and many who were paralyzed or lame were healed. So there was much joy in that city.

But there was a man named Simon who had previously practised magic in the city and amazed the nation of Samaria, saying that he himself was somebody great. They all gave heed to him, from the least to the greatest saying, 'This man is that power of God which is called Great.' And they gave heed to him, because for a long time he had amazed them with his magic. But when they believed Philip as he preached good news about the kingdom of God and the name of Jesus Christ, they were baptized, both men and women. Even Simon himself believed, and after being baptized he continued with Philip. And seeing signs and great miracles performed, he was amazed.

Now when the apostles at Jerusalem heard that Samaria had received the word of God, they sent to them Peter and John, who came down and prayed for them that they might receive the Holy Spirit; for it had not yet fallen on any of them, but they had only been baptized in the name of the Lord Jesus. Then they laid their hands on them and they received the Holy Spirit.

There can be the water without the Spirit, but the water speaks of the Spirit and his coming.

Acts 9:17 describes what happened to Saul after his experience on the road to Damascus: 'So Ananias . . . said, "Brother Saul, the Lord Jesus who appeared to you on the road by which you came, has sent me that you may regain your sight and be filled with the Holy Spirit." And immediately something like scales fell from his eyes and he regained his sight. Then he rose and was baptised.'

His conversion, his new birth, and his being filled with the Spirit were all part of the same great wonderful action.

Acts 10:44. This passage describes the giving of the Holy Spirit to the Gentiles. 'While Peter was still saying this (preaching to Cornelius and the other Gentiles at Caesarea on the Mediterranean coast) the Holy Spirit fell on all who heard the word. And the believers from among the circumcised (the Jewish believers who were there) who came with Peter (to see what would happen) were amazed, because the gift of the Holy Spirit had been poured out even on the Gentiles. For they heard them speaking in tongues and extolling God. Then Peter declared, "Can any one forbid water for baptizing these people who have received the Holy Spirit just as we have?"' It is all part of the one coming which the water symbolises; the coming of the Holy Spirit as a person to dwell in their lives.

The point in Acts 19 is the same. What is the baptism with the Spirit? Whatever term you use – baptism or conversion or new birth, regeneration, being saved – it is God through his Son in his Spirit coming to take up his abode in a human being's life and heart and coming to stay forever.

You can call it a baptism of love. 'Hope does not disappoint us, because God's love has been poured into our hearts through the Holy Spirit who has been given to us' (Rom. 5:5). As the Christmas carol says, 'Love came down at Christmas.' The love that came down at Christmas has stolen into our hearts. That is the baptism, the coming of love. And, of course, the coming of love, which is the first of the nine fruit of the Spirit (Gal. 5:22,23), has to do with character. Why has Jesus Christ come to dwell in your heart? Is it so that you might have specially thrilling, subjective experiences and manifestations of the Holy Spirit? No. Is it so that you can be a great preacher or a great witness? Not primarily. He has come so that he may form his image in your life. Ultimately he has come so that people you live with will see the authentic Jesus in you, notably in the kind deeds you do. That is it. And of course that is evangelism too, because when people see Jesus they either want him or they do not. So when you allow Jesus to grow up in you and let the fruit of the Spirit begin to appear and develop, people seeing Jesus in you will react in one or other way. Those who react favourably will say, 'Ah, there's something in him, there is something in her that I want.' There is nothing in the world that so builds up character the way love does, because love of other people sorts us out ourselves.

Do you see what I am saying? Conversion and the new birth, and the baptism of the Spirit are all to do with the one thing. It is the coming of God, the coming of Jesus, the coming of the Holy Spirit to your life. Is there progress? Is there development? Are there subsequent experiences? Oh, yes! But whatever names you use, do not try to say that God has half-come and that he is going to whole-come the next time. Now, this is more important than some Christians realise. This is where so many people go astray. God is one, and God coming into my heart is one.

But did you know that God can sometimes hide himself very wonderfully? Sometimes we take him in and say, 'Sit there' in some garret in the top of our house or some cellar in the bottom. 'That's your room. In there and don't come into the living room.' We confine him, and what is called the filling of the Spirit is not more of the Spirit poured in, but rather the Holy Spirit let out of his little cubby-hole under the stairs. That is one of the most practical things I could ever say. That is the secret.

There are so many reasons for this. Let me explain what this does psychologically. People who believe they have got half a God, half a Jesus or half a Holy Spirit are constantly straining and craving for something more. You can visualise them on their knees, agonising and weeping for God to come to give them some special experience. But all the time he is sitting there in their hearts saying, 'If you would let me out I would give you what you like.' But you see they are absolutely diverted from the thought of letting him out all through the house by straining at the horizon. They are looking for him away there. They become craving, discontented souls, whereas they have got all there is of him already.

It may take courage to open this door and say, 'Lord, I think you can go in there.' Or 'I think you could slip upstairs and see what's around there and spread your influence there.' But it has all to do with him within. From a psychological point of view that is very different. There is no more than Jesus, and you have got him all – but you don't realise it. It is like having a big fat bank account on which you are constantly able to draw. That is a very imperfect illustration, but you see the point. You draw on him more and more, but from within. The filling is *from within*, once he is there.

Here is a formula. It is an old one. There is only one baptism, but there are many fillings. There is an anointing of the Holy Spirit that can come upon us specially for special tasks. Every time a man preaches the gospel he needs a fresh anointing. But if God blesses him preaching on a Sunday morning, he cannot become complacent and assume that that anointing will do for night. For it will not. God will desert him in a kind of a way, and he will know when he stands again in the pulpit. But that is really another subject! Character is the first thing and love builds up character into maturity. The gifts are for service.

You see this in John the Baptist's life. Look at Luke 1:80. 'And the child grew and became strong in spirit.' And this is all the clearer in the Lord himself, in Luke 2:40: 'And the child grew and became strong, filled with wisdom; and the favour of God was upon him.' Later we read: 'And Jesus increased in wisdom and in stature, and in favour with God and man' (Lk. 2:52). That is character, growth in character. Then we read about him again: 'And Jesus, full (or filled) with the Holy Spirit, returned from the Jordan, and was led by the Spirit for forty days in the wilderness, to be tempted by the devil (as preparation for his service)' (Lk. 4:1). The filling of the Spirit and the fullness of the Spirit have very often to do with service, because the filling of the Spirit can be an experience of the power of God coming upon us for a specific task. And when you are not engaged in a specific task for the Lord the Holy Spirit of Jesus can lie dormant, even quiescent, in your heart. He rests in us, and then when we need his special power, when we need his special comfort, there he is. He has never left us.

Now, look at Acts 2:4. Here we find the Spirit coming to the disciples especially for service and growth in character. 'And they were all filled with the Holy Spirit and began to speak in other tongues, as the Spirit gave them utterance.' If you read on you will find that the tongues they spoke in were the languages of the pilgrims who had come to Jerusalem for the Feast of Pentecost. So when the Holy Spirit came upon the church first of all he gave them the power to speak in tongues they had never spoken – in Persian, in Greek, and a whole lot of other languages. The Holy Spirit enabled them to preach the gospel of God in these languages so that they could hear the gospel in their own tongue. That was the initial filling for service.

Then, in Acts 4:8 we see 'Peter, filled with the Holy Spirit' giving his defence as he speaks of the power of the gospel to the crowd that is standing by. In verse 13 we see the boldness of Peter and John. That doubtless has to do with their character, but it is also related to their service. The Holy Spirit comes and fills us both to build us up in character and to fit us for service. After Peter and John came back from prison we read that 'when they had prayed, the place in which they were gathered together was shaken; and they were all filled with the Holy Spirit and spoke the word of God with boldness' (whether it was in tongues or not does not matter). They spoke the word of God with boldness so that people heard them preaching the gospel (Acts 4:31).

Acts 6:3-5 has more to do with the character of the first deacons. 'They were full of the Spirit and of wisdom . . . full of faith and of the Holy Spirit.' But the filling of the Spirit in Acts 7:55 has to do with Stephen's service, his witness before those that were about to martyr him. 'But he, full of the Holy Spirit, gazed into heaven and saw the glory of God . . . .' Similarly in Acts 9:17, Paul was filled with the Holy Spirit and soon began to preach the gospel in Damascus. In Acts 11:24 we are told of Barnabas 'a good man, full of the Holy Spirit and of faith.' I think this related both to his character and to his service. That is certainly true of Acts13:9: 'Saul, who is also called Paul, filled with the Holy Spirit, looked intently at him (Elymas the magician)', and spoke to him in the power of the Holy Spirit.

You see, a true Christian character is bound to be used by God. Mind you, the extent to which it is used may partly depend on your faith in believing that your life is telling. You can be a very good Christian yet your life does not tell because you are not believing that it will. It is not easy when we are all so imperfect, but you need to believe that your life is going to tell. And before you can do that, you have to be sure that Christ is in your life, really in you and that you are joined with him; and that you are not pulling down the blinds and hiding him because you are ashamed of him. You are not to flaunt him, not to flash your light, you are to let it shine. You are just living your normal ordinary Christian life and letting your life tell, and you are believing that it is going to tell. You are not going to ask to see what it is telling, who it is telling, what the result is in people's minds and hearts. You see, you cannot do that. If you are a gardener you have to learn to put the seed in and leave it. All you do is water and feed it and leave it. You do not poke in it and keep looking to see if it is coming up; you leave it, and it will grow. But it will take time. It is exactly the same here.

So this is the sequence. He is in you. You are not hiding him. You are glad he is there, and you are enjoying him. You are yielding yourself progressively to him, letting him have his way with your life. You say to him: 'Go anywhere and do what you like because I can trust you. You are kind and gracious and considerate. Sometimes you will ask me to do something that I don't understand, and it may frighten me to death, but I'll still trust you, even when I don't understand.' And all the time, since you have not pulled down the blinds and drawn the curtains, you believe people are seeing what's going on. And they will!

THE HOLY SPIRIT

11: Apostles and Prophets

Somebody was saying to me this morning about a friend, 'Oh, if there is more of Jesus to be had, she'll go anywhere.'

But there isn't more of Jesus to be had. You may say, 'We haven't got all of Jesus.' But yes, in a sense we have – when he comes to dwell in our hearts. It is not a part of Jesus, not a divided Jesus, not half a Jesus we have. We may not yet have experienced his potential, but it is all there. It is all *given*, because the Holy Spirit has been given to us. It is one of the mysteries of the Christian life how modestly and quietly the Lord can live in our hearts and put up with an awful lot and never assert himself – until sometimes we could think he had fled. I am sure there are some young Christians who may sometimes think, 'I am not a Christian after all. He has gone. He can't be here. I can't feel him. I feel so sinful. I have slipped. I have fallen. I have made a mistake. He can't be with me. He is gone. Help me!' Yet they really wanted him with all their hearts in the first place when they invited him in. Is he so fitful? Is he so easily offended? He is grieved by our sins and our fallings and all that kind of thing, but offended and run out? Never! He is there 'for keeps'. He is there not only for time but for eternity. He is determined to change you. He says, 'Oh you have tripped up again. Come back to me and say you are sorry and I will enfold you in my arms again and we will go on and you will do better next time. Trust in my grace and not yourself.' But he will never go. He will never run out on you. That is impossible. There he is, in his personality, in his being with all his grace, all his fruit, to bless you and cause you to grow in grace and in spiritual stature.

Let me say one thing more before we go on to the question of the gifts. Because the idea of the 'baptism of the Spirit' must be reserved for the new birth, that is not to say that we may not have second experiences and third and fourth experiences too; though very often a *second* experience can be quite singular and dramatic. We may come to a point when we become dissatisfied with our Christian life and find that while we have received Christ into our hearts and he has given us all of himself, we realise there is more, we are able to yield to him. As we have already suggested, we say to him: 'That's your room. Now, don't you keep running all over the house. You stay there. That is your place.' And we keep him in his attic. There comes a time when we say, 'Lord, here are the keys. Go everywhere. Have me all. Fill me' (from within, of course). You can call that consecration or dedication if you like. That can happen very dramatically.

It does not always happen so; some people just grow in grace.

For instance, I used to know a man who told us he was converted as a young lad, but he never had any joy. He was involved in Christian work because his family were, but he never had any joy in the Lord. He went through all the motions, even to taking part in open air meetings. Then one day somebody took him and put him into the middle of the open air ring and said, 'Go on; give your testimony.' Well, he did not have much testimony to give, because he had no joy in his life, but he opened his mouth to say the most that he could. He had hardly opened his mouth when his whole soul was filled and flooded with joy, and he could have danced, let alone given his testimony!

Now, we must turn our attention to some of the gifts of the Spirit. The first gift of the Spirit to the church (1 Cor. 12:28; Eph. 4:11) is that of *apostles*. The Greek word is a compound one: *apo-stellō* meaning to send away or send out. An apostle is a sent out one. But there are several aspects to the New Testament's use of the term apostle. The first is that he is one who has seen the risen Lord. One or two scriptures are relevant here. In 1 Corinthians 9:1,2, Paul says: 'Am I not free? Am I not an apostle? Have I not seen Jesus our Lord?' Apparently Saul of Tarsus had never seen Jesus in the mortal flesh. We are not sure about that, but the likelihood is that he had never seen him until he was trudging up the road to Damascus. He got the shock of his life. The one he despised and whose followers he wanted to imprison and kill, like Stephen who had been stoned to death because he was a Jesus man – Saul of Tarsus sees and hears that very Jesus from heaven!

Luke 24:45 is also relevant here. 'Then he opened their minds to understand the Scriptures (and that must of course be the Old Testament Scriptures for the New Testament ones weren't written then). Thus it is written (here is Jesus himself expounding the Old Testament), that the Christ should suffer and on the third day rise from the dead, and that repentance and forgiveness of sins should be preached in his name to all nations, beginning from Jerusalem. You are witnesses of these things' especially that on the third day he rose from the dead. Again, Jesus says in Acts 1:8: 'But you shall receive power when the Holy Spirit has come upon you; and you shall be my witnesses.' Note that it is the risen Jesus who is saying this, before he ascended. Then notice what happens in Acts 1:21-23: 'So one of the men who have accompanied us during all the time that the Lord Jesus went in and out among us, beginning from the baptism of John until the day when he was taken up from us – one of these men must become with us a witness to his resurrection. And they put forward two, Joseph called Barsabbas, who was surnamed Justus, and Matthias.' And Matthias was chosen as the twelfth apostle. That establishes the first definition of an apostle. He is someone who has seen the risen Lord. As we see, that included Paul and Matthias (1 Cor. 15:8 and Acts 9:5).

But there is a second aspect: apostles are a unique company of the servants of God. They are built in, over Christ, as the foundation of the church (Eph. 2:20). I often think that people studying the Scriptures fail to see the significance of this verse. Look at it carefully. Paul is writing here to the Ephesians, Gentile Christians. He is saying to them, you Gentiles are no longer strangers and sojourners (second-class citizens to the Jews), but you are fellow citizens with the saints, members of the household of God, built upon the foundation of the apostles and prophets (prophets here I think means New Testament prophets), Christ Jesus himself being the chief cornerstone (the only foundation of the church). That is the second aspect of an apostle. He is one of those who are built into the foundation of the church. They are a unique company never to be repeated. There will never be another apostle Paul or John, or Peter, or James. Part of the reason is that they were used by God to write his holy Word, and God's holy Word is now completed. At the very end of Revelation 22 the Spirit through John warns the saints about adding to the Word or subtracting from the Word. You must not add to the Scriptures, nor take away one jot or one tittle of the Hebrew letters from them. So the apostles are unique in a double sense. They are in the foundations of the church, the next stones built above the foundation stone Jesus Christ. But they were also uniquely used of God to communicate his holy Word, the saving truth of the blessed gospel.

But then there is a third, wider context in which the term 'apostle' is used. You can take the word from the Scriptures and apply its simple definition to anyone who is sent out by the Holy Spirit to do any particular task. You could say that any missionary, any minister or any lay servant of God anywhere who is sent out to do a task is an apostle. You can use the word today in that sense if you wish. Some have used the word 'apostle' as others would use 'elders' or 'deacons'. But we must remember that Scripture speaks of apostles in those first two particular and unique ways: apostles who have seen the risen Lord and who are in the foundation of the church; and apostles who have been used for the transmission or the revelation of God of the full gospel.

We turn now to the second gift, *prophets* (Rom. 12:6, compare v.3;1 Cor. 12:10). It is interesting that in 1 Corinthians 12:10 prophets are mentioned sixth not second (as in Romans 12 and Ephesians 4). Prophets are mentioned following the utterance of wisdom, faith, healing and miracles. Now, what shall we say of prophets? Are they also a unique company? Look back to Ephesians 2:20. They are also the foundation of the church. In that sense they also belong to a unique and never-to-be-repeated company. But that does not of course exclude the use of the term in Scripture for others. We must look at that now.

What are prophets? Some people think of prophets primarily, some even exclusively, as fore-tellers. That is often their office, but they are primarily *forth*-tellers, that is speakers forth for God. Priests speak to God for men; prophets speak to men from God.

You know that Christ is prophet, priest and king. He is prophet (Deut. 18:15) in that he comes to declare God's word fully and finally. He is God's last word to man. Then by his death and rising, his ascension and work of intercession in heaven on the ground of his sacrifice for us, he is our High Priest. He is speaking to God for us and pleading our forgiveness and continuance in his fellowship. So prophets speak to men from God and priests speak to God for men.

Look at Deuteronomy 18:15. The first prophet spoken of in the Scripture is Abraham, and perhaps the next significant prophet is Moses himself. See what the Lord through Moses says about that: 'The Lord your God will raise up for you (Israelites) a prophet like me from among you, (and of course he is prophesying of Christ's coming to declare the word of God) from your brethren (and Jesus of course is one of their brethren; he is of the tribe of Judah and of the house of David, he is a Jew of the Jews).' To see the significance of this, look at Hebrews 12:18: 'For you have not come to what may be touched, a blazing fire, and darkness, and gloom, and a tempest, and the sound of a trumpet, and the voice whose words made the hearers entreat that no further messages be sent to them . . . but (you have not come to Mount Sinai) you have come to Mount Zion and to the city of the living God, the heavenly Jerusalem, and to innumerable angels in festal gathering . . . and to Jesus, the mediator of a new covenant . . . .' You see the beautiful contrast? Back to Deuteronomy 18:17-22. 'And I will put my words in his mouth, and (like the prophet Jeremiah) he shall speak to them all that I command him. And whoever will not give heed to my words which he shall speak in my name, I myself will require it of him. But the prophet who presumes to speak a word in my name which I have not commanded him to speak (a false or a lying prophet) but who speaks in the name of other gods, that same prophet shall die. And if you say in your heart, "How may we know the word which the Lord has not spoken?" (a fair question) – when a prophet speaks in the name of the Lord, if the word does not come to pass or come true, that is a word which the Lord has not spoken; the prophet has spoken it presumptuously, you need not be afraid of him.'

These are prophets in the primary sense, those who are in the foundation of the church. I suppose this means also that they were inspired to speak God's holy word in the sense of giving revelation of the truth as we have it in the New Testament. But the New Testament speaks also of prophets in a secondary sense in Acts 2:11; 1 Corinthians 14:1; Acts 19:6; 21:9; 1 Corinthians 11:4,5. There are prophets in the church who may be moved to prophesy ecstatically, and their prophecies need to be interpreted. There are others who will prophesy in the language that is understood by the people. But it is the common experience that where the word of God in its fullness is known most prophecy, forthtelling and foretelling, comes from the exposition of the Scriptures. So, you see, as with guidance, so with regard to what is called prophecy, the Word has it all! The Spirit of prophecy cannot possibly give to anyone anything that is not in perfect agreement with the Holy Scriptures; and indeed it is from the Holy Scriptures, pondering Scripture, poring over it, and by the Holy Spirit applying them to our contemporary situation that the true purpose of the Spirit is made known.

I want to say a word about prophetic insight in the secondary sense. One of the insights that God has given us here, I believe, is one that is necessary to the revival of the church in our land. It began with a feeling that one wanted to understand the deeper things of the atonement of the death of Christ, until one began to see that there were different dimensions in the death of Christ; that Christ died to deal with our *sins*, what we had done wrong; that Christ died also to deal with our *sin*, our natures that had gone wrong; lastly, and most significantly, that Christ died to deal with the source and author of sin, Satan himself. I believe this is the message of the hour. I believe the next decades in our land's history will prove that an absolute essential of the Christian faith, if there is to be a movement of the Spirit and our nation is going to be turned back from disaster and loss: Satan, or the third dimension, has to be exposed and expounded to the church.

One of the things we have seen and are seeing, and I believe we will see in days to come, is a growing number of Bible-hungry young people longing for the deeper things of the Word of God, savouring them, applying them to their own lives, and to the nation. In the midst of it there are a great many in the church who will have absolutely nothing to do with what we call a conservative evangelical ministry. You will hear people all over the place discounting us as behind the times, in a backwater, obscurantists and so on. But all the time – and this is something that has happened within the last thirty, forty years in our islands – there has grown up a whole literature on the Scriptures by conservative evangelical scholars, equal to the quality, insight and ability of any liberal scholars today. And these scholars are increasing in insight, in stature and conviction. Although a great many of those in the church will not listen, and despise and condemn, at the same time the church in general becomes colder, more lifeless, more helpless, more hopeless, more taken up with other things than the Word of God and society reaches a new low in morality.

There is pollution and a frightening increase in world population. We are devouring resources. And in the midst of a situation which even the sanest and most balanced scientific and intellectual prophets would say is dire and frightening, we believe that God has purposes of grace for these years towards the end of our century. We look to see God working yet more wonderfully and mightily. The time will come when it will be possible to put so many conservative evangelical ministries on the map of Scotland, to go no further afield, that the map will be covered with men. There are still large barren areas in our beloved Scotland; there are hungry souls, sheep looking up unfed. But the day will come. Wait and see it.

Some of you young folk are called to this responsibility and this privilege, to see the day when there will be a turning to God, a hunger for his Word, a repenting of sins, a turning back to that which is holy and righteous and good and pure. Then – this is my hope – the nation will be at least partly purged and cleansed, and wickedness will be curbed, and a great new missionary expansion take place. This I see is coming. Why am I so sure? What makes me most sure is that I see God is doing a deep work. When you build a skyscraper you dig deep. And for a long time behind the barricades you see nothing. You think, what is going on behind these railings, these barricades – nothing? Oh no, they are digging deep to build high. That is what God is doing. And this is part of that gift I believe, the gift of prophecy that God will give to the church today, to declare God's Word and make men listen and turn. Are you going to be part of this? Then, as the apostle Paul says, 'Desire spiritual gifts, the higher gifts, that of prophesying.'

THE HOLY SPIRIT

12: Evangelists, Pastors and Teachers

The gifts of the Spirit are distributed among the believers, this gift to that one and this to another. It is quite clear that the first gift to the church was apostles, then prophets. Apostles in the primary sense are those who had seen the risen Lord and who are in the foundations of the church; and indeed – in the case of the apostles Paul, John, James and Peter – have given to us a great deal of the New Testament revelation, the fullness of the truth about the gospel of the Lord Jesus Christ. They therefore were not only very important people in the history of God's redeeming work but possessed unique ministries never to be repeated again.

The prophetic element must always be in the church. The more we know the Word, the more we have studied and swept through it and seen the rhythms of God's workings in history, the more we saturate ourselves in the Word and understand it and the relation between the two testaments, the more we shall be able by the help of God, by his Spirit, his prophetic Spirit, to understand what God is doing throughout history. That will help us to have some conception of what God is purposing to do in our time. So we press our eyes to the window and look out to see where Christ's church is likely to be going with God's help to the end of this century. It may be a very, very significant time in the purpose of God, as well as in the history of man. J.A. Motyer speaks about the prophets 'having an awareness of God working in history'.

We should remember that prophecies with regard to the future of this old world give two extremes: promises of movements of God's

Spirit, including an outpouring of God's Spirit on the whole nation of Israel (Rom. 11) before the end of the age. On the other hand there are prophecies of the apostasy that is to come upon Christ's church and of days of persecution. You cannot read the Revelation of John without seeing that. So days will grow darker and days will grow brighter. The days are bound to grow brighter for those who are the Lord's, as people travel on with the Lord because he seems to get better and better as we know him more. Otherwise the days will grow darker unless from time to time God may be pleased to pour out his Spirit.

So the prophetic element is very important, and we need constantly to study God's Word and cry to him in prayer to help us to see where he is going. This is part of the purpose of congregational gathering for prayer and part of the reason why I put so much stress upon it. What we are trying to do, I hope humbly and yet very determinedly, is to see where God is going. You see, he loves to work quietly for a time, and nobody thinks anything is happening. They sneered and laughed at poor old Noah for about a hundred years, hammering home the nails in his ark. They said, 'You silly man, building a great battleship in the middle of the country.' But the Flood came!

So we need to discern God's working in history, even in a dark day. Can you see God working in his church today? Do you *want* to see it? I can see him working in his church today, and I am more hopeful than I was thirty, forty or fifty years ago, far more hopeful that God is going to do great things, whatever else may happen in the world.

Paul says that there are apostles, prophets, and next, *evangelists*. We turn first to 1 Corinthians 12:7-11, 28-30. In this chapter you will not find evangelists or evangelism in any explicit sense. But of course, one could imagine evangelism taking place in the exercise of most if not all of these gifts. Don't you think?

Now to Romans 12:4. Where do you see any reference to evangelists and evangelism here? Here also evangelism is not explicit as a particular gift of the Spirit or as an office within the church – because it belongs to all Christians. Evangelism isn't really what many evangelical people think it is: to do with placards, missions and special opportunities and all that goes with a great big circus. We are not excluding large meetings; doubtless God puts it into the hearts of some men to do something like that. But it really is very interesting that there is no reference in either of these passages to anything as explicit as evangelism or evangelists.

But in Ephesians 4:11 we find the word we are looking for. God's gifts to the church are that some should be 'apostles, some prophets, some evangelists . . . .' The most significant reference to evangelists in the Scriptures apart from this is in 2 Timothy 4:1: 'I charge you in the presence of God . . . preach the Word.' This is how evangelism is most often expressed in the Bible: 'preach the Word', which for us embraces everything from Genesis to Revelation. It is absolutely tragic that for so many, from the Bible has been extracted what is called the 'simple gospel'. It is sometimes almost fiercely set over against the rest of the Bible, so that if you read the rest of the Bible, people will say, 'That's not the gospel.' It is *all* gospel – good news, with the background and preparation of the bad news of course. It is all good news: it is the revelation of God, from Genesis to Revelation. So it is 'preach the Word'.

Now, all that is included in the Bible is the very Word of God, and belongs to a category absolutely distinct from the very finest of other writings. There are some very fine writings, for example in the Apocrypha. I have suggested as some writers have, that Paul very likely had read the book of Wisdom, and especially the fifth chapter where he doubtless got the idea of the metaphor of warfare, weapons, and all that kind of thing. But it doesn't belong to the Word of God. When you read literature outside the Bible, I think most people with average intelligence and certainly spiritual sensibilities would be able to tell that it was of a different quality and character. It does not have that glow about it that marks it out as the authoritative word of God. Scripture is not merely good devotional or spiritual or religious writing, but a word that has the stamp of the authority of the Almighty God upon in. Preach that then.

Paul continues: 'Be urgent in season and out of season, (with your heart always on fire with love for people. You cannot be a Christian without loving people. If you have a disdainful, contemptuous or fearful spirit with regard to people, there is something wrong with your Christian life. The more you love Christ, the more you learn to love people, all kinds of people; loving them even in their sin, as he did us) convince, rebuke and exhort (says Paul to this young servant he is sending out to be a shepherd to the sheep), be unfailing in patience and in teaching . . . .' But what about evangelism? 'As for you, always be steady, endure suffering, do the work of an evangelist, fulfil your ministry.'

Now, could anybody in the whole world doubt that from these references in Scripture it is perfectly clear that evangelism has to be seen in a teaching context? Do you see that? Is that so apparent to you that there is nothing to argue about?

2 Timothy 3 ends magnificently with a comprehensive statement on the sufficiency of Scripture to equip the man of God. In his last extant chapter Paul now charges Timothy, the young servant of God, how he should use the Scriptures. The charge is solemn because it is given before God and Jesus Christ who is to judge by his appearing in his kingdom, those who will then be living and dead. It is this which makes our calling so responsible, not only the coming judgment but the fact that the Judge who is to come is before us now, and we are being judged by him, however kindly, every moment. We are subject to that constant judgment that metes out rewards and punishments day by day, presaging the final summation, which will leave nothing out; but, with effortless accuracy, will appoint each to perfect felicity or everlasting despair. And even within those adverse realms, what nuances of reward and retribution, pleasure and pain there will be as the harvest of this earthly life!

The manifestation of Christ in his glory to establish a perfect kingdom will settle all for ever – yet not arbitrarily, but according to what we have done, whether it be good or evil. To live in the light of this is not too strict, for not to do so is to be dangerously lax and to flirt with, if not disaster, at least dismay. Each, then, must work at his God-given task.

The Christian minister's task is to proclaim the Word. But that is a comprehensive task. Does rightly to divide the Word of truth demand a lifetime of leisured study, a sequestered occupation whence the minister emerges like a scholar to make sage pronouncements and then retire again to the quietness of his study? Not on your life! For all his need of balanced judgment, he must be among people. The task is urgent. Is he not a dying man preaching to dying men – bringing home to them, whether it is convenient or not, the judgment under which they live, convicting, exhorting with all patience and teaching? The Christian minister is always on duty, standing between a true understanding of the saving word and the life of man to which that word has to be constantly, faithfully, relevantly and effectively applied. It is a full-time task, with time off only to sharpen the scythe to do a better, that is a more fruitful, job.

How men professedly called to the ministry of the Word can turn aside to other tasks, however Christian, which are properly the tasks of the laymen, we do not know. Say what they like, it is a dereliction of God-given duty, if indeed God ever chose them for it. The apostles knew this at the peak of the Pentecostal effusion (Acts 6:1-7). Nor can it be justified for a moment that Christian ministers should desert their calling (unless it was never their calling, in which case let them say so and decline its emoluments) on the grounds that Christian laymen are not rising to their duty in society. For it is the Christian minister's task to prepare laymen to know and do their duty with as much urgency as the minister must do his. It is not his to do the layman's job for him. This would seem to be elementary. You can tell that many men were never called to the ministry when you see how readily they abandon it for other tasks and come down to something lower. So many ministers have other preoccupations which seem to claim so much of their attention. Recreation? Yes, but if we live near enough to these verses in Timothy our tensions will be resolved and our all will be devoted to proclaiming the Word with passion and with patience.

Paul continues: 'The time is coming when people will not endure sound teaching' (2 Tim. 4:3). The urgency charged in verses 1 and 2 is now related to the growing trend of refusing sound teaching. If we ask when this takes place, the answer is surely that it happens whenever and wherever sound teaching is offered; for there are those attracted to the Christian cause on account of a variety of its products. When faced with it stem and root they prove to be cut flower enthusiasts, who love beautiful blooms but will have nothing to do with the toil and soil of the garden. It is only when sound teaching is pressed upon them that they realise that there are elements in the Christian faith with which they profoundly disagree, and they proceed to campaign for their elimination. Away with all this teaching, they say. It is this fact which so often shakes Christian ministers, who out of the goodness of their hearts tie themselves in knots trying to reconcile the objections of nice people with the orthodox faith they have to declare. They should have more sense, or at least learn it from Jesus, who when Nicodemus challenged the necessity of the new birth simply hammered its truth the more firmly home. 'We speak of what we know, and testify to what we have seen; but you receive not our witness.' (Jn. 3:11). The only hope of making you see it, Nicodemus, is that, ignoring your objections, or better still out-arguing them, we drive home the truth – to your softening or hardening.

What is this desire to compile a list of ear-tickling teachers but a ruse of the devil to frustrate the purpose of the sound teaching which alone builds Christian character? There is nothing in the world the devil hates so much as Christian character produced by the teaching of Scripture applied to our lives by the Holy Spirit. That is why he will do anything he can to turn the Christian church into an entertainment agency. It does not matter to him whether the entertainment is secular or sacred, as long as it neglects character-building teaching. A great deal that neglects or even refuses such teaching today is called sacred. It may be that, in effect, the greatest enemies of the gospel are those who offer it to the world on superficial terms – as though that is all they themselves see in it. Christian entertainment takes the place of worldly entertainment, and the worst feature of it is that it feels smug about the change because it is sanctified by Christian language. Yet the effect is as fruitless as if it were secular. What matters whether it is in a beetle-drive, bingo or evangelistic hall where men escape the mighty challenge of the Word of God? The loss is all the same. Indeed, it is less hypocritical in the former than in the latter.

It is not for nothing that it is the 'given' part of salvation – justification – that superficially evangelistic folk stress, the part where man simply opens his empty, soiled hands for the gift of forgiveness and Christ's righteousness. But what about the working out of that righteousness, from the heart to the finger tips? That is what we may call the 'doing' part of salvation (although all our salvation is from God). It takes courage to embark upon this 'doing' and work out salvation in sweat, blood, toil and tears. Yet who has Christ who does *not* embark on such an enterprise? A merely superficial evangelistic emphasis that purveys the diluted stuff that passes for the gospel, knows not the Christ of the cross. We already see some of the fruit of this in evangelistic novels and films which portray the Christian life as a kind of hallelujah paradise and are totally devoid of the realism of the New Testament. 'Come to Christ and get your problems solved.' Fair enough! But we must also say, 'Come to Christ and get a new set of problems that will break your heart a thousand times over. And find your solutions only yonder, on the further side of the grave.' It is a heart-breaking life for those who will have it, but it is a heart-mending life too. It is John 12:24 yet again: 'Except a corn of wheat fall into the ground and die it abides alone. But if it dies it brings forth much fruit.'

But in the end a minister must fulfil his own God-given ministry. He may still hope that others will see its fruits and emulate it, with all due modifications for his own personality and his own situation. But whatever happens he must not be swayed by statistics, numbers, or popularity. It is not a scoreboard he must consult, but the face of Christ mirrored in the Scriptures. That face is a wondrous mirror of sorrow and joy, pleasure and pain, beauty and gauntness. It welcomes and warns, but its magnetism will eventually be greater than its repulsion. At least this is the test of a minister truly called, that a thousand crosses, all very rugged, will never drive him away from his only help and hope. Thus Paul with tender ruthlessness bids Timothy maintain that guardedness which is possible only to the sober, resisting all subtle blandishments to relax with the world, yet ever bravely willing to suffer the evils which are the penalty of resisting the seductions of the Devil, doing the work of an evangelist fully carrying out his service.

What is the work of an evangelist? It is to make known the good news of Christ. All of it? Yes, all of it which is given to men. But this work must have a beginning. You cannot initiate man into all the glories of the faith at once. Yet a whole Christ must be presented from the start, lest at any point in the believer's pilgrimage he turns and says, 'Oh, I didn't bargain for that.' Does someone object that this blurs the distinction between the teacher and the evangelist? Well, is that not a good thing? What is the good news but the word of God to man in Jesus Christ? What is the teacher to teach but the good news, all of it. The line is often too clearly drawn. Indeed Donald Guthrie, one of our leading evangelical scholars, writes that, 'There was probably a good deal of fluidity in the use of terms describing various offices, and there is no need to suppose that the terms were uniformly used.' This seems to be borne out by the apostle's concluding remark in verse 5. He says, 'Fully carry out your service' or 'make full proof of your ministry.' What is this but a warning lest he produces converts who are drawn by half a gospel, sooner or later to be repelled by the other half?

'But,' you say, 'the gospel is not made up of two contrary halves.' No, but it does contain profound paradoxes that will be fully resolved only in glory. It therefore behoves the Christian minister to make sure that in his presentation of the truth the cost is as prominent as the gift; the suffering as faithfully proffered as the glory. Yet that is not really the way to put it. The suffering is the *way* to the glory. This has been obscured in evangelicalism by the almost exclusive stress upon the gift. It is a gift with a purpose, to be used to an end. And there is the rub. It is all very well to come to Jesus and drink from the wells of his salvation, but that makes us strange bedfellows for the worldling. Has your evangel made that plain? And what about the Devil? Does your evangel include that?

What then of pastors and teachers? Before we look at the work of the pastor we must look at the pastor himself. By definition he is the under-shepherd of the flock. His primary task is to feed the flock by leading them to green pastures. He has also to care for them when they are sick or hurt, and seek them when they go astray. The importance of the pasture depends on the value of the sheep. And if you pursue the pastoral metaphor a little further, Israel's sheep were reared, fed, tended, retrieved, healed and restored for sacrifice on the altar of God. Many who are called pastors, having lost the end in view, or never having seen it, become pedlars of various sorts of words, gulling the people or leading them into their own power. When they fail to gather a clientele for their own brand of merchandise, they up-tail and away and leave the flock, for they are not really interested in the flock of God.

This is one of the marks of a new character and quality of ministry in our land, that ministers seeking a congregation do not make up their minds on the basis of the character of the manse. Nor does the decision depend on how convenient education is for the children, although the children need education. It does not depend on anything other than this that God calls a man, and lays his hand upon him, and puts it into the heart of a people to desire him, and when they call him they mean him to remain with them and be pastor and shepherd and teacher to them until God – and no one else – should call him away. The fruit of that kind of ministry is abundant.

There are two great influences in Scotland today. One is undoubtedly the Universities' and Colleges' Christian Fellowship, working in the colleges and universities of our land, with its literature and the influence of its servants, godly travelling secretaries. The other is the quality of ministries given by God who sets men down and makes them remain and teach the Word until people have grown up in that Word. And the most fruitful ministries in the land today are of those who have been fed and brought up on the Word of God by solid, systematic teaching. I have absolutely no hesitation in saying that of all the gifts of the Spirit this is the gift that God would give to his church in our land today.

I am concerned with the present and our own land – with our own church and God's calling to us. Apostles are gone, and the prophets, though I believe there are still prophetic elements in the church. Evangelists there must be, and the laymen are the evangelists. You are the evangelists. You will all be out in the world tomorrow, one way or another. You are the ones to touch people's souls for Jesus Christ, and you will do it according to how you have received the Word of God as it is taught, as it is fed to you by faithful shepherds of the flock. Can you see therefore the burden that is on the heart of any pastor?

The fruit of such a ministry is seen in a thousand ways. It is particularly seen in the character that is inculcated in those who receive it and respond to it. But, naturally, it also creates problems.

It is only when we delve deeply into the Word of God that a great many problems that are not lying on the surface begin to be seen. If this work is summed up as the ministry of the whole Word to the whole flock, it is not confined to the pulpit. Obviously not. But all the rest follows and flows from the whole ministry of the Word.

When I first came here there were some who told me that the success of my ministry would depend on my visitation. I believed that and acted upon it for a few years and gave myself to it to the point of exhaustion. But I proved that the more I visited some people the less they came to church. That is not to despise visitation. It is a great grief and sorrow of my heart that there is not more of that done. What brings people to church is the Word of God, the living Word given to them to feed their souls. And it is the fruit of that ministry which builds churches and produces ministers, evangelists and missionaries that God would scatter throughout the world.

It very often happens that when we discuss in private the word that has been given, and the problems that it has raised or part-solved in somebody's life, the best advice to be given is to go back and sit under it more and more. It is not in private conversation that souls are straightened out so much as in further study and listening to the Word. How often have people said that they have spent a week wrestling over some spiritual or moral problem, and coming to church have had it all solved in the ministry of the Word! If only we would trust the Holy Spirit more, he would guide us into all the truth. That does not mean that we will know everything, so that we become walking theological encyclopedias. But he will lead us to know all the truth we need to live Christ's life to the fullest extent in our personal situation.

So, it seems to me that evangelism, pastoring and teaching belong very closely together, and are to be bound up within the local church situation. Thus pastors, teachers and evangelists will together produce Christians of character and quality. Then evangelists will be sent into the world with burning, flaming hearts, bringing people to Christ, showing his love in their ordinary daily situation, and thus building Christ's church.

THE DEVIL

1: The Devil's Origin, Nature and History in the Old Testament

The Bible indicates the origin of the Devil more by hints than by direct statements. He was one of the sons, or angels, of God (see Job 1 and 2), apparently one of the brightest of them. He seems to have fallen away on account of his preoccupation with his own beauty and glory, and with his ambition to unseat the God of glory from his throne in order to take his place. This we learn from two prophetic passages, Ezekiel 28:11-19, and Isaiah 14:12-15, which should be studied carefully to see to what extent the prophets are taken by the Spirit beyond the tyrant rulers they inveigh against (the king of Babylon in Isaiah and the king of Tyre in Ezekiel), and to what extent they portray the head of all evil, Satan himself, in his origin and fall.

Ezekiel seems to go further back than Isaiah, to Lucifer's beauty and wisdom, which corrupted him, until his evil intent was exposed and he was cast out of God's presence. In Isaiah he has already fallen, the reason being given in terms of self-will: 'You said in your heart, "I will ascend to heaven; above the stars of God (whatever 'stars' mean there) I will set my throne on high: I will sit on the mount of assembly in the far north; I will ascend above the heights of the clouds, I will make myself like the Most High"' (Is.14:13, 14).

'I will make myself like....' It sounds pathetic, doesn't it? A creature, however high and fine, trying to ape the uncreated God, is foolish, and that is just what the Devil is – foolish; but he hedges himself round with such consummate powers of deception that we are not supposed to notice it.

Someone once took exception to Malcolm Muggeridge speaking of the Fall of man as a joke, and it may be that only a humorist would dare to see it like that. But from one point of view we should all be humorists here, for the right attitude to the Devil is that expressed in Psalm 2:4: 'He who sits in the heavens laughs; the Lord has them in derision.' The difficulty is that we associate humour with frivolity. That is unfortunate, for we often read far more sense and wisdom in the humour columns of newspapers than elsewhere, certainly more than in political columns – and often more than in religious articles! In that second psalm the enemies of God and of his people were saying 'Let us burst their bonds asunder, and cast their cords from us' (v. 3) and God, says the psalmist, laughs at the diabolical hopes of the Devil's whole crew.

This diabolical folly is perhaps not entirely unconnected with the status of angels as fallen, in comparison with the status of man. Psalm 8 helps here, as does its quotation in Hebrews 2. We speak of man as the 'crown of creation' because he alone of the creatures of God, so far as we can see from the Scriptures, is made in the image of God. When God came to earth he came as man, not as angel or lower creature, and it is men who are to judge the world including angels, says Paul (1 Cor. 6:2, 3). And the Spirit of Jesus through John says of men and women (not of angels) that, 'He who conquers, I (Christ) will grant him to sit with me on my throne, as I myself conquered and sat down with my Father on his throne' (Rev. 3:21). That honour is granted to no other creature.

Furthermore, the writer to the Hebrews says that angels, though 'winds and flames of fire', are serving spirits, and are sent to minister to the heirs of salvation as their underlings (Heb. 1:14). We speak of 'ministering angels', which means serving angels. This language must be taken seriously when we come to consider the spiritual forces of evil. We must not be confident in ourselves with regard to them (as fallen creatures under their sway, we are at a serious disadvantage) but we can be confident in another Man, to whom angels are 'small fry'. Jesus never argued with the Devil, but answered him shortly, and bade him go. He would not even suffer him to stand in his presence but commanded him to get behind him. By his authority we must similarly resist the Devil (1 Pet. 5:9).

This leads us back to the beginning of Satan's activity in history, as recorded in Genesis 3. Derek Kidner is inclined, for all the serpent's 'malevolent brilliance', to regard him as a mere tool of 'a more formidable rebel'. He adds that Genesis 3:15, the *protevangelium*, the first promise of the Saviour as the seed of the woman who shall bruise the serpent's head, compels us to do so. Nor, he says, does Satan come to Eve in his own authority, but through a subordinate, as Satan came to Jesus through Peter (Matt. 16:21-23). By coming thus in a more compromising guise, Satan avoided any compulsion of his victim and strengthened the appeal to the victim's own pride, that he was acting on his own initiative. It might be added that the Devil hides himself behind any messenger whom he sends to appeal to his intended victims, whether the appeal is from without, through another person, or from within through the alleged reason of the messenger himself. Thus he is able to do his nefarious work as the deceiver under cover.

Yet the serpent's plausible appeal must be seen in the light of the sheer grace of the first two chapters of Genesis, which are crammed with God's free, generous provision, with only one prohibition, 'Don't touch that tree!' If ever man was without excuse for sinning it was then, for Adam before the Fall was without bias. It was as easy for him to do right as to do wrong. If there was bias at all, because of God's goodness, it was to do right, not wrong. Therefore, notwithstanding the Devil's hellishly deceptive powers, coming as he did with his disastrous serpentine intrusion into that ideal situation, Eve's astonishing entertainment of him, as if she had taken leave of all her sense of God's lavish and careful provision, can be seen only as the most wicked and heinous departure from all that God had made her and expected her to become.

No recoil upon the Devil, to blame him, can minimise the enormity of Eve's and Adam's sin. It stands in all its heinousness, responsibility and gross ingratitude. For this creature, the serpent, was actually suggesting to Adam and Eve the complete discrediting of the one who had given them life with all its gracious gifts and benefits. This parent

sin is the sin of sins, equalled only by that primal sin of Lucifer whic[ ]
stands out like a blot against the light of what God had made him.

It is important here, therefore, to hold two things firmly togethe[r]
One is the essentially deceiving nature of Satan, whose wiles mu[s]
always be taken into account, so that we sinners never bear the blam[e]
alone for our sin (*cf.* Jesus with Peter, Matt. 16). The other is the fu[ll]
responsibility of man for listening to voices which are completel[y]
contrary to his knowledge and experience of God. One of the mo[st]
important points, which will emerge later, is that Satan certainl[y]
wants us, when condemned, to bear the whole blame for our si[n]
doubtless hoping that he can thus bow himself out of our ken and l[et]
sin within us carry the full condemnation, as if there were not a Sata[n]
at all.

Man's first sin was engineered by the Devil himself with gre[at]
ingenuity. At the same time, he brazenly contradicted all that God ha[d]
said, done and given to Adam. As we follow the story through fro[m]
that first sin, we perceive two elements reacting upon one another an[d]
combining with one another in different degrees: Satan's responsibili[ty]
and man's responsibility.

Take Cain and Abel. Cain obviously did not give his best to God
to put it mildly! Abel did, thereby putting Cain at a disadvantage. Ca[in]
was cast out of God's presence for wanting to be more than he ha[d]
any right to be or could be. The Devil was therefore on the defensiv[e]
as those are who think they are insufficiently appreciated. Like the[m]
he became exceedingly aggressive, and made Cain so mad (althoug[h]
Cain would not have attributed his madness to the Devil but wou[ld]
have thought it was his own) that he murdered his godlier brother wh[o]
put him at a disadvantage. Yet it was really Cain, through the Dev[il]
who put himself at his own disadvantage by daring to offer God le[ss]
than his best. The results of this and of Cain's subsequent yielding [to]
evil, are seen in all that followed in Genesis 4, until we have polygam[y]
and murder once more.

In Genesis 4 we also find the beginning of pastoral life, of musi[c]
musical instruments and tool making. What of these? Are they evi[l]
There is no need to condemn them, or anything else that has its rise [in]
an evil society, but we have to note nevertheless, that these things [o]

emerge in a particularly wayward and sinful community. We know that music, great gift of God though it be, both in itself and by what can accompany it, is capable of drawing men away from God until the gift of God becomes an idol and substitute for God. As to crafts, the first tool made by the first artificer was apparently used for murder. That does not make tools evil, but it remains a fact that it was evil people who devised these things.

The question we must ask is, 'Does so-called civilisation lead us ethically forward or backward?' Of course, we do not condemn any advance in human knowledge and achievement, but a great deal of the ingenuity of genius has led man away from God rather than to him. The restlessness of the creative urge is particularly susceptible to self-will, fostering aims and ideals which so far from nurturing a divine discontent that leads on to humanly edifying accomplishments, seems rather to assert an arrogant impatience with both God and his laws.

The modern Hungarian artist Vasary, who works with what he calls colour shapes of the circle, square and triangle, claims that his new art medium, which he asserts has infinite possibilities of permutation, will lead to a new perfection in art. It is obvious that in his disarming conceit he regards himself as a new kind of god in the art world. You can hardly expect such a man to be a devout believer. You cannot satisfactorily *be* a god and *have* one!

Aesthetics are a great problem which we cannot go into in detail. I believe, however, that the coming of Jesus Christ to our lives ought to increase our aesthetic appreciation. Yet that aesthetic appreciation is fraught with the greatest possible dangers, for here evil genius can so easily, plausibly, and seemingly worthily but deceptively creep in. We build glorious cathedrals to the glory of God, but they are mostly for our own pleasure, especially when we turn them into tourist attractions, as we turn their music into sacred concerts. Do we not see the work of Satan here? And ought we not to seek to expose him so that we may learn to enjoy these things in the presence of God in a spirit which will not lead us astray as it has led countless others astray?

Now to Genesis 6. After this, the world became so bad that God repented that he had made man. It is an awful indictment that 'The

Lord saw that the wickedness of man was great in the earth, and that every imagination of the thoughts of his heart was only evil continually' (v. 5). 'And the Lord was sorry that he had made man on the earth, and it grieved him to his heart' (v. 6). What had brought God to this conclusion? Was it that the wickedness of Cain's progeny had grown gradually worse? This is true, of course, but there was more to it than that; there was a new daring assault on man, or rather, once again, on woman.

It is difficult to get away from the assumption that the sons of God who took the daughters of men to wife in Genesis 6 were angels, who thereby fell from their own estate. A good case has been made out for this view by Selwyn, which Alan Stibbs supports and Derek Kidner seems to incline to. They argue that 1 Peter 3:18, 19; 2 Peter 2:4, 5 and Jude 6, all refer to an invasion of the human scene by angelic beings seducing women. The results of these illicit unions seem to have been grotesque, giant creatures, the Nephilim and Anakim who strode the earth in antediluvian times. 'Delitzch holds that "the sons of God" were men invaded by demon spirits; this could reconcile two views!'

However, we read subsequently of such creatures in Israel's history, such as Goliath in David's day. They cannot be descended from creatures destroyed by the Flood, and there is no evidence that any of these creatures was preserved in the ark. But what fallen angels tried once, they might easily have tried again. Suffice to say that although all the antediluvian creatures were destroyed and only the godliest line preserved, that line itself soon fell into heinous sin; and although it is easy to attribute the wilfulness of Babel merely to the results of sin planted deep in the heart of man without further encouragement or aid from the Devil, is it reasonable to assume that he was no longer as active in the strategic sins of men? Certainly, in the fulness of time, the act of these who proposed to build the tower of Babel defied once more the God who had not only warned the antediluvians of their danger through wickedness, but had in the end destroyed them for not heeding his warning. Whence came such sustained, obdurate defiance and hardened opposition to the will of God, an opposition that had to be answered by God's confusing their language and scattering them over the face of the earth? He who does not see the evil one at work in this has surely missed the point of Genesis 3:15, and much else.

Notice that as we look back to the various acts of the Devil and his agents following his removal from the presence of God, we see that God had an answer for each one. Not an improvised answer either, as if he had been caught napping, but an answer both masterly and strategic; part, indeed, of a long-term policy.

Thus the Fall is answered by the first promise of a Redeemer, not from sin, but from Satan. This remark gives the opportunity to emphasise one of the main theses about the Devil: in the practical life of sanctification we, alas, too often leave the Devil out of account, and reckon with the results of his work rather than with himself. That has proved disastrous for Christian life and warfare. It is as if the Criminal Investigation Department were forever going for petty criminals and never seeking the master-mind behind them!

The destruction of the godly seed of Abel is answered by a new seed, that of Seth. The rise of a horrid race of wicked men through these strange marriages is answered by the judgment of the Flood and the salvation of Noah and his family in the ark of salvation (1 Pet. 3:20ff.). The tower of Babel is answered, not only by the judgment of the confusion of tongues and the scattering of the peoples, but by the call of a new man, Abraham. Nor had God his sorrows to seek with Abraham. If you gather the strands of evidence, it seems clear that Abraham disobeyed God in dragging his whole family from Ur to Haran, where he 'stuck' until God took his father Terah away.

The next test for Abraham was that, through his own questing spirit, he went too far south, down into Egypt (which, surely pictures Satan's domain). God subsequently gave Abraham's family their fill of the south, as predicted in Abraham's dark experience in Genesis 15, where it was prophesied that his descendants would be slaves in a land not theirs for four hundred years, and would then come out with great possessions and 'come back here to the land of the Amorites' (15:16).

There are many intriguing strands of Old Testament history which invite us to ponder the precise interactions of God and the Devil in the perfect outworking of the divine plans. Take the barrenness of Sarah, and that of Rebekah (like the barrenness of Hannah later, and of Elizabeth). That seemed to hinder, although only for a little, the sovereign purposes of God, as is seen in the unfolding life stories of their sons, Isaac, Jacob, Samuel and John the Baptist. The Almighty God seemed to be using Satan like an obstacle in an obstacle race, and this simply showed his power (and dare we say it, reverently, his cleverness) in surmounting the barriers to his will. It is this heroic attitude to the problems of evil which enables us to see the whole thing as a holy 'joke'. You may not like Malcolm Muggeridge's word but do you see his angle? Or is your God so small that you have him labouring hard against Satan until the issues are almost in doubt? I hope not.

Then we have God's choice of that twister Jacob in preference to the happy pagan Esau – a much more lovable character. Instead of the earthy Esau we have the wily Jacob and his oily sins. But he had faith (no credit to him); and Satan can do what he likes with a cunning rascal like Jacob, but if faith is planted in his heart, he will get out of Satan's clutches, as his brother would not, and eventually will be used of God: there was a Peniel. Yet Jacob had many sins,' not least in respect of his favouritism of Joseph, which led at last, through the famine, to Satan's attempt to remove his people from the land God had given them through Abraham. But as we have already remarked, God foresaw that, and had his good purposes already 'in the bag'.

By the way, is not frequent famine in the land of Canaan (something hardly known in fertile Moab) a recurring sign of the pressures of the enemy on God's people, and sometimes, indeed, a sign of judgment on them for their sins? The reasons for Israel landing in Egypt are complex in the extreme, but within the sovereignty of God and his over-arching purpose, there is a place for Satan's wiles and the sins of Israel, man and family. In the sequence of these interweaving events my selection may not be yours if you were sweeping through the Old Testament, and I may be leaving out some which you think, even on my thesis, ought to go in; but the selection is not as important as the need to see Satan lurking at every turn, trying to do despite to the long-term purposes of God, yet always through what appears to be mere human folly only. No, all the blame is not man's; these attempted set-backs to the purposes of God are too persistent, consistent and cumulative not to belong to a planned campaign. 'An enemy hath done this.'

Of course, it was sin that got Israel into Egypt – but it was Satan, more. And for four hundred years it seemed that the purposes of God were frustrated, until the divine strategy seemed to lie fallow. Yet it was not so, because Satan, being the restless creature he is, is never content with even his most spiteful actions against God, and so, as usual, he went too far, and caused Israel to be so oppressed by Egyptians that their cry came up to God and he heard it. The pressure of Pharaoh against Israel and Moses, all the things that went wrong, such as the decree against the male children of the Hebrews, were calculated in the economy of God to lead to a direct confrontation and show-down one day.

Paul has the last word on that drama of events (Rom. 9:17), which is, that God raised up Pharaoh to show forth his power in overcoming and destroying him because he dared to oppose the sovereign will. That was a rebuff for the Devil, but he did not have the sense to see it. Or was it that he could not go against his own freely chosen self-destructive nature? The Almighty God has nothing to fear from him if he is brave enough to suffer the wounds the Devil tries to inflict on him in the battle. He *is* brave enough!

Take all that complaining of Israel in the wilderness, and their oft-repeated plea to go back to salubrious Egypt. Strange how the land of bitter bondage took on such an attractive aura in the wilderness, and how they weighed against solid food, – bread and flesh, and the miraculous water from the rock, which was Christ, – the mere condiments and seasoning of food, – garlic, leeks, onions, cucumbers. On the other hand, they just as perversely refused to go into Canaan because of the giants. What could be clearer than that Satan wanted to destroy the nation in the wilderness because he was unable to keep them in bondage in Egypt? He put into their hearts even to seek another captain to lead them back into Egypt. Satan was working overtime, hindering, hindering, hindering! But there was always another generation to come, even if all these adults had to die the death of judgment in the desert.

Then there were the hindrances which the new generation suffered in going into Canaan by the back door, round the Dead Sea (not straight up as they ought to have gone from Kadesh). Edom would not let them pass through, nor would Moab (both related to Israel, for all their vileness), so Israel circumambulated them; whereas the Amorites, who originally invaded the Transjordan and were not related to Abraham, refused to let Israel through and were destroyed.

Then Moab, still doubting Israel's intention to make for Canaan and leave the nations on the east side at peace, procured Balaam to curse them, because they feared Israel would double back and destroy them. It would be impossible not to be amused at the Devil here. He planned to get Balaam to curse Israel, but it was the Spirit of God who came upon the unfortunate Balaam, until he prophesied all God's gracious will for Israel in the most superlative terms. The Devil's agent could do nothing but mouth his enemy's sentiments! That is one of the great jokes of the Bible. You cannot be a real Christian without a sense of humour. It is from God, and he who does not have it fails to see major elements in the divine personality and in his holy strategies.

Now Israel is in the land, and Satan and his enemies get short shrift, and a goodly part of the land is taken and the enemies liquidated. But Satan is not idle, at least not in his head. He is planning. Israel will tire of driving enemies out: he will see to that. He will take away their desire for the Lord's blessing, and the middle portion of the land will satisfy them (which was a fraction only of what God promised Abraham and his seed for ever, see Gen. 15:18). And it is not a far cry from a failure in zeal to possess their possessions to accommodating themselves to the pagans still in their midst. By the end of the book of Judges, despite great deliverers such as Gideon and Samson coming on the scene, they departed from the strict instructions of their religious life given at Sinai until 'every man did that which was right in his own eyes' (Judg. 21:25). But it was Satan's eyes they saw with, not their own, and how he must have chuckled at that!

So 1 Samuel opens with fat old Eli and his wicked sons. But there is a youngster at Shiloh in the sacred tent: Samuel.

Samuel is one of the greatest figures in Old Testament history, especially when you consider the spiritual degradation and declension out of which he raised Israel, and what his schools of the prophets did to counteract the sins of the first kings of Israel (as Elisha's schools did later to counteract the later sinful kings of Israel and Judah). You can depend upon God's all-foreseeing eye matching the hour with a man – which makes us wonder sometimes if he has deserted us as a nation; there is no man for the hour! But God raised Samuel for the hour, a personality fully able to foil the Devil's latest attempt to destroy the faith.

Satan retired to plan something new. (This is perhaps always the meaning of his withdrawal, after he has licked his wounds; he never learns.) He took a major trick, one whose repercussions ring down the ages of subsequent Old Testament history. The conquest of David and the peaceful prosperity of Solomon are undoubtedly types of Christ's kingdom to come, yet the private sins of these monarchs with their women (adultery and idolatry go together, whichever is the former), sowed seeds which ultimately brought the whole kingdom down. Was this not a major defeat for God? Not at all! He had not only foreseen it, but had already purposed to use it to his glory in creating a godly remnant, in and out of the land, that he might ultimately bring his purposes to a perfect and fruitful point in another man, Christ Jesus. He had begun with one man, Abraham, a type of one to come, who was to be the first in a new and everlasting order of humanity – Christ, the firstfruits of the resurrection.

This spacious purpose embraced the captivities (Assyrian and Babylonian) and all God's use of the wicked nations which he raised to be the rod of his judgment upon his people; the people, indeed, to whom he made eternal promises. Integral with his promises to them, was the warning that if they rebelled against him in the land he would drag them out of it. The wicked nations therefore concluded, when he had done so, that the Lord had cast his people off. (That's what Moses feared they would think, see Exodus 32:12, Numbers 14:13.) Much later, when Rabshakeh, Sennacherib's servant, taunted the Jews before the wall of Jerusalem, he said to them, 'Moreover, is it without the Lord (their Lord!) that I have come up against this land to destroy it? It was *your* Lord who said to me, "Go up against this land and destroy it"' (Is. 36:10). Well!

God punished all these nations for the punishment they meted out to his own people, although it was in his sovereign will that they should first be used to thrash them. Unfair? Not at all! God does not give quarter to his enemies. Does he need to? Have they changed and become godly? Nay, verily; they thrashed Israel and Judah out of sheer wickedness, and enjoyed every moment of it, even while God wept for his own in their afflictions. When God had used his enemies, the enemies of his people, he owed them nothing but to destroy them.

Yet he used the captivity in Babylon to accomplish a great purpose of humiliation in his people, and a new devoutness. In the fulness of time, as the Jews had been taken away in at least three deportations, they returned over a period of almost a hundred years in three returns, remnants of remnants of remnants, a demoted bedraggled people, to cling to the rock of Zion for more than four hundred years; no longer a nation, but under foreign occupation practically all the time, by Persians, Greeks, Selucids (Syrians), Egyptians and Romans; until a babe was born of a peasant maid in a Bethlehem outhouse.

But the Devil is not such a fool as we sometimes think. He knows he has to be cunning to survive, let alone try to win. He was watching all these four hundred years of the Jews' chequered humiliation, and well knew the babe who was to be born. The peasant maid of Nazareth, that backwater village (it is still an Arab stronghold within the state of Israel), was, as we know, a princess of the royal line of Judah, whose lineage can be traced through the Old Testament to the New. Not only so, but the babe's birth was different, not only in that his mother was a princess of Judah (albeit under the sorry disguise wrought by hundreds of years of humiliation and foreign oppression), but because he was the very Son of God. He was virgin-born, conceived of the Holy Ghost.

Poor Satan is hard put to it to beat that! As God produced a new man, Abraham, in answer to the Devil's ancient triumph at the tower of Babel, so now there was a new man, but of another, unique order, to start a new race of everlasting manhood. That must have been a tremendous shock to the Devil, and he tried his best to destroy him. That awful journey of poor Mary to Bethlehem for the census at a most inconvenient time, the decree of monstrous Herod to destroy the infants, the flight to Egypt, the very land which Satan had used as a prison to hold ancient Israel – isn't God daring? – there he hides his Son in the very land of Egypt (no more godly than ever)!

Then there was the long journey back to Nazareth. Satan saw the boy in Nazareth; although he could do nothing about his perfect boyhood, did he not try? Perhaps he supposed the youngster could not harm the Satanic kingdom in that backwater, and so he seems to have left him alone. But the Devil must have had a trying moment when the youngster came to Jerusalem at the age of twelve! We have no record of any disturbance to Satan's kingdom, beyond the lad's perfection, for eighteen years. Even at the age of thirty (Satan may have speculated) a man is not going to rise suddenly and make a major attack on him. Would he not have tried before that, or have shown at least some sign of trying it? He would have been at least the obvious ring-leader of trouble against Satan's kingdom, to give him practice in that costly art! So the Devil may have argued to allay his own most terrible fears.

The astonishing thing about the divine tactic is that God waited thirty years to do in three (or was it three days, or even six hours?) a work which put Satan at a permanent, indeed an eternal, infinite disadvantage with God. Despite all his desperate efforts in an all-out bid, either to prevent Christ being put on the cross or, alternatively, to defeat him on it (perhaps the division in the Devil's mind confounded him), Satan could not prevent Christ dying that death which procured multiple benefits for man, nor prevent him from being raised from the dead, the first man to pass through human life unscathed by sin, and, therefore, necessarily immortal, indestructible, and impervious to Satan. Satan stood helplessly by and could not even pinprick the risen glorified Christ.

Of course, he can still do much hurt to Christ's children, but if the eternal seed (1 Jn. 3:9) is planted in their hearts, they are rendered indestructible too, albeit the indestructible is planted in mortal, that is to say, destructible bodies. But inasmuch as Jesus says, 'He that believeth in me shall never die', something happened by that death and resurrection and the subsequent planting of the divine seed in men's hearts which can never be undone. Satan is now at a permanent disadvantage with God. For the Almighty God has now a foothold in man which Satan had laboured hard throughout the Old Testament

ages to prevent, perhaps often not knowing quite what hi
malevolence wanted to do, but just blindly resisting God's will. Onl
God knew how skilful the enemy's strategies had been, but he als
knew that they were hopeless. And he had now this wonderfu
foothold in man because he had known all the answers before th
Devil and his agents had had time to ask the questions.

All that we believers now suffer from Satan is understandable onl
on these terms. Satan, having suffered his second major defeat – fina
and irretrievable at that (the first was his removal from God'
presence for seeking to usurp the place of God) – is exceedingly mad
Since he has gone too far to be converted or changed, he is determine
to do his damnedest to hurt Christ, through his people, until Go
finally banishes him from their reach.

A large part of the book of the Revelation deals with this, but th
word we want is that great one in the twelfth chapter, whose trut
should be on the finger tips of our faith. In its final statement it reads
'Woe to you, O earth and sea, for the Devil has come down to you i
great wrath, *because he knows that his time is short!*' (v. 12).

Two things emerge from all this. One is the hurt which God allow
himself and his people to suffer in order to fulfil his purpose of creatin
and redeeming a people worthy of his Son. The other is the fact tha
the achievement was never in doubt, because God was using Satan,
mere creature, however irretrievably ruined, perverse and malevolent
to do a thing of quality, that would alone satisfy the Father's heart t
all eternity. The ferocity and subtlety of the Devil in all he seeks to d
against Christ and Christians is the price Christ and we have to pa
for the quality work of establishing the kingdom of God in the hearts o
men, the crown of creation. If we lose sight of this, nothing is sure
than that we shall be swept out of the battlefield, or will have to op
out of it through sheer demonic pressure. Fortunately, with the Bibl
in our hands and the Holy Spirit in our hearts to bring its trut
contemporarily and urgently to sight, there is no need for that, for w
are not, or ought not to be, ignorant of his devices, wiles an
stratagems. It is ours not only to study the Word of God prayerfull
but, believing it utterly, to use it for what it is, the sword of the Spirit
We must learn how to go over to the offensive against the Devil. W
shall come to that in due course.

THE DEVIL

2: Christ's Victory over the Devil

The most important fact to know about Christ's victory over the Devil is that he procured it for man. Our Saviour had no need of it for himself, which is proved by his resurrection. Death could not hold him, because he died as he had lived, sinlessly. Given the death of Jesus, his rising was a foregone conclusion.

Why had Christ no need of a victory over the powers of evil for himself? These powers were tremendous, were they not? They seemed so, and to us fallen creatures they are, but they are of a different substance from him. The Father is the uncreated God; the Son is the only begotten of the Father, co-creator with the Father and with the Holy Spirit; whereas the most powerful and resplendent angels are but creatures. As creatures, they are under the Creator's power every moment of their existence. He can snuff them out like a candle any moment he chooses. God has no difficulty of power, control or authority over them.

Why then, we may ask, does he not utterly destroy all fallen spirits? The simple answer is that God is so great and wise that he can use them to evoke his glory, and yet never be touched by their evil. Then when he has used them to the full, he will cast them into the place prepared for them, which they richly deserve.

The beginning of God's use of evil was to allow it to arise, by giving angelic beings the faculty corresponding to free will in man. Some angels misused it, and enticed man to sin; then God had both the Devil and fallen man on his hands. The whole purpose of redemption is

---

to show that God is well able to cope with both the Devil and falle
man in such a way as to save man from the Devil; that is, annul hi
power, and at last put him where he belongs, in the place prepared fo
him – and not to his liking!

One of the amazing mysteries of our God is the extent to which h
allows evil, sin and suffering in his universe. God, we said, could hav
snuffed out the Devil at the first sign of his presumption; or could hav
left him in existence, destroying the man who fell, then creating
second, natural Adam, in the hope that he would not succumb. Bu
God chose rather to suffer both the Devil and man (and man'
progeny) until his own time. That led to all the trouble we have bee
skimming over in the Old Testament. Yet in it all, God is weaving
purpose, starting with Abraham, until he became a nation, sufferin
the nation's tantrums until it was reduced to a pathetic remnant. Ther
even later it was reduced to the fine point of a really new man, Jesu
Christ, who comes on the scene to tackle the Devil in the reality c
human flesh.

This One, God the Son, is also truly and properly Man, one of u:
tempted in all points like as we are, sin apart. It is he who tackles th
Devil. If the Devil can get him down, that will be not only a defeat fc
God's second man (Adam being the first), but will be a defeat for Go
himself. For this man *is* God. Defeat is therefore unthinkable; althoug
we must not think of the contest ideally, but practically. This is
matter of flesh and blood, however divine its humanity. This victor
cannot be gained in a purely spiritual realm, much less in the realm c
pure thought. It is a matter of God's creature, a fallen angel, havin
become God's enemy, now venting his diabolical spleen and jealous
on God through this Man. He must be dealt with, and can be dea
with only in this way.

I have said that the Devil tried his damnedest to get Christ down.
the Creator is to triumph over his mere creature gone wrong, he wi
have to do it in a human body, and will have to stand all the vengef
wrath poured out upon that one, frail, ordinary human body. That bod
is the battlefield of God and the Devil. Satan had already notched u
one supposed victory over God on the battlefield of human flesh – ov
Adam and Eve. But, of course, that victory was a dangerous precede
for Satan, for it is not good to enter a new battle flushed with a form

victory; it tends to make one less careful. Not that Satan was all that ignorant of what he was up against, he had already tested Christ severely; but he had not yet begun to know the resistance that flesh and blood can put up against him when it is indwelt by the pure Spirit of God. God is no fool. He knew what he was doing and what he could do. Most important, he also knew Satan's limitations (which is probably more than Satan knew!). That is something to think about when we fear the raging Devil: his limitations. All evil, sinful creatures are limited.

I want now to compare what Satan knew about Christ's toughness at the beginning of his three-year trial, in the temptation, with what he had yet to learn of his resistance on the cross. The initiative in both trials was divine (the Devil initiates nothing).

It seems to me that Jesus approached the temptation after his baptism in a way opposite to his approach to his death on the cross. The first was a sort of practice round! We might compare the two roughly with Satan's two assaults on Job; the first merely external, albeit very painful, but the second wracking his own person in the most excruciating way. In the first, Satan was allowed to strip away from Job the dear delights of his life, his wealth and his family; in the second, he attacked him not only in body, but in mind and soul, and with every demonic weapon he knew.

The same can be said of Jesus; only more so. In the temptation, Jesus resisted Satan absolutely and on all counts, scarcely exchanging words with him, certainly only as few as would send the Devil about his business. But in his death he allowed himself to be sifted to the uttermost. Satan was given leave to do his worst to him.

It may be that Jesus was not ready for the final test on the cross until the end of his three years' ministry. It does say in the Letter to the Hebrews that our Lord learned obedience by the things which he suffered, and was thus made perfect (although *never* imperfect) in a realm of perfection which he had not known hitherto (5:8, 9). I know that that refers to the cross, but need we exclude his three years' testing from its references?

The temptation may be viewed as the test of Christ's persona integrity. But on the cross he was being tested as the prototype Mar the test case on behalf of a host of others who were to follow him int immortal manhood, if he proved successful. It is a new Man who i being tested, where the former man, Adam, failed. If this Man Chris Jesus can get through human life from beginning to end entirel without sin, then, since he is not only a life-receiving but a life-givin, Man (1 Cor. 15:45), a whole kingdom of such men will eventually b able to get through, notwithstanding their sinfulness. He is their File leader, the Pioneer, as Hebrews 2:10, 12:2, Colossians 1:15, an Revelation 1:5 all show.

A new race has been born in Christ, one which can overcom Satan's attacks. It is not simply that God has gained ascendancy ove Satan (that was never in doubt), but now men in Christ will prove t be of better, finer essence than even the best of the angels. But th only way for this to be proved is for the two beings (the Creator an rebellious creature) to engage and become locked in an almighty, fin; struggle, in which Jesus proves his divine essence, in a fully huma body, to be categorically superior to Satan's diabolical stuff, angel an spirit though he be, with no human limitations. But Jesus must prov this by giving himself completely into the Devil's hands in order th; Satan may try him totally and do his hellish worst on him. That i exactly what Jesus did: he gave himself into Satan's hands. Th courage of that act is beyond all praise; and the result we know.

The greatness of this victory gained in Christ's flesh over Sata cannot be over-magnified. Christ's resistance to the Devil on th cross was not the resistance of keeping the enemy at bay, as in th temptation, but of letting him have his way and will with him, to ru right through him, looking for flaws but finding none.

The difference between the temptation and the cross may b compared to the difference between smearing a poisonous ointment o the surface of the skin, and eating the stuff! Christ's system resiste both; but it called for more resistance to withstand the second than th first. In the latter case (to change the metaphor), Christ's resistanc had to hold out to the end because the Devil was allowed by God t sift his holy Son (remember the fine flour in Leviticus 2:2, 6:15) to th finest, sheerest, floury grain of his perfect character.

We sinners know nothing of this. We have not endured that degree of testing. We all succumb to Satan's blandishments long before we approach anything like ultimate resistance. No man but Christ knows what ultimate resistance is and what it costs. It is beyond our imagination to understand all that that body, mind and soul went through in resisting Satan to the very last. But he did resist to the end, and remained unscathed, and emerged perfectly unsullied. Remember, being sinless did not make him less sensitive and susceptible to suffering, but more. Even his sanity was preserved (and many Christians die with their minds completely gone), so that his words as he was about to bow his head (it did not slump, he *bowed* it,) are not only among the sanest ever spoken, but among the sublimest ever recorded. 'Father forgive them, they know not what they do.' 'Father, into thy hands I commend my spirit.' 'It is finished.' And by that time, I believe, Satan was already paralysed and powerless.

We are reminded of Joshua, the high priest in Zechariah 3, when Satan stood to accuse him as the representative of the Jewish remnant returned from captivity. Joshua was dressed in the filthy garments of Israel's centuries of sin. Satan stood ready to condemn. (He can be very pious when he likes!) And the Lord said to Satan, 'The Lord rebuke you, O Satan!' Then the angel of God proceeded to remove Joshua's filthy garments and put new robes on him. What was Satan doing the while? We do not know; he is not even mentioned. Either he had fled with shame or fright to conceal his powerlessness, or, worse, was standing there, the picture of misery, because he could not lift a finger to hinder the holy angel's good work on the high priest. It is a heartening picture.

As with Joshua, so with Jesus on the cross, only more so. He outmanoeuvred, outwitted and out-suffered all that was launched against him, and in the final moments of his life virtually said to Satan:
> It is finished. You are beaten, and you know it! Satan, you have not a single trick left up your sleeve. There is not a weapon left in your armoury. There is not another thing you can do, or think of doing to try to get me down, or my Father, or his Spirit. You are utterly beaten and helpless, and you know it. I am still King, more King than ever now, for I have endured all your mad rage and calculated

ingenuity, although you tried to drag poor mankind, with me, furth
into your infernal clutches. You have failed!

Now, like the King I am, I commit my Spirit to my Father. (I ha
work to do in another realm, 1 Peter 3:19.) Meantime, I will let y
have my body in death to give you one more chance to master n
If my body does not come up from death, Satan, you have won. E
I would have you note, and I think this is ominous for you, tha
am not dying at the moment you decide. I have sufficient enduran
to remain in mortal life probably for hours yet. *I* am choosing t
moment of my death, and that will be when I am fully assured tl
I have conquered you.

Then, like the king he is, he bowed his head with divine dignity, a
calmly handed over his spirit to his Father, that he might undertake,
the first instance, before his resurrection, the work described in
Peter 3:18, 19. Nothing could have been more regal, controlled a
assured. Christ strode out of mortal life, like the hero of a play leavi
the stage at its close, the master of the whole drama, and certai
master of the accursed Devil. No language, no music, no divine
could do justice to the magnificence or significance of that deed. It
beyond words, and beyond all grasp of human reason, yet we are a
to understand it in its significance for us, even if we have to stre
our minds a little to do so.

Let me develop the picture of the actor leaving the stage. Imagi
him, having finished the drama on one stage, leaving it w
consummate assurance and striding downstairs to another, the und
world where the chained spirits of fallen angels are incarcerated.
him march on to the stage and pronounce upon these damned spi
their deserved doom.

Even while they were taking his body down and reverently laying
in the tomb, even while John was lovingly leading broken-hear
Mary away, and all present with any finer feelings were weeping th
hearts out at the dreadful mistake that had been made, Christ v
busy proclaiming doom to the fallen angels who kept not their f
estate. And as Balak, king of Moab, was helpless before
prophecies of Balaam, so the Devil has to stand back and see t
multiple work of redemption completed for man. Christ brir

redemption from the guilt, penalty and shame of our sins, redemption from the inbred power of our sinful nature and from the author of both of these, the Devil himself. He can do nothing about it. He is bound, defeated, rendered utterly helpless to do any more harm.

What king is this, what victor this, reigning royally from a tree? No words can match his glory. We can only wonder and wonder again at what a Man has done to the Devil.

Let us see the essential nature of the deed, and make a comparison of the categories involved in it. It was, of course, the creature versus the Creator. But see the unequal elements in the struggle: it was the Creator, with the seeming disadvantage of having become a man, living and fighting within the limits of manhood. Jesus played absolutely fair to his manhood. We do not believe that in the whole of his human life he acted even once solely as God. He acted only in faith and by faith as the human Son of his Father. He never stepped out of the God-given limitations of his human nature. Whereas Satan, who attacked him, had no such limitations. He was altogether spirit, and although a created spirit, yet had all the advantages that angels now have over men because of the limitations of flesh and blood, time and space. It is an unbelievable victory, and yet it is fact, and all done in flesh and blood.

That is what we have to fasten on. *A man has beaten Satan*; and being, also, God in human flesh, his victory is not only of qualitative but of categorical importance. A man has passed through the whole of human life unscathed by sin, and is therefore able to bear the sins of other men because he had none of his own. Because he remained personally sinless throughout, death could not hold him. He must rise from the dead, to live as a man for evermore.

Could Satan possibly have conceived the tremendous thing the resurrection of this Man would be and do? Surely not. It was not a mere reviving like that of Lazarus – poor Lazarus died again, he was still mortal. No, Christ became an indestructible man, without limitations of time and space, able to appear in the upper room, and on the shore of Galilee, in a moment of time, and disappear at will with effortless ease and with delightful mystification to his disciples. Not much wonder that Jesus had a merry forty days, appearing disappearing and reappearing to them!

We know, of course, what Christ was doing. He was appearing t let them know that it was truly himself who had risen from the dea ('Come, Thomas, put your finger into the wound'), and he wa disappearing to teach them that he was with them all the tim although invisibly. What a thought! A Man impervious to Satan an sin, who could dart behind Satan's back and get the advantage of hi before that darting spirit had time to gather his wits! Do we real take this in? Do we really believe it? Talk about ghost stories! The was never anything as hair-raising as this, and yet so comforting, fc all this was done for us. This is for us. 'Thanks be to God who give *us* the victory' (1 Cor.15:57).

That is what we are coming to: *our* victory in his. But let me say th now: to say that Christ's victorious death was for us men, is not t limit its scope, although it is to concentrate it. It does not narrow it. is true, of course, that Jesus' death was first of all an offering c himself to the Father. 'Lo, I come to do thy will, O God' (Ps. 40:6- Heb. 10:5-9). The Son is showing his filial submission and obedienc to the Father in giving himself up to death, even the death of th cross.

This was not the first time the Son had shown his submission, i equality, to the Father. If we take in the implications of the perfe bliss which prevailed within the heavenly family circle before th worlds were made (Jn. 17:5, 22, 24), the Son's attitude of son submission to the Father was part of that perfectly consiste relationship which existed between them from the beginning. But it on earth that it is now seen, and on the cross! Why? Because t wants to show us some of the secrets of the divine working. Thi which seemed to be the private part of Christ's death in relation to th Father, was also for us, to show us how to submit. Therefore, concentrate on Christ's death for us is not to limit it, because wh affects man as the crown of creation affects the whole universe. Th manifestation of the sons of God will lead to the recreation of th whole world (Rom. 8:18-25).

Wherever in time, or out of it, we set the fall of Lucifer, and whatever significance we give to it, it was the Fall of man which brought the whole creation to ruin around him (Gen. 3:14-19). If Jesus died for man, then that multiple work was going to take care of the work of saving all saveable creatures in the universe (fallen angels being unsaveable). Nothing can be greater, no contemplated deed can be more significant for the whole created order, than that which takes place as the victory of God over the Devil in human flesh.

I cannot stress this sufficiently in view of what I hope to say in the next chapter. Most of our excuses for not taking up the cudgels against the Devil are expressed in such terms as, 'The spirit indeed is willing, but the flesh is weak' (Matt. 26:41). But it is important to notice that if Jesus used the word 'flesh' there in anything like the same sense as Paul generally does, it does not mean human nature, but what Satan and sin have imposed on human nature. That, and its author, are precisely what Jesus died to save us from, here and now.

THE DEVIL

3: Our Victory over the Devil

We come now to the practical part of our theme. The general biblica
order is doctrine first, then practice, as in Ephesians chapters 1-3, an
chapters 4-6. This does not confine all doctrine to one division, and a
practice to the other; they interweave and intermingle in the mos
stimulating way possible. There is an order, none the less, and w
have followed it in this study. Now we are to take up the subject a
practically as we can.

The question is: 'What are we going to do about what Christ ha
done for us?' Is there any part of it that we enter into, yet do nothin
about but accept? Yes. I have already spoken of the three dimension
of the death of Christ: for our sins, with our sin, and to gain victor
over Satan. I suggested that we reverse the ascending order, of sin
sin and Satan, at least for this subject of the Devil, since he is th
head of all evil and ought to be dealt with before we deal with sin a
nature and sins as deeds. Nevertheless, we shall keep to ou
ascending scale, of sins, sin and Satan.

Many professing Christians regard the first dimension of Christ
death, the forgiveness of sins in justification, as the whole. It i
fundamental, of course, not least in that we have no part in
whatsoever. As the hymn writer Cecil Francis Alexander says:
> There was no other good enough
> To pay the price of sin;
> He only could unlock the gate
> Of heaven, and let us in.

Or, as Acts 4:12 says, 'And there is salvation in no one else, for there is no other name under heaven given among men by which we must be saved.' But it is but a third part of our redemption. And there is a profound paradox within it, for this is where Christ comes near enough to identify himself with our sins, and yet stands most apart from us, because he alone is pure enough to do the deed. Only the sinless can bear the sins of others and rise from the dead without them. He had no sins of his own to keep him in death or in bondage to the powers of evil. The result of this part of Christ's work for us (and we repeat that it is a part, although primary and fundamental) is that God declares believers in Jesus to be 'righteous in Christ' (Rom. 5:1).

Yet salvation is not only a matter of what God declares us to be (although what he says is bound to be at least potentially true, and will become actually true), but is also a matter of what God does within us, which has to do with our sanctification. This second dimension involves Christ dealing with our sinful nature. What God does in us is to send the Spirit of his Son into our hearts, the Spirit of the Christ who has done for us on the cross a complete work. We have, therefore, not only the fruit of his work in our hearts, but the Worker of the work, who is there to work *in us* what he wrought *for us* on the cross.

We have already said that we can have no share in the objective, justificationary part of salvation. We can only accept it humbly. But the sanctificationary part we must share in, because the Christ who died to remove our sins (our actual transgressions) also died with our sin-nature, to slay it for us, that he might give us, strange as it may seem, the death of that fallen nature as a potent, usable gift.

Paul labours hard to show this in Romans 6. When he says we are 'dead indeed unto sin', he means that the seed, or germ, or principle (1 Jn. 3:9) of Christ's death to our sin-nature is planted within us, in the core of our personality. There, nourished by God's Word, it begins to grow until it supplants the old Adam, because it is working as a potency of holy death to sin, a sin-killer. We are thus able to mortify sin and live to righteousness. Then we have a moral power to obey God's commands, for we find a response of both desire and ability within our own hearts.

This is the part of Christ's death into which we not only can, but must follow him. He died for us who could not die safely for ourselves (as sinners we would have gone down into eternal death). He did so in order to give his death to us as a seed of the Spirit that we might die our own death to sin after him, drawing on the power he has gained. And, of course, the same Spirit who unites us to Christ in his death, also unites us to him in his resurrection to life everlasting (Col. 3:1-3). It is, therefore, a spiritual fact that we are dead indeed to sin through him. This does not mean that sin is dead within us but, in our new, Christ-centred personality, we are dead indeed to sin and do not practise sin any more; as John says in his epistle (1 Jn. 2:28-3:10).

This fact, of course, has to be believed before it can be practised. Christians who say they do not understand it cannot make it work in their lives. They say, 'But how can I be dead indeed to sin when I feel the motions of sin in my members?' We do not look to the old Adamic nature, still there, and expect to see anything but the motions of sin in its members! You are looking in the wrong direction, to the wrong person. Look at Christ within you, not at Adam within you. If the seed is there, even if it is as tiny as a mustard seed, it will grow, given nourishment.

This is what Jesus keeps telling us in the mystery parables of the kingdom (Matt. 13). But unless we believe that Christ crucified and risen is within us, we shall not be disposed to draw upon his mighty, gracious resources. I could have a cheque for £100,000 in my pocket and not know it! Unless I know it is there, believe the fact when told, and take and use it, it will do me no good. In the same way, faith must believe the fact before it can act upon it.

However, it is the third dimension with which we are now concerned. Jesus not only died to remove our sins and slay our sin-nature in order that he might give us his new, resurrection life, but he died to slay the dragon, to bruise the serpent's head, to defeat finally in his human body the one who sowed the evil seed of sin within us. He must defeat Satan where Satan defeated Adam, in a human body. To this end God gives us the Spirit of that Jesus who not only wrought the first dimension, bringing peace, and the second, bringing sanctifying power, but the third, bringing victory and power over the original evil itself. The embryo of Christ's life, which begins to grow within us, is therefore the seed of the incarnate, crucified, risen and glorified Christ, who conquered Satan in a human body like ours. This victory he plants within us for our present, personal and continual use.

It is one thing for Christ to gain victory over Satan in his body, it is another for us to gain victory over him (Col. 2:15, Heb. 2:14, 1 Jn. 3:8, Phil. 2:5-11)! All the Easter hymns trumpet forth the glorious fact that Christ has conquered the Devil, but few go on to shout about what he did it for: solely and only to give his victory to us, that we might conquer the Devil and destroy his works in our hearts, in the church, and even in the world. 'But thanks be to God,' says Paul, 'who gives us the victory' (1 Cor. 15:57). 'This is the victory that overcomes the world,' says John (and, we may add, that overcomes the flesh and the Devil, too), 'our faith' (1 Jn. 5:4). What is faith, but the operation of the Spirit of God within us, enabling us to exercise the gift of faith in innumerable practical situations?

Look at the subject of Christ's victory as dealt with in Revelation 12. The victory of Christ over Satan is declared (vv. 7f.); then a loud voice in heaven declares the fact of that victory. But the eleventh verse goes on to tell us what effect this has upon the saints and what power it places at their disposal: 'And they (the saints) have conquered him by the blood of the Lamb and by the word of their testimony (to that fact), for they loved not their lives even unto death.' This is the staggering fact: the death and resurrection of Christ not only gives him victory over Satan, but enables him by the Spirit to give us victory over him, too. Indeed, that is what Christ did it for, that we might have the mastery over both the Devil and demons.

I want to speak of this in two particular areas: the life of Christian sanctification, and that of Christian warfare. It has always grieved me that some who teach the message of sanctification have done innumerable Christians the serious disservice of leaving the enemy of souls out of account as far as the life of sanctification is concerned. I have written of this in *Towards Spiritual Maturity*. To deal with two dimensions only of Christ's death leaves the enemy out of account, which is exactly what he wants.

Many Christians have been taught the truth of death to sin in Romans 6 and have tried to make it work in their lives. Believing that, in Christ, they were dead indeed to sin, they have looked for a life of Christian victory over sin, and have been deeply disappointed. The more determinedly and tenaciously they have held to this truth as their only hope of salvation from sin, the more they have seemed to be defeated, until they have begun to wonder if there was a jinx working against their attempts to lead a holy life. There is!

Some have thought that they have not been properly taught in the Word, and yet, however complex the whole body of teaching in Romans 6, the main ideas have seemed to them simple enough. Some have been driven to the conclusion that the Word is clear enough, but that it does not work in practice, which is a fearful conclusion to have to come to about God's Word. There is only one answer to the problem: the Devil himself has intruded into the situation.

Look at it in this way: while we are dead in trespasses and sins, the Devil has nothing to worry about; we are his and are lying safely in his arms. But when we are awakened to our need of a Saviour and flee to Christ, he has lost us. Yet he can still do us harm, keeping us ignorant of the wonderful truths we have been discussing, about being dead to sin and alive to God.

We may see these, and stand upon them, and wait to see their practical effect in an upsurge of holy power in our lives. Then Satan is desperate, because we are not only awakened to the need of forgiveness and receive it, but also to the possibilities of living a holy life. Then Satan, who had been able to stand back and let our sinful nature erupt freely on its own, is now obliged to come into play himself.

This is how he does it, since his nature is to deceive: he hides himself in the folds of our sinful nature, and as fast as we seek to mortify the flesh, so fast he stirs it up and makes it work overtime to defile us. Then our last state becomes worse than our first.

The point is this: Satan has been obliged to come into active play to prevent you from living a holy life. But if you keep merely mortifying the flesh without taking cognisance of the fact that the Devil is working personally in it, then the application of the power of the second dimension of the death of Christ, to sanctification, in order to deal with what is really the third dimension, victory over the Devil, will be useless and futile. Second gear will not do third gear work! You need to know that the Devil himself is waging war against you personally, and that Christ died to give you power to whip round on him, like Jesus when he turned on hapless Peter, named the Devil and commanded him to go: 'Get thee behind me, Satan.'

Now you are able not only to detect him, but to expose him and command him to go, which he must do if you command him by faith in the power of the blood of the Lamb. By that blood he is once and for all defeated. If in one case only this does not work when intelligently applied, then Christ's death would prove ineffectual. That cannot be.

Detection is the great problem. Or, perhaps it is the willingness to detect him. One of the greatest works of Satan is to cause people to believe that he is unreal, and they tend to laugh him out of existence. 'You don't really believe in ghosts, do you?' He is no ghost, but a spirit too spiritually substantial to be regarded so quixotically. This is, unfortunately, why you do not read much about him in modern Christian literature. But Bunyan knew! Listen to him:

> One thing I would not let slip. I took notice that now poor Christian was so confounded, that he did not know his own voice; and thus I perceived it. Just when he was come over against the mouth of the burning pit, one of the wicked ones got behind him, and stepped up softly to him, and whisperingly, suggested many grievous blasphemies to him, which he verily thought had proceeded from his own mind. This put Christian more to it than anything that he met with before, even to think that he should now blaspheme him that he loved so much before. Yet if he could have helped, he would not have done it; but he had not the discretion either to stop his ears, nor to know from whence these blasphemies came.

We must have both the discretion to know he is there, and the courage to deal with him. But our sense of sin inhibits us. Yet in the fight against evil we must not fail to attribute blame to the Devil, however co-operative we have been with him in our sin. If we initiate sin, that is one thing, but if he does it, after we have been wonderfully saved by spiritual knowledge, then he must bear his full share of blame. This is what pseudo-pious souls will not see.

As we plunge further into the subject of Christian warfare, we see that the life of sanctification is itself the beginning of Christian warfare. God cannot use unholy saints; they are a contradiction in terms. As long as we remain unholy, because sin is not mortified within us, we shall never rise up in battle against the foe. He has beaten us on the level of inbred sin because we have not taken seriously enough, by faith, the fact of the seed of God within us. When we do, Satan comes into play. A holy child of God is of great potential danger to the Devil and his kingdom.

How are we then to deal with Satan? There are three stages in the training of a Christian warrior. The first, paradoxically enough, is the art of strategic retreat. That is, we must learn that God allows Satan his evil days (Eph. 6:13) when he is let out on a long leash to try the children of God. The first fact we must learn is that when he is let out like a roaring lion we must know where to run for shelter – to Christ. We have no shelter from Satan but in Christ. He alone can challenge him. Take such a passage from the Psalms as this: 'Be merciful to me, O God, be merciful to me, for in thee my soul takes refuge; in the shadow of thy wings I will take refuge, till the storms of destruction pass by' (Ps. 57:1).

Then, having learned how and where to run in the evil day, we come to the second stage in our military training, the art of unyielding defence. Most of the warfare passage in Ephesians 6:10-18 deals with the art of defence. The armour is defensive: the breastplate of righteousness, the feet shod with the gospel of peace to enable us to stand our ground, the shield of faith to withstand the fire-tipped darts of the wicked one, and the helmet of salvation to protect the head.

After a thorough training in the art of unyielding defence, we must learn to attack the enemy, for you can hardly call the sword of the Spirit, which is the Word of God (Eph. 6:17), a weapon of defence! Here we learn to assail the enemy, not run from him or stand our ground against him, but run *at* him, and learn to rout him and drive him from the field by the great weapon of all-prayer (Eph. 6:18).

For example, we are confronted with the evil one who, in our church, in our school, or even in our home, is sitting pretty, making havoc of our attempts to do the Lord's work by making inroads into the hearts of others. He is entrenched and in command – or have we realised this is the situation? I am amazed at how many Christians would never dream of attributing to the Devil even the most sorry spiritual situation. I know there are those who too readily attribute to the Devil what appear to be matters of sheer human sin and wickedness, but there are, none the less, situations so obdurate that we can only conclude that the Devil himself, or one or more of his powerful demons, is in control.

What are we do? Sit back moaning and accept the situation? Never! Not if we know whose we are, whom we serve, and whom we are fighting for, and with. We very soberly recognise a work to be of the Devil. We do not ignore or absolve his agents, we concentrate upon him, not them, and this enables us to love and pity his deluded agents, to 'love your enemies.' Jesus was not letting Peter go 'scot free' when he turned to him and said, 'Get thee behind me, Satan!' He was saying, 'O Peter, you have let Satan use your lips.' Our Lord loved Peter out of his sin, and yet hated the Devil much more for seeking to employ the man he loved so much.

When we detect and recognise Satan, what do we do? Do we turn to God to ask him what he can do for us in the situation? If we do, he will answer, 'Have you forgotten what I have done for you? I can do no more than I did nearly two thousand years ago. Have you tried that power?' 'What power?' 'The power of Jesus' victory over Satan.' Listen: 'And they overcame him by the blood of the Lamb,' not only by the fact of Christ's victorious death, but by their testimony to that victory, thus entering into that dimension of experience of Christ's death in which he defeated Satan.

What do we mean by entering into that 'experience of Christ's death in which he defeated Satan'? It is not easy to understand, or to do, but it is possible. In fact, for Christ's servants and soldiers it is necessary.

Take the teaching of the apostle Paul in 2 Corinthians 4:10-12 and relate these verses to, say, Paul being stoned (presumably) to death at Lystra. He says in 2 Corinthians 4:7 that we have this treasure (the life of Christ) in earthen vessels (human bodies) 'to show that the transcendent power belongs to God'. We are 'always carrying in the body the death of Jesus, so that the life of Jesus may be manifested in our bodies' (v. 10). 'For while we live,' he goes on in verses 11, 12, 'we are always being given up to death for Jesus' sake so that the life of Jesus may be manifested in our mortal flesh. So death is at work in us, but life in you' (that is, in others).

Here, then, are two distinct but related results of sharing the experience of Christ's costly but victorious death: personal resurrections for ourselves, and, because we live and go on witnessing to others, resurrections (new births) for others. Thus we have in the course of our Christian life many resurrection experiences out of what appear to us to be certain deaths (there cannot be a resurrection without a death). Not only so, but since in the evil one's intention our deaths are to prevent us being used in respect of others, we not only emerge from our deaths victorious, but others are brought from the death of sin into the risen life of Christ, and are thus born into Christ's kingdom.

It is not enough in a dire spiritual situation, where the enemy has been detected, simply to mouth the words of Ephesians 6, or Revelation 12, and calmly, objectively, detachedly call on Christ to give victory. The only way to enter into an experience of Christ's victory over the powers of evil is to be willing to enter into a vital, costly experience of Christ's death as his victory over Satan.

This is where we follow Christ into his experience, although we do not enter into his action for us in the forgiveness of sins and justification. We do not share in that latter work, but stand by it and let God do it all for us. But as in sanctification (Christ's work wrought in us) we have to enter into an experience of death to sins so in gaining victory over Satan we must enter into that dimension of Christ's death which procured his victory over the enemy. This is partly what Paul is speaking about in Colossians 1:24 when he says, 'I rejoice in my sufferings for your sake, and in my flesh I complete (fill up) what is lacking in Christ's afflictions for the sake of his body, that is, the church.' What can this mean but that we need to have our own share in the sufferings which Christ completed for us? – in our own interest and in the interests of others.

This is what Moses was doing up the mount when Israel gained victory over Amalek (Exod. 17:8-13). This was prevailing prayer (*cf.* Eph. 6:17, 18). The holding up of Moses' hands in prayer was really his entering into the victory of Christ over Satan (Christ's death being certain; he is the Lamb slain from before the foundation of the world. Moses may therefore be said to have drawn on the power of Christ 'on account' as it were). While Moses held up the hands of prevailing prayer, Israel was in the ascendant, and when he let them down, Amalek gained ground.

To keep up the hands of prevailing prayer is costly and we are able to pay the price only because it has already been fully paid. Jesus speaks of this in the binding of the strong man (Matt. 12:29; Mk. 3:27). We know that Satan is still at large, although his activity is restricted since Christ's death, but he roves about like a lion which, it sometimes appears, no one can tame. This is because the victory of Christ is hidden from the world (see the mysteries of the kingdom in Matthew 13).

At one impulse of the death of Christ in any believing man's experience, Satan can be bound, gagged and utterly defeated. We saw earlier how God took command of situations in which Satan was about to work havoc, and by one word Satan was obliged to stand by helplessly and see all his plans absolutely ruined. The same is true with any situation where Satan seems to be in control. We are to bind the so-called strong man Satan, and then spoil his goods. That is to say, we are to invoke by costly experience the death of Christ as victory over Satan, and see him driven into a corner, to stand helplessly by while God undoes situations of his creating and radically changes them.

Think of the Shepherd Psalm: 'You prepare a table before me in the presence of my foes, with all dainties and all pleasant ministrations to my needs' (Ps. 23:5). And my foes can do nothing about it, because they are rendered powerless by my sharing in Christ's victory over them! This could lead us into deep waters. I am quite sure such trafficking in the crucifixion power of God always lies behind true revival. And what is more needed to-day? Are we prepared to pay the price of it?

Consider what we learn in Daniel 10. Daniel was in an agony of prayer, for the Lord was leading him into prophetic truth. The Lord came to comfort him by reminding him that from the beginning of his prayer his words had been heard. 'And', says the angelic being, 'I have come because of your words (of prayer). The prince of the kingdom of Persia . . . ('prince' here undoubtedly means demon spirit in control of the king or prince of Persia, the opposite of guardian angel; perhaps, rather, call him a Satanic guardian angel) . . . withstood me ('me' is the holy angel) twenty-one days; but Michael, one of the chief princes (an archangel, Jude 9), came to help me, so I left him (Michael) there (presumably wrestling) with the prince of the kingdom of Persia and came to make you understand what is to befall your people (the information God wanted to give Daniel) in the latter days' (10:12b-14).

Daniel's prayer, which God had heard instantly, had presumably to continue until he had wrestled himself into a victorious agony of prayer for the angel who was on his way with the enlightenment God was to give Daniel as to the future. Michael the archangel was called in to help the angel, whose progress had been barred by the demon spirit ruling the heart of the prince of Persia. What took place between the forces of the holy and the unholy angels was decisively determined by the kind and quality of Daniel's prayer, which at last brought victorious light and power to bear on the sons of men.

Before human situations, dominated by evil spirit forces, can be changed, mortal men, praying in the Holy Spirit in the deeper dimensions of the victorious death of Christ, must come to grips with them there, whether they understand the spiritual mechanics of what they are doing or not (*cf.* Job chs 1, 2, 42). But educated Christians should know the spiritual mechanics by which these things are done!

Therefore, unless we have some conception of the two kingdoms at war in the heavenlies, we shall not realise that there are battles respecting seemingly human situations which can be fought only by our touching the heavenly spheres and intelligences, good and bad. That is why Paul says so emphatically that we wrestle not against flesh and blood. Our fight ultimately is not with men – although men may be the agents – but with principalities and powers, with the world rulers of this present darkness, and with the spiritual hosts of wickedness in the heavenly spheres (Eph. 6:12).

All this may terrify some, and they may not want to know it. But the fact is, we have been given the victory over all these powers of evil through Christ, and it is ours under God and in Christ, saturating ourselves in all his blessed potencies, to use it.

THE SECOND COMING

1

You have asked me to give these three addresses on the second coming of Christ; and I must lead in to them with a word about looking towards Christ and his first coming, as seen from the beginning of time, indeed, from hints in Scripure, before that, since he is the pre-existent One.

Who Christ is, his coming, and indeed, the creation itself, all have to do with the nature of the eternal Trinity. You do not really begin to understand biblical doctrine and the divine purpose in creation and redemption until you have wrestled with questions concerning the Godhead and relationships within the Trinity (co-equal as the three Persons of the Godhead are). Creation and redemption are rooted in the relationship between the Father and the Son. This is where man as a creature pre-conceived by God comes in. The fact that the church, consisting of saved sinners, is to be the Bride of Christ and have a relationship with Christ as intimate and exalted as his Bride, or his Body, indicates that the coming of Christ into the world for his own is a matter of the highest divine strategy.

First of all, then, man is made uniquely in the image and likeness of God – no other creature is such (even angels are small fry in the ultimate economy!); thus the fall of Adam (following the fall of the angels) was an event of major importance, warranting God's judgmental response to it. As Donald Mackay put it, there came a new creative fiat by God to be taken as seriously as the original fiat of creation. If I remember him rightly, Mackay means that the second half of Genesis 3 defines a radically different creation from that of

Genesis 2, as far as Satan, the world, the woman and the man are concerned. The world is now a sort of mal-creation of which travail in childbirth for woman, thorns and thistles in the ground and hard labour (as distinct from pleasant and fruitful labour, 2:15) for man, are some of the obvious instances (Gen. 3:14-19).

But the most important verse is Genesis 3:15 in which God makes a universal declaration with unique import for the rest of history. He says: I will put enmity (this is not merely the result of the Fall as a fact, but what God purposes or wills, morally and ethically, to do about it) between the Satanic world empire (snatched by duplicity from the dominion of man, Gen. 1:26) and the seed of the woman. For the rest of history, starting from that point and sweeping right through the Old Testament, we see the enmity and conflict as Satan and his crew try to prevent the promised and ultimate seed of the woman, Jesus Christ, from coming to the earth to save man and recover for him his dominion lost by the Fall.

This is why it is important for us to trace at least a few of the promises of Christ's coming in the Old Testament. Take Deuteronomy 18:18,19: 'The Lord said to Moses, "I will raise up for them (Israel) a prophet like you from among their brethren; and I will put my words in his mouth, and he shall speak to them all that I command him. And whoever will not give heed to my words which he shall speak in my name (this looks right forward to the final judgment), I myself will require it of him."' Notice, by the way, that Peter on the day of Pentecost, quoting these verses in Acts 3:22-25, points further back to Abraham in Genesis 12:1-3 as the beginning of the covenant God made with him and his posterity and all the families of the earth, although that covenant of grace could equally well be said to go right back to Genesis 3:15, the first promise of the Saviour. See this again referred to by Zechariah (John the Baptist's father) in Luke 1:72,73: 'to perform the mercy promised to our fathers and to remember his holy covenant, the oath he swore to our father Abraham . . .' and thence back to Genesis 22:16-18 and to Genesis 3:15.

Peter then in Acts 3:24 looks back to Samuel and to 'all the prophets' as prophesying Jesus' coming. Luke also describing the walk to Emmaus (Lk. 24:27) attributes to 'all the prophets' prophesyings concerning his coming.

Then we have Christ's first coming announced by David (Psalm 40:6-8) incorporating words put into Messiah's mouth by the Spirit: 'Sacrifice and offering thou dost not desire, but ears hast thou prepared for me (the Hebrew is 'dug out'). Burnt offering and sin offering thou hast not required. Then I said "Lo, I come: in the roll of the book it is written of me, I delight to do thy will, O my God; thy law is within my heart"'. That this is so is confirmed by the writer of Hebrews (10:5-8) as having truly come to pass in the incarnate experience of Jesus Christ.

Then we have Christ's birth prophesied in Isaiah 7:14: 'a virgin shall conceive and bear a son, and shall call his name Immanuel (God with us)' just as we have the most intimate and meticulous details of his passion and death in, *e.g.* Isaiah 53 and Psalm 22. We can trace this further, at almost any length, taking in such prophecies as that of Micah 5:2 concerning the place of his birth, Bethlehem; or his second birth by resurrection, Psalm 2:7 (quoted in Acts 13:33, Heb. 1:5); his triumphal entry into Jerusalem, Zechariah 9:9, along with other references to his resurrection, *e.g.* Psalm 16:10 and his ascension in Psalm 68:18.

But one of the most important things for us to understand in considering Old Testament prophecies of the coming of Messiah is that some of them necessarily telescope two comings. It is important now that the first coming has taken place, to distinguish, as far as we can, the one from the other. We should view the prophetic scene, especially in the Old Testament, like ranges of mountains with folds upon folds that in the dimness look like one massive outline but yet contain long valleys between their massive shoulders. Indeed, this is one of the major reasons why the Jews of our Lord's day missed him; they were unable to integrate two main strands of prophecy, one very popular which saw Christ as their coming King, Champion and Vindicator; the other which saw him as the Suffering Servant (see the Servant Songs in Isa. 41:8-20; 42:1-7,18; 43:5-10; 49:1-9; 50:4-11; 52:13-53:12). It is this failure (and refusal) to integrate the two which the apostolic writer draws attention to in the Acts (3:18) – 'But what God foretold by the mouth of all his prophets, that his

Christ (the anointed One) should suffer, he thus (to the amazement of all) fulfilled' (see also 17:3; 26:23, for the same assertion!).

The many references to Messiah as the Suffering Servant undoubtedly have to do with his first coming; but those concerning the prophesied glory of his royal kingdom more naturally point to his second coming. But there is a great tension between the prophetic ideas of the Sufferer and the King, the Lord reigning from the tree or from the throne. This poses the vexed question, how far do the Old Testament prophecies concerning the work of the One crucified/reigning Redeemer refer to the church on earth and how far do they refer to the church in heaven? How far do they portray the victories of Christ in the gospel age, and how far do they usher in the eternal or heavenly state after his coming in judgment? And can we define, in relation to all these prophecies, when he comes the second time – whether before the millennium (Rev. 20:2–7) or after the millennium, or whether there is a millennium at all (although that is hardly a fair question since a-millennialists simply have other ways of explaining the millennium)? This is essentially what happens to the church (both in earth and in heaven) in relation to Christ between his two comings during the gospel age when Satan is bound (but, it should be explained, bound only to those who have faith in Christ's victory and who therefore exercise it to the binding of Satan).

But to return to Old Testament prophecy, I sometimes wonder if Christ himself gives us a key to the partial solution of these vexed problems, when in Nazareth in the synagogue, he reads from Isaiah 61: 'The Lord has anointed me to bring good tidings to the afflicted; he has sent me to bind up the brokenhearted, to proclaim liberty to the captives, and the opening of the prison to those who are bound; to proclaim the year of the Lord's favour.' There he stopped; the words that follow, which our Lord apparently did not read are 'and the day of vengeance of our God'. Luke 4:20 goes on, 'And he closed the book, and gave it back to the attendant, and sat down . . . .' You know why he did not read 'the day of vengeance'? Because the vengeance (judgment) was not yet. That is why Jesus said to Nicodemus, 'For God sent the Son into the world, not to condemn the world, but that the world through him might be saved'; and to Zacchaeus, 'For the Son of man came to seek and to save the lost'.

May not the distinction between his coming with favour and then vengeance afford us a touchstone upon which to test what belongs to his first coming, and what to his second coming?

I recall how impressed I was when I first heard the book of the Revelation characterised as mainly a book of judgment. No one could say that all it writes about are end things, because after that marvellous introductory vision that floored and flummoxed John when he saw the glory of the Jesus on whose breast he had leant, John in his vision heard about the church – universal in terms of the seven churches of Asia (chs. 2, 3). Nonetheless, Revelation is a book mainly about end things, or things leading up to the end. What do you think? Or do you simply repeat what you have heard or read, and close your mind to all other views? The one thing I think is really unholy in this realm is close-minded dogmatism.

I say this, not because I do not want to make up my mind about so many areas here; I do, desperately, the older I grow and the more I become dragged into involvement with the strategies of Christ's church, in our own country and further afield. But I have made up my mind several times about the second coming and had to change it too because of what I regard as the sheer weight of devout biblical scholarship. I was brought up on pre-millennialism, largely because that was all that the only Bible book shop in Aberdeen sold. It took me years to get it into my system that there was not one scriptural text to justify or even suggest a secret rapture. That is really a figment of the imagination in comparatively modern times – apart from the rather grim fact that that belief has now terrified far too many generations of children of pre-millennial parents who have had to force themselves to make unreal or premature 'decisions' for Christ out of sheer panic that Christ would come secretly in the night and take away their parents, and they would wake in the morning to find them gone. A cruel and unnatural suggestion! I can vouch for the truth of it, because dear Christians that I have associated with for many years now were ultimately and happily delivered from that snare! This in itself does not discountenance pre-millennialism (there is a non-dispensational pre-millennium). But if you are a pre-millennial dispensationalist, you are very far behind the times with regard to devout, modern biblical scholarship. The evangelical church throughout the world (largely with the exception of the so-called

Bible Belts in America, along with their influence elsewhere, of course) has moved on, generally speaking, to an a-millennial position, perhaps largely due to the influence of William Hendriksen and Martyn Lloyd-Jones.

But I think it true to say that increasingly in conservative evangelical or Reformed circles there is a conviction growing that perhaps a post-millennial position is probably nearer to what the Scriptures really teach. You have pre-, post- and a-: 'Pre-post-e-rous', as some earlier wag remarked!

This post-millennial view has made considerable advances recently, due partly to Iain Murray's book *The Puritan Hope*; I must tell you, whoever you are and whatever your viewpoint, that you can hardly be regarded as competent to judge which position is nearest to biblical truth until you have at least reckoned with that book.

Although Iain Murray would probably not use the description 'post-millennialist' of himself, he goes back to the Puritans of the 17th century, and shows that the majority of them looked towards the end of the age for a millennium of gospel grace before the coming of Christ in super-abundant measure, especially after the conversion of Israel (Rom. 11:25,26,). Both verses 12 and 15 of Romans 11, rightly read and understood, seem to promise a far greater and more widespread movement of the Spirit after Israel's conversion rather than before it. Iain Murray brings forward quotations from many of the great and godly men of different centuries; but perhaps his most striking point is one which is in perfect keeping with the point I have been making, namely our Lord's division of the sentence in Isaiah 61:2 into two, which prophesies respectively his coming to 'proclaim the year of the Lord's favour and the day of vengeance of our God'.

Surely a collocation of scriptural passages on the Lord's second coming should lead us all to agree that the last event in time is the coming of the Lord as the Judge of the earth! C.S. Lewis puts it in theatrical terms: he says that 'when the author comes on to the stage, that is the end of the play'. Surely the very idea of our Lord returning to the earth in a domestic setting violates our deepest scriptural knowledge and our spiritual instinct concerning the last day (the end of the age) when 'the Son of man comes on the clouds of heaven with power and great glory and sends out his angels with a loud trumpet call'; 'the day of the Lord will come like a thief, and then the heavens will pass away with a loud noise, and the elements will be dissolved with fire, and the earth and the works that are upon it will be burned up' (Matt. 24:30-1; 2 Pet. 3:10).

In opposition to the extreme post-millennial side asserting that this describes gospel age events symbolically represented, Tasker on Matthew 24, says:

> In this very difficult section the evangelist has brought together sayings of Jesus which foretold the downfall of Jerusalem and the final coming of the Son of man in judgment. As the language in which these events is expressed is partly literal and partly symbolic, and as Jesus would seem to have regarded both of them as 'comings' in judgment, scholars have found it extremely difficult to say with any degree of certainty which parts of the chapter contain an answer to the question of the disciples, When shall these things be? (*viz.* the destruction of the temple buildings mentioned in verse 2), and which parts are a response to their supplementary question, And what shall be the sign of thy coming, and of the end of the world?

> It would seem that the disciples, by placing these two questions in juxtaposition, associated very closely in their minds the impending fall of Jerusalem and the coming of Jesus which would mark the end of the present age.

Might it not be a good thing for us then in our search for the nearest to a satisfying understanding of the scriptural prophecy concerning the Lord's actual second coming, to start with that end event, that final event as prophesied? Accepting that as cataclysmic and final (for it is the last judgment) we can then look back to what is said in Scripture about events between the two comings, and see if we cannot make simpler sense of the course of future history or from the beginning of the age of grace, the gospel age, until the end.

Certainly one good principle to follow would be for us all to put far more emphasis on the clear passages of Scripture, and not base our case so much on the difficult, dark and obscure passages, especially those which can bear so many different interpretations, of which perhaps the two most striking are Matthew 24 and Revelation 20.

Consider this extract from J.A. Alexander's Commentary on Mark 13 written in the nineteenth century. After a survey of views, he says:

> Even this incomplete enumeration (of hypotheses of whether Jesus is speaking of A.D. 70 or of the end of the world) will suffice to show the vast variety of plausible hypotheses devised to facilitate the exposition of this difficult and interesting passage; a variety susceptible of only one solution, namely, that the prophecy itself has been but partially fulfilled, and that the unfulfilled part, from the very nature and design of prophecy, cannot be fully understood, or even certainly distinguished as literal or figurative, until the event shall make it clear. Every prediction which has been fulfilled was equally mysterious beforehand, for example those of Christ's first advent, scarcely one of which was not susceptible of two or more interpretations till he actually came, and the same thing may be looked for in the predictions of his second coming. It is the part of wisdom, therefore, not to attempt what is impossible, (the anticipation of things yet to be developed), but to ascertain, as far as may be, what has been verified already, and to be contented, as to the remainder, with careful explanation of the terms employed, according to analogy and usage, and to be contented with a reverential waiting for ulterior disclosures by the light of divine providence shining on the word. Among the incidental but important questions raised in this discussion, one of the most difficult and interesting has respect to the apparent nearness of the two events as here predicted, (A.D. 70; end of world (age)) and the mode of reconciling this representation with the truth of history and our Lord's omniscience. This is a difficulty not confined to any one hypothesis, but pressing more or less on all which recognise a real prophecy with two distinguishable themes or subjects.
> To this point as well as to the general question (upon what hypothesis or principle the passage is to be explained) there will be constant reference in the following detailed examination of the chapter.

But, you see, I have already quoted Matthew 24, and even that passage (which many think could refer to a cosmic, final coming of the Lord in great power and glory) is said by committed post-millennialists like J. Marcellus Kik (no mean exegete and a name to be reckoned with in Reformed scholarship) to be a cosmic description of a spiritual coming, an event or experience prior to the final coming, as he believes also in the case of 2 Peter and Revelation 21-22, which most people believe describe the heavenly state. You see how difficult the whole thing is, and how it behoves us to seek to be very simple, main-line and basic about it, and as objective as we can be.

I remember once discussing the second coming with Martyn Lloyd-Jones in the Green Room of the Music Hall in Aberdeen. He said to me 'I never say more in public than that he is coming.' But he asked me, nonetheless, if I had read Hendriksen's *More than Conquerors*, obviously recommending it, and he has since declared himself to have been always an a-millennialist.

We will explore this further, but since Christians are of very different persuasions on the matter we might profitably begin by laying down what we do agree on! Don't you think that would please the Lord, who is with us now, and who will bless us here and hereafter according to our obedience to his will, in loving one another and seeking the unity and peace of this fellowship (Eph. 4:1-3)?

Whatever the truth be about the Lord's coming, and whenever and however he will come; if he tarries his coming for even a few years, the hope of our land could be in our hands more than we know. One thing I am certain of, God requires of us particularly our years at university as Christian students. Let me put the possibilities to you in this way. Something was done around the CU's of Scotland in the 1960's which for one thing has put on the map of the north-west coast of Scotland from Fort William to Cape Wrath, a line of evangelical ministers with perhaps no more than one or two little places missing. Some years ago I remembered a godly man saying to me, after holidaying there, how utterly dead the north-west was. Others of different denominations have said the same. Dead Sabbatarianism and legalism with drunkenness and immorality to a high degree. But you cannot say all the ministers in these places are dead now!

Take the schools of Scotland: the advance that has been made in Scripture Union in schools and in Crusaders and similar classes is phenomenal, and a great deal of that has emerged from those who were in the University and College Christian Unions. You do not know your potential as you sit here and absorb the truth of God! Therefore, if we are to make a concerted effort on behalf of our land, and ultimately God is pleased to turn the tide of ungodliness and wickedness, we must be united in the Lord on things that are assuredly verifiable, and of first importance.

What then do we agree on concerning the coming of the Lord? First, that he is coming: 'I will come again and receive you unto myself, that where I am there ye may be also'; 'this same Jesus shall so come in like manner (clouds *etc*.) as ye saw him go into heaven'. The Apostles' Creed (which I would think sums up biblical truth regarding the matter truly and acceptably), says, 'from heaven he will come to judge the quick (the living) and the dead.'

That obviously bespeaks the general resurrection at the end of the age which Jesus speaks of so plainly in John 5:29 when he says all will come forth: 'those who have done good to the resurrection of life, and those who have done evil (and it is our character as we have lived it out that will tell, then), to the resurrection of judgment (which is final damnation)'.

I hope we are agreed that he is coming thus. We will not ask when just now, or how, since, although there are signs of the times, none knows the day, not even the Son, only the Father. What do we do until then (or until we are taken away from this earthly scene)? You know what Paul said to the Thessalonians who were so preoccupied with the thought of our Lord's soon coming, and certainly thought and hoped he would come in their day – Paul himself hoped for that (2 Cor. 5:5). He said, 'You're not looking for the Lord's coming! You're just shirking your work and expecting other people to feed you. You're just looking for sensation'. The way to prepare for the Lord's great and glorious coming is to serve the Lord who is with you now in your heart, your home, at your work, and in the world where he is busy looking for his own among the flotsam, the debris of human society.

Occupy! not speculate, or wonder, or argue, or gape, but get busy. What doing? Well, to answer that properly ought to provide the practical justification for your asking me to deal with the second coming. What does Jesus mean when in the parable of the pounds he says, Occupy, or trade, or do business till I come. The purpose of this parable is to correct those who thought the kingdom of God was to appear immediately (Lk. 19:11–27). The word in the original which occurs only here in the New Testament is *pragmateuomai,* be pragmatic, practical, active! Isn't that interesting? The parable (which is perhaps the nearest to an allegory of all Jesus' parables) goes on to say that the king's servants who were each given a pound to trade with hated him so. On coming back, he called his ten servants to see what they had gained by trading. And that word is a compound of *pragmateuomai, diapragmateuomai,* meaning to augment (the pound) by trading. That can only mean the growth of the church by the teaching of the gospel. Paul says, 'I charge you in the presence of God and of Christ Jesus who is to judge the living and the dead, at his appearing and his kingdom, preach the word; be urgent in season and out of season, convince, rebuke, and exhort, be unfailing in patience and in teaching . . .'(2 Tim.4:2).

That is a truly balanced view of our task, just as balanced as the challenge in the two letters to the Thessalonians which deal so particularly with the second coming. There, reminding them of his nursing care of them when he came with the Gospel, Paul also says he sought to please God, not men, in what he taught and how he behaved. He laboured night and day (tent-making by day and preaching and teaching by night, or *vice versa?*) not to make himself burdensome to them. Behaving with meticulous propriety he exhorted and encouraged them, like a father his children, to lead a life worthy of God and, he says, they accepted the message as the Word of God, not the word of men, to them. Later he said that although the day of the Lord's coming would surprise men, they ought not to be surprised because they should remain awake and be sober, encouraging one another and building up one another in the faith, and – particularly – admonishing the idle.

In 2 Thessalonians he says they should not get excited thinking that the Lord would come before the man of sin appeared, and the apostasy set in. He deals very hard blows at those who are idly preoccupied with the second coming, enough to stop work and allow other kindly Christians, even the Christian fellowship itself, to feed them. So that the right attitude towards the second coming is that of getting on with the Christian job.

But what is the job? It is a combination of two jobs, which need to be finely balanced and are so perfectly poised and balanced in the Scriptures (*cf.* the significant passage quoted from 2 Tim. 4:1-2 about preaching the gospel and the reference from the Thessalonian letters). The two jobs are, evangelism and edification – and in that order. Without evangelism the church on earth would die out. Without edification (Bible teaching applied to building Christian character and building Christian fellowships) the church becomes so weak and vulnerable that ultimately the very impulse to evangelise dies out (apart from entertainment evangelism which should surely be beneath our notice as dishonouring to the dignity of Christ), the wood, hay and stubble being burned up in judgment.

Of the two, exclusive concentration on evangelism proves to be more disastrous, largely, I think, because too much concentration on an evangelistic message seems to generate in so many an opposition to thorough and systematic Bible edification, and that really menaces the health and certainly the strength of the church. On the other hand, the great danger of exclusive Bible teaching ministries is that the church goes into a holy huddle and opts out of its evangelical responsibility, and becomes virtually dead. I do not think there is a word to be said in favour of such a condition any more than about a frothy condition – except this, that 'sound dead' if it should ever be quickened and come alive again (like crowds of excellent people who years ago ran out of the Taylorite Brethren movement and have enriched various branches of the church ever since) has a tremendous lot to offer. Only the Spirit in a fellowship can recover and maintain the balance, and such a fellowship is really and truly the only one which is preparing for the Lord's coming biblically. We must therefore never set these two, evangelism and edification, over against one another adversatively, but always see them complementarily.

What, then, am I wanting to say to you? The prospect of the return of Christ must make a difference to the way we live now – this is the consistent testimony of Scripture. But what difference? We should be growing *up* in ourselves and we should be going *out* to others, in love and faithful witness to our returning Lord. Never let the complex patterns in the tapestry of the biblical teaching on the second coming divert you from the main picture. Live for him now, and you will be ready to welcome him when he comes!

THE SECOND COMING

2

In the previous study I suggested that as a simplification of the issue of the Lord's second coming we accept from Scripture the finality of his coming for salvation and judgment. This is surely right If we think of the Old Testament ages as preparing for and pointing to Christ's first coming to deal with sin (that is the barrier to God becoming our God and we becoming his people – *i.e.* taking us to his heart and home); then we ought to think of the time between his two comings as that in which he is gathering the rest of his elect ripening the fruit of his redemption in successive generations, with a view to the climax, consummation and final show-down between good and evil as Christ brings to completion that for which he came in the first place.

If we can all agree on this, that Christ comes at the end, not 'pre but 'post' (the a-millennialists and non millennialists are as 'post as the post-millennialists as far as this is concerned!), then we car seriously get down to considering what we may learn from Scripture concerning the pattern of activity and events leading to that so called 'far-off divine event'.

We can take the words of Hebrews 9:26b-28 as a guide and look at the words which New Testament writers have used to enshrine the idea of Christ's second coming. There are three words principally *parousia* = his presence; *epiphaneia* = his visible manifestation which comes from the word *phainō*, to shine (although the church has used this term to commemorate the presenting of the Christ-child to the Gentiles, in the persons of the magi, supposedly on the 6th January or, as it is, the twelfth day of Christmas); and thirdly *apokalupsis* = unveiling.

The first, *parousia,* is the commonest term of the three (we find it four times in one chapter, Matt. 24:3,27,37,39; once in the resurrection chapter, 1 Cor.15:23; four times in 1 Thess. 2:19; 3:13; 4:15; 5:23; three times in 2 Thess. 2:1,8,9; twice in Jas. 5:7,8, concerning patience; thrice in 2 Pet. 1:16;3:4,12; and in 1 Jn. 2:28; eighteen times altogether). The second word, *epiphaneia,* is found in one phrase along with *parousia* in 2 Thessalonians 2:8; it is also found in 1 Timothy 6:14; 2 Timothy 4:1,8; Titus 22:13; all of which are translated 'appearing'. The third word *apokalupsis* is found in 1 Corinthians 1:7 'waiting for the unveiling of the Lord'; in 2 Thessalonians 1:7; and 1 Peter 1:7,13; 4:13. The word as it is used in Revelation 1:1 (the title) clearly does not refer to the one particular event of his coming, his birth, but to the whole grand unveiling from incarnation to consummation.

It is interesting that none of these three significant words suggests motion, progressive or travelling motion in the sense of expressing arrival or entry: if I may use theatrical terms, the coming of the Lord is viewed not so much as a return to the stage of history, but rather as being on stage when the curtain goes up. There are, of course, expressions of motion-like prepositions in 2 Thessalonians 1:7, 'from heaven', and the ordinary word for coming, *erchomai,* as in Matthew 16:28 and 24:30. Fair enough, but the prevailing idea is of Christ appearing in the sense of being visibly present. Of course he is coming from heaven, from the right hand of the Father, where he now intercedes for us; but he is still here, is he not, by his Spirit in our breasts and in the midst of this very Christian fellowship?

I do not want to exaggerate this as if I alone had made a great discovery; but it interests me. You see, in a sense, the transfiguration was a sort of rehearsal for the grand outshining at the consummation, because although Christ's mortal form was not invisible to the disciples, it was as if God gave answer to Peter's embarrassed prattling (he did not know what he was saying) by – if I may say so reverently – switching on Christ's glory! Not that I believe the whiteness of his raiment and his general incandescence was his eternal glory (it could not have been his *redemptive* glory before his death); but it was the glory of his perfect manhood with all his manly human virtues in full and perfect evidence in their ultimate dimension – personal glory! Personality is glory! None the less (and I keep using this term 'switch on' because of its vividness and also because I think it is perhaps as near a visible conception of what will happen as we have), he was switched on, and the disciples saw him as he really was (and is). They saw all that was hidden in his apparently normal manhood, dressed in ordinary clothes, shining through.

But, then, we are surely to regard that final event as not only instant ('in the twinkling of an eye', 1 Cor.15:51-54), but cosmic and changing all things. 'Behold, I make all things new.' As Christ in his first coming makes all things new in the lives that receive him by repentance and faith, so, when he returns in power and great glory in the total sense, he will make all things new (Rev. 21:5). This is where I can hardly agree with Marcellus Kik (although I am greatly attracted to his general thesis and to much of his teaching), that the expressions for Christ's coming in *e.g.* Matthew 24:29–31; 2 Peter 3:10–13, are, as he says, like many Old Testament cosmic and cataclysmic references, to be understood as hyperbolic or symbolic, not literal. Think what is taken away from the prospect of our Lord's coming if you do not take this literally: 'the heavens will pass away with a loud noise, and the elements will melt with fervent heat and the earth and the works that are upon it will be burned up. Since all these things are thus to be dissolved, what sort of persons ought you to be in lives of holiness and godliness, waiting for, and hastening the coming day of God; because of which the heavens will be kindled and dissolved, and the elements will melt with fire. But, according to his promise we wait for new heavens and a new earth in which righteousness dwells.' What is that symbolic of? The complete disintegration of the human personality and human society? It could describe the destruction of Babylon (Rev. 18:10, 21); but does even that do justice to these catastrophic terms?

But, enough on the actual event of the coming. We must now try to see if we can make acceptable sense of the welter of biblical statements concerning what transpires between the comings, what leads to his coming. We will take the different main views in turn and look at them as briefly and comprehensively as possible.

Pre-millennialism goes back to the early fathers in the Christian church. A fair summary of it would go something like this: the present world will endure six thousand years, corresponding to the six days of the creation. Towards the end of this period the sufferings and persecutions of the pious will increase, until finally the incarnation of all wickedness appears in the person of the Antichrist. After he has completed his destructive work and has boldly seated himself in the temple of God, Christ will appear in heavenly glory and triumph over all his enemies. This will be accompanied by the physical resurrection of the saints and the establishment of the Kingdom of God on the earth. The period of millennial bliss lasting a thousand years will correspond to the seventh day of creation – the day of rest. Jerusalem will be rebuilt; the earth will yield its fruit in rich abundance; and peace and righteousness will prevail.

At the end of the thousand years the final judgment will ensue and a new creation will appear in which the redeemed will live for ever in the presence of God. Comparatively simple! This, generally speaking, remained the pre-millennial view for many centuries, right into the nineteenth century. One wonders what pre-millennialists today think of this in relation to modern dispensational modifications of it.

Let me give you another pre-millennial summary which perhaps clarifies the pre-millennial view: remember it is of the ages preceding its nineteenth century dispensational turn.

The coming advent of Christ to the world is near, and will be visible, personal, and glorious. It will be preceded, however, by certain events such as the evangelisation of all nations, the conversion of Israel, the great apostasy and the great tribulation, and the revelation of the man of sin. Dark and trying times are therefore still in store for the church, since she will have to go through the great tribulation. The second coming will be a great, single, outstanding, and glorious event, but will be accompanied by several other events bearing on the church, on Israel, and on the world. The dead saints will be raised, and the living transfigured, together they will be translated to meet the coming Lord. Antichrist and his wicked allies will be slain; and Israel, the ancient people of God will repent, be saved, and restored to the Holy Land. Then the Kingdom of God, predicted by the prophets, will be established in a transformed world. The Gentiles will turn to God in great abundance and be incorporated in the Kingdom. A condition of peace and righteousness will prevail in all the earth. After the expiration of the earthly rule of Christ the rest of the dead will be raised up; and this resurrection will be followed by the last judgment and the creation of a new heaven and a new earth.

With that view a lot happens historically after Christ's coming: this is the point at issue! Now, although much of that will find acceptance with informal pre-millennialists, yet if we impose the dispensational pattern of Darby, Kelly, Trotter, Scofield, Bullinger, Grant and others, you will see how different it is. It gives virtually a new philosophy of the history of redemption in which Israel as a nation plays a leading role and the church is but an interlude! The dispensationalists' guiding principle prompts them to divide the Bible into two books, the book of the Kingdom and the book of the church. That last sentence is a startlingly simple and comprehensive way of describing the dispensational plan because it goes into almost a maze of covenants and dispensations which leads to various versions of the view, and much division within pre-millenarianism itself! There are really two second comings, one *for* and the other *with* Christ's church, two or three resurrections (if not four), and also three judgments. There are also, as indicated, two peoples of God, Israel on the earth and the church in heaven, which according to some will eternally separate!

Now let us look more closely at this dispensational view and its philosophy of history. God deals with the world of humanity on the basis of several covenants and seven dispensations. Each dispensation tests man and because he fails, it ends in judgment. There is, for example, the dispensation of the theocracy of Israel, the Kingdom of God, with its golden age under David and Solomon. Instead of increasing, because of unfaithfulness that kingdom of Israel failed altogether, and was carried away into exile although the prophets predicted a future blessed hope, through Messiah. But when at last Messiah came Israel refused their king, and instead of establishing his Kingdom their king withdrew to a far country, postponing the Kingdom until his return. In the interim the church, founded by Christ, is gathered out of Jews and Gentiles in the dispensation of grace of which the prophets never spoke, and which has nothing to do with the Kingdom and the dispensation of law; but sharing Christ's sufferings and forming the body of Christ, the church will as the Bride of Christ one day share his glory. Christ is not the king of this church, but its head; he is king of the Kingdom – a different entity! The church's task is to preach the gospel of free grace which is a different gospel from that of the Kingdom. The preaching of the gospel of free grace will prove in the end a failure, and will not effect conversions on a large scale (incidentally, it was protest against this pessimistic view that drove Billy Graham to become the great evangelist he has become). At the end of this dispensation Christ will suddenly return; it is imminent now, at any time, and will lead to a far more effectual and indeed universal conversion. No predicted events now precede Christ's coming. It is called the *parousia,* when Christ will appear to rapture (secretly) his saints and meet them in the air; all the righteous saints will be raised from the dead, and the living saints will be transfigured 'in a moment, in the twinkling of an eye'.

While Christ and the church and even the Holy Spirit are absent from the earth, seven years will intervene, divided into two parts, each of three and a half years (based on Revelation 11:2,3,9); when the gospel of the Kingdom will again be preached (because it will virtually be the age of the Kingdom) primarily by a believing remnant of Jews; there will be many conversions but many will still continue to blaspheme God. During the second half of these seven years there will be a period of unparalleled tribulation, Antichrist will be revealed and the bowls of wrath (Rev. 16:17) will be poured upon the earth (the church, of course, is safely in heaven). At the end of this period the Lord will come, not now secretly and for his church, but openly in power and glory with them; the living nations are judged, the sheep among the nations separated from the goats, the saints that died during these seven years are raised up, Antichrist is destroyed, and Satan bound for a thousand years. The millennial Kingdom is now established, a real, visible, terrestrial and material Kingdom of Jews with the restoration of the theocratic Kingdom, including the re-establishment of the Davidic kingship. In it the saints will reign with Christ, the Jews will be natural citizens and many Gentiles will be adopted as citizens. The throne of Christ will be established at Jerusalem, the centre for worship in the whole world, and temple worship will be reinstituted. After the millennium Satan will be loosed for a little season and the hordes of Gog and Magog (Ezek. chs. 38, 39) will assemble against the holy city. The enemies are devoured by fire from heaven, Satan is cast into the bottomless pit where the beast and the false prophet are, the wicked dead are raised up and judged at the great white throne (Rev. 20) and there will be a new heaven and a new earth.

Now, if any of this sounds at all garbled to pre-millenarians, it is really because the full blown pre-millennial views are various. There is a great variety of opinions with indefiniteness and uncertainty at many points. I, personally, am glad that I can see two sides of this. I was reared up on it and knew most of its intricacies pretty intimately and was often tied in knots over them.

Let me point out in a word or two some of the major objections to this view, apart from one's general bewilderment (not to say suspicion) of its complexity.

It is based on a literal interpretation of the prophetic future of Israel and the Kingdom of God, but after Christ comes. But we are lost in what is virtually confusion of the natural and the spiritual, and of the material and the eternal. For instance there would be the church walking the earth, or ruling over it, in resurrection bodies, but converted Jews on the earth with natural ones. Is that conceivable? What does that do to such simplicities as John 5:28,29? 'The hour is coming when all in the graves will hear his voice and come forth, those who have done good to the resurrection of life, and those who have done evil to the resurrection of judgment?' Who dare separate that into two distinct events?

The second major objection is as follows: the notion of the postponement of the Kingdom because the Jews refused their Kingdom, and the church (New Testament only) seen as a mere parenthesis is surely ridiculous, and makes for a permanent division of the people of God even in heaven! Calvin correctly speaks of the 'church' in his Old Testament commentaries when he means the Old

Testament church, Israel. But perhaps the general bewilderment at pre-millennial dispensational complexity and its confusion and uncertainty with regard to so many of its interpretations is the strongest argument against it! Yet, this is what vast numbers of Christian folk in America particularly, fervently and implicitly believe. We even get it among believing space men during the moon visitation programme!

But, of course, there is also as I said a much simpler scheme of the non-dispensational pre-millennialists. They do not accept the secret rapture but believe the church will pass through the tribulation and will be on the earth during the rise and reign of Antichrist, and therefore they reject the two-stage coming of Christ before the millennium, and hold that Christ will appear openly to take away his saints and to overthrow Antichrist and establish his millennial kingdom on earth. But you see, here is Christ a thousand years before the end of the age! It simply won't do!

Now for a brief look not as you might expect at post-millennialism, but at so-called a-millennialism. A-millennialism is really a misnomer because it does not deny the notion of a thousand year reign so much as give a very different 'non-blissful' interpretation of it: the millennium, although those who hold this view do not like to call it that or use that term very much, is the time between the first and second comings of Christ. It considers both the saints in heaven during that time and the saints on earth. It believes quite simply that the church and the world will go on (Satan being bound by faith in Christ's victory), until the one, simple, all-inclusive divine event of Christ's invisible power and glory takes place. It was this view that earlier I characterised in Lewis's theatrical terms as 'when the author comes on to the stage, the "play" is over'. I came to that view first through C. E. Alexander of Liverpool, who when I found it hard to jettison my literalist views of Old Testament prophecy (such as Zechariah 14, the mount of Olives split in two, and other vivid, even lurid passages) told me to read the 19th century German commentator Hengstenberg; and when I got him on Revelation 20 (which is surely the most difficult chapter in the whole Bible) he made things so clear and simple that I swallowed the a-millennial view and therefore took large doses of Hendriksen, as in his commentary on Revelation, *More than Conquerors.*

Curiously enough, modern conservative scholarship has very little positively to say on a-millennialism, compared with screeds on and against pre-millennialism. Perhaps that is partly due to the a-millennialist's radical simplicity. You have just this great gap between the two comings of Jesus Christ, however long, and all the details which pre-millennialists turn into programmes and dispensations are regarded largely as different descriptions of the one divine all-inclusive event which brings both full and final salvation and eternal judgment to men.

Louis Berkhof whose *Systematic Theology* has pages on pre-millennialism has only a few sentences on a-millennialism. One sentence of his I think is hardly fair: it says that from its name, a-millennialism is purely negative. But its name really belies what it holds; for as we have said it does have a view of the millennium – that it is the time between the first and second comings of Christ. More important, over against the pre-millennial confusion of earthly and heavenly, and natural and spiritual, it holds that the kingdom of Jesus Christ (as distinct from the church) is represented in the Scriptures as an eternal and not temporal kingdom, and to enter that kingdom in the future is to enter the eternal state (the 'everlasting kingdom' *cf.* Isa. 9:7; Acts 14:22, *etc.*). This is a view which is as old as Christianity itself, had many advocates among the church fathers of the second and third centuries, and ever since has been widely accepted. It is either implied or expressed in the great historical Confessions of the church and has been the prevalent view in Reformed circles until the late 16th and 17th centuries when post-millennialism came into view.

Now, we are to look at post-millennialism again later and then try to give some judgment on these three views as they are currently regarded, but before I close I want to complete the picture, and give a summary of the post-millennial view.

Louis Berkhof writes that post-millennialism holds 'that the gospel which will gradually spread throughout the whole world, will in the end become immeasurably more effective than it is at present, and will usher in a period of rich spiritual blessings for the Church of

Jesus Christ, a golden age, in which the Jews will also share in the blessings of the gospel in an unprecedented manner.'

'"It will be a period in the later days of the Church militant, when under the special influence of the Holy Spirit, the spirit of the martyrs shall appear again, true religion be greatly quickened and revived, and the members of Christ's churches become so conscious of their strength in Christ, that they shall, to an extent unknown before, triumph over the power of evil both within and without" (A.H. Strong). The golden age of the Church will, it is held, be followed by a brief apostasy, a terrible conflict between the forces of good and evil, and by the simultaneous occurrence of the advent of Christ, the general resurrection, and the final judgment.'

Now, I should say at once, because of the optimistic tone that I have used in describing it, that there is a perversion of post-millennialism, and it is that from which we would totally dissociate ourselves, because it is simply a social gospel view of the inevitability of progress in the world, the world inevitably getting better and better by sheer, fatuous, a-moral optimism, and by a process of moral and philosophical evolution. The historic post-millennial view has nothing to do with that; it is by the powerful preaching of the true gospel that this blessed state, it is said, will come.

The key verses for this view (which is abundantly expounded in Iain Murray's book, *The Puritan Hope*) – and I bid you turn them up with me – are Romans 11:12,15,25,26. The subject of Romans 11 is God's future and greater purpose for Israel as a nation. It is impossible to take a sweep of Romans 9-11 and not see this. Scholars have looked at particular passages and verses and even single words in these three chapters, particularly in chapter 11, so narrowly that they have sometimes missed the point of their whole body of truth.

Notice particularly Romans 11:11-15. The question of the Gentile nations arises in this context: Israel's temporary rejection of her king and God's temporary rejection of her allowed the Gentiles to be saved. It was God's purpose – the Jews had no such intention – to allow this to happen so that the Gentiles (and we Christians are mainly Gentiles) might be saved. God has, among other things, another purpose in view in saving the Gentiles: to make the Jews jealous. Now, we have got to get a grip of that before we can understand this passage: his purpose was to make the Jews jealous: it is as plain as that. Ultimately, God's purpose in making the Jews jealous by the conversion of the Gentiles, will succeed; and Israel, as a people, or as a nation – Handley Moule uses the word 'race' because not necessarily every Jew on earth, but the race of Israel – will come to Jesus Christ and be saved.

'So, I ask (says Paul), have they (the Jews) stumbled so as to (in order to) fall? By no means (God forbid)! But through their trespass (in rejecting Christ – let me comment as we work through this) salvation has come to the Gentiles, so as to (*eis* in the Greek, with a view to) make Israel jealous. Now, (this is the critical verse along with v.15) if their (the Jews') trespass means riches for the world (and what can the 'world' mean there but the Gentiles?), and if their (the Jews') failure means riches for the Gentiles (that is clear enough), how much more will their (whose? Surely, the Jews') fulness (full inclusion) mean (for the Gentiles)!'

Now, take the two intervening verses between 12 and 15, *i.e.*, 13-14. 'Now, I am speaking to you Gentiles. Inasmuch, then as I am an apostle to the Gentiles, I magnify my ministry in order to make my fellow Jews jealous' (You see, it is so exciting because Paul has such a love for the Jews; the beginning of Romans 9 shows that, like Moses, he would almost wish himself to be accursed to save the Jews, he loved them so much. But God said, 'Not you to the Jews; Peter to the Jews; you to the Gentiles.' But he cannot take his love for them out of his heart, for he will not let go the Jews until God deals with the whole problem in his final visit to Jerusalem. I think one sees in his later writings how he drops his preoccupation with them. But this is another story for people better able to deal with it than I.) 'and thus save some of them. For if (and here in v.15 the truth of v.12 is repeated more succinctly) their rejection (God's rejection of them because of their rejection of Jesus) means the reconciliation of the world (that can only mean the Gentile world), what will their (the Jews') acceptance mean (by God) but life from the dead?' (For whom? Surely the Gentiles). We will come back to the end of that because there is a vital point there.

Verses 25, 26: 'Lest you be wise in your own conceits, I want you to understand this mystery, brethren: a hardening has come upon part of Israel, until the fulness (and I reject as many do, the translation of the RSV. 'the full number' for a reason I will give later) of the Gentiles come in, and so all Israel will be saved.'

Now, in general with regard to the belief that the Jews as a race, or as a nation will yet be saved, listen to Handley Moule. He is commenting on Romans 11:25-27.

> This is a memorable passage. It is one of the most definitely predictive of all the prophetic utterances of the Epistle. Apart from all the problems of explanation and detail it gives us this as its message on the whole, that there lies hidden in the future of the race of Israel, a critical period of overwhelming blessing. If anything is revealed as fixed in the eternal plan, which never violating the creature's will, yet is not subject to it, it is this. And thus, the promise of coming mercy such as shall surprise the world sounds all the more sovereign and magnificent. It shall come; so says Christ's prophet Paul, not because of historical antecedents, or in the light of general principles but because of the revelation of the Spirit. He speaks of that wonderful future as if it were in full view from the present: ALL ISRAEL SHALL BE SAVED.

Then Moule goes on:

> Believest thou the prophets? The question asked of Agrippa by St Paul, comes to us from this prediction of his own. And he answers, 'Lord, we believe.'

Moule continues:

> Our Master knows that for us in our day it is not easy. The bad air of materialism and the profound and stolid fatalism which it involves, is thick around us. And one symptom of its malign influence is the growing tendency in the Church to limit, to minimise, to explain , if possible away from the Scriptures, that which is properly and distinctively superhuman, whether of work or word. Men bearing the Christian name, and bearing it often with

loyal and reverent intention, seem to think far otherwise than their
Lord thought about this very element of prediction in the holy
Book, and would have us believe that it is no great thing to grasp,
and to contend for. But as for us we desire above all things to be of
the opinion of Him Who is the eternal Truth and Light, and Who
took our nature, expressly, as to one great purpose, in order to
unfold to us articulately His opinions. He lived and died in the light
and power of predictive Scripture. He predicted. He rose again to
commission His Apostles, as the Spirit should teach them, to see
'things to come' (John 16:13). To us, this oracle of His 'chosen
vessel' gives us articles of faith and hope. We do not understand,
but we believe, because here it is written, that after these days of
the prevalence of unbelief, after all these questions, loud or half
articulate, angry or agonising, 'Where is the promise?' the world
shall see a spiritual miracle on a scale not known before: ALL
ISRAEL SHALL BE SAVED. Even so, Lord Jesus Christ, the
Deliverer, fill us with the patience of this hope for Thy chosen race,
and for the world.

Now, you see, such a phenomenal event as this, if God gives time
(and that is a suggestion we will look at in the final study) will have
a profound effect in the whole Gentile world. That is really the post-
millennial thesis developed from the 17th century; that the Jews as a
race, or nation, or people are yet to be saved. And after that? Have
another close look at these two verses, 12 and 15, and think! I was
going to quote from John Murray on this, whom I have mentioned
before, but I will quote from Iain Murray, and then from Spurgeon as
quoted by him:

> The glory of Christ has indeed been declared in the earth in past
> ages. In the apostolic age, 'His lightnings enlightened the world:
> the earth saw and trembled.' Ps. 97:4. The Reformers and Puritans
> beheld him as the conquering king and it made them strong. The
> eighteenth century Church knew his power and longed with
> Charles Wesley that 'the world might taste and see the riches of
> his grace'.

> The same was true in revivals of the last century. 'It were worth
> living ten thousand ages in obscurity and reproach,' declared one
> minister in Ulster, 'to be permitted to creep forth at the expiration

of that time and engage in the glorious work of the last six months of 1859.'

Now listen to Spurgeon:

The fulness of Jesus is not changed, then why are our works so feebly done? Pentecost, is that to be a tradition? The reforming days, are these to be memories only? I see no reason why we should not have a greater Pentecost than Peter saw, and a Reformation deeper in its foundations, and truer in its upbuildings than all the reforms which Luther or Calvin achieved. We have the same Christ, remember that. The times are altered, but Jesus is the Eternal, and time touches him not . . . . Our laziness puts off the work of conquest, our self-indulgence procrastinates, our cowardice and want of faith make us dote upon the millennium instead of hearing the Spirit's voice today. Happy days would begin from this hour if the Church would but awake and put on her strength, for in her Lord all fulness dwells.

He ends with a prayer:

Oh! Spirit of God, bring back thy Church to a belief in the gospel! Bring back her ministers to preach it once again with the Holy Ghost, and not striving after wit and learning. Then shall we see thine arm made bare, O God, in the eyes of all the people, and then myriads shall be brought to rally round the throne of God and of the Lamb. The Gospel must succeed.

This is the theme of many of the Puritans, as Iain Murray has brought out: the Gospel must succeed on the earth. This temporal world cannot end with seeming failure, even for the church. You see, Christ's death was not for himself. Christ did not need a victory over the Devil; he could have snuffed him out like that. God had no need of a victory over the Devil; it was gained for us – FOR US! And, do you not see, it will not succeed unless it succeeds *in men*. The Gospel must succeed. 'It shall succeed' (says Spurgeon); 'it cannot be prevented from succeeding; a multitude that no man can number must be saved.'

Now, no one is suggesting that that is anything like the last word, nor will it be when we conclude our next study. But I suggest to you in all solemnity, and with the authority of these verses we have read in Romans 11 if nothing else – no, nothing else – just as the meaning of these verses and what they say is not all that easy but must be understood – that it is imperative for everyone of us to know the truth, so far as God will enlighten our hearts and minds and consciences.

So I am saying to you: go to bed with that tonight! After all, you know, God has set us as representative of seven universities in Scotland, not to say churches and other Christian groups. We cannot possibly be insignificant. I do not believe we are, poor little worms as we are! Let us ponder this and see, see if God will not stir.

I have got some notes here about what Billy Graham said to me in my home years ago, after he had been living with a pre-millennialist who tried to get him to see that only a few could be converted because it was too late in the day and the Lord would come and he ought not to be involved in large scale evangelism. He sat in my room and wrung his hands, and, although it may have had nothing to do with that, when he returned home throwing off the shackles of pessimistic pre-millennialism he had his first great campaign in America when so many crowded to Christ. And I suppose all of us know some significant trophies of grace who were won through dear Billy after that. You see, it *does* make a difference what you believe about this!

THE SECOND COMING

3

I could not really honourably put you off dispensational pre-millennialism, which was my intention, until I had expounded it, whether you understood it or not. I think it only fair for you to know a thing before you judge it. That should obtain in other disciplines and it must also obtain here. All I would say is that I am glad if you see and agree with me on this, that Christ in his second coming could not possibly come a thousand years before the end of the age. That crystallises one of the most objectionable points of the whole pre-millennial view: Christ could not possibly come a thousand years before the end of the age. We can therefore, set that view aside and have done with it.

This leaves two other views, which in some respects are not so very different from each other. You could say the difference, put simply, is the degree of optimism with regard to the future before Christ comes which is associated with a-millennialism and post-millennialism. That is the question. This is the important thing which is really of vital importance to the UCCF, to your Christian life and to the prospect for Christ's church in Scotland and in the world, namely, what is our expectation in days to come? What is yours? Nothing could be more important than that.

The main issues between these two views (a-millennialism and post-millennialism) are to my mind clear, and easily and simply expressed. They are whether you believe in the conversion of Israel as a nation before Christ comes and whether, following that, you believe there will be a great Gentile revival thereafter before the apostasy and the emergence of the man of sin which last is, of course, something that all the views accept.

Now, read Revelation 20:7-11: this must be what leads to Christ's coming. He comes in answer to this to deal with the resurgence of evil. Revelation 20:1-3 speaks of Satan being bound, whatever is meant by 'bound'. Verses 7-10 say that when the thousand years are ended 'Satan will be loosed from his prison and come out to deceive the nations that are at the four corners of the earth, that is, Gog and Magog, to gather them for battle; their number is like the sand of the sea. And they marched up over the broad earth and surrounded the camp of the saints (whether you think of that geographically or not, does not matter at the moment) and the beloved city; but fire came down from heaven and consumed them, and the Devil who had deceived them was thrown into the lake of fire and brimstone, where the beast and the false prophet were, and they will be tormented day and night for ever and ever.'

Now read 2 Thessalonians 2:1-10: 'Now, concerning the coming of our Lord Jesus Christ and our assembling to meet him, we beg you brethren, not to be quickly shaken in mind or excited, either by spirit or by word (interesting terms – many people are, by both), or by letters purporting to be from us (spurious letters), to the effect that the day of the Lord has come. Let no one deceive you in any way, for that day will not come unless the rebellion (the apostasy of 1 John 4:3) and the man of sin is revealed, the son of perdition who opposes and exalts himself against every so called god or object of worship, so that he takes his seat in the temple of God, proclaiming himself to be God. Do you not remember that when I was still with you I told you this? And you know what is restraining him so that he may be revealed in his time (there are a whole lot of things there we must not touch upon). For the mystery of lawlessness is already at work, only he who now restrains it will do so until he is taken out of the way (and we are not going into that either!) and then the lawless one will be revealed, and the Lord Jesus will slay him with the breath of his mouth and will destroy him by his appearing and his coming (*epiphaneia* and *parousia*). The coming of the lawless one by the activity of Satan will be with all power and with pretended signs and wonders, and with all wicked deception for those who are to perish, because they refuse to love the truth and so be saved.'

There is, then, this apostasy, whatever you would like to call it, before, leading to and inviting as it were, Christ's coming in power and glory.

But let me go back again to the two main issues (and they can be clearly and easily expressed), whether there will be a conversion of Israel as a nation before Christ comes, and whether following that (with reference to the verses in Romans 11) there is time for, or there will be, a great Gentile revival before the inevitable apostasy. Mind you, with regard to those who believe in both the conversion of Israel as a race or nation and a great revival following that, some are so enthusiastic (and we can understand that if there is time at all, the whole world will be amazed at the conversion of the Jews! Think of what this would do. What would the television do about that?), that they tend to minimise the apostasy, and really play it down. Yes, they admit it because it is in Scripture and they cannot deny it, but they say it will be a comparatively small thing. Now, you see from the passages I read, and there are others, it cannot be a small thing.

Back to our question: do we believe that there is a spiritual future for the Jews as a nation? Do not quibble about whether every Jew in the world would be converted. All-inclusive terms in the Scriptures seldom mean absolutely every soul. But do we believe that there is a spiritual future for the Jews as a nation? The other question is in vv.12,15.

If you are interested in my present opinion, ever since I read the Scriptures, particularly this Romans passage, but other passages too, I have always believed that there was a spiritual future for Israel as a nation. Even their physiognomy has been preserved during two and a half millennia of dispersion. I know that some mix their blood with Gentiles and lose their distinctiveness, but for most of them the stamp remains. Even those who have no religious faith at all, often have a character, a rock-like character which is deeply impressive. Even now, some people with a Jewish background know the tribe from which they came. I once asked a lady, 'Do you know your tribe?' 'Yes', she said, 'I am of the tribe of Levi.' 'How, in the world do you know that?' 'Well it has been handed down.'

Amazing! Their distinctiveness has been preserved for over two thousand years while they have been scattered over the face of the earth, so that they can come together as a nation, as they did in 1948, and people the land again. Let me say this: those who cannot see that as a miracle – including Israel's survival in the land for nearly three decades – need their heads examined! I think Handley Moule, whom I quoted the other day and could quote again if you needed it, sees such a belief as a matter of faith.

What I want to do now, is to set this in biblical context by means of a Bible study on faith. We are going to turn to Genesis 12 and read, not the first three verses, as one often does, but the first four verses.

Genesis 12:1-4, 'Now the Lord had said to Abraham, Go from your country and your father's house (he was partially disobedient here, as we know from Acts 7, Stephen's speech) and go to the land which I will show you. And I will make of you a great nation, and I will bless you, and make your name great, so that you will be a blessing. I will bless those who bless you, and him who curses you I will curse; and by you all the families of the earth will be blessed (or bless themselves). So Abraham went as the Lord had told him.' That (v.4) is the obedience of faith.

Take Genesis 15:6, which everybody knows. Abraham was complaining in the earlier verses that he did not have a child. How could he be the father of many nations when he did not have even one child? The Lord said, 'Oh, I'll attend to that. Go out of your tent and have a look at the sky. Look towards heaven and count the stars, if you are able to number them.' Then he said, 'So shall your descendants be.' 'And Abraham (and this is quoted three times in the New Testament) believed the Lord (when he told him that) and it was reckoned to him as righteousness.'

17:1: 'When Abraham was ninety years old the Lord appeared to Abraham and said to him, I am God Almighty, walk before me and be blameless and I will make my covenant between you and will multiply you exceedingly. Then Abraham fell on his face (why did he do that? He was submitting to God's Word, wasn't he, and worshipping God, and accepting what God had said to him about the covenant of grace); and God said to him, Behold, my covenant is with you and you will be the father of a multitude of nations. No longer shall your name be Abram, it shall be Abraham, for I have made you the father of a multitude of nations. I will make you exceedingly fruitful, I will make nations of you. And I will establish my covenant between you and your descendants after you throughout the generations for an everlasting covenant, to be God to you (this is what one finds in the Bible, he wants to be God to us) and to your descendants after you . . . .'

Verse 15: 'And God said to Abraham, as for Sarai, your wife, you shall not call her Sarai but Sarah shall be her name. I will bless her and moreover I will give you a son by her (and she was ninety at the time, or round about); I will bless her and she shall be a mother of nations; kings of people shall come from her . . . . Then Abraham fell on his face and laughed and said to himself, Shall a child be born to a man who is a hundred years old? (I don't believe Abraham disbelieved the promise, but he thought, how in the world can it be this way?) And Abraham said to God, "O that Ishmael (who would have been a lad of about eighteen by this time) might live in thy sight." God said, "No, but Sarah, your wife shall bear you a son (ninety though she is) and you shall call his name Isaac and I will establish my covenant with him for an everlasting covenant with his descendants after him."'

God is asserting what he would do. Look at Romans 4:16, breaking into the argument. 'That is why you depend on faith, in order that the promise may rest on grace (Abraham's descendants) not only to the adherents of the law but to those who share the faith of Abraham, for he is the father of many nations, in the presence of God in whom he believed, who gives life to the dead and calls into existence the things that do not exist.'

This passage is introductory to the passage about the child who was born to Abraham when his wife was nearly ninety. 'In hope he believed against hope' (Lord, I believe, help thou my unbelief. It is often in the midst of doubt and unbelief that God plants his gift in our hearts that persists and overcomes unbelief. Do not be surprised if you have doubts and questions. But if there is something deeper in you, rooted in you, that cannot disbelieve, that refuses to deny the information God has given you, then recognise that it is God fighting with the Devil in your soul), 'that he should become the father of many nations; as he had been told, So shall your descendants be. He did not weaken in faith when he considered his own body which was as good as dead, because he was about a hundred years old, or when he considered the barrenness of Sarah's womb.'

No distrust made Abraham waver. That is not to say there was no doubt or questioning or fear; we know that he laughed when God told him what would be. See the struggle in the man's heart and life, and yet the faith prevails. 'No distrust made him waver concerning the promise of God, but he grew strong in his faith and he gave glory to God.' You see, if you look at your doubts, your questionings, your fears and are taken up with that psychologically and spiritually, you will almost forget that God is there. Do not look to what you fear, what you doubt and what other people doubt for you. Look to God alone! This is what Abraham did. Look to God's word in the Bible and in your heart.

Abraham gave glory to God, fully convinced that God was able to do what he had promised. Now, this we so often doubt. If it is true what Paul writes in those two verses in Romans, then we have got to believe it. We have to believe that God was able to do what he had promised through Paul; even if we don't like it we have got to believe it. That is why faith was reckoned as righteousness. 'Ah, but', says Paul 'the words that were written were written, not for his sake alone, but for ours also.' You students take note!

Hebrews 11:11. 'By faith, Sarah herself (not Abraham here) received power to conceive, even when she was past the age since she considered him faithful who had promised.' Sarah's faith! 'Therefore from one man, and him as good as dead, were born descendants as many as the stars of heaven and as the innumerable grains of sand on the seashore.'

Back to Genesis 22 to complete our Bible study on faith. The first three verses – this is Abraham taking his adolescent son Isaac to

Mount Moriah: 'After these things God tested Abraham and said to him, Here am I. Take your son, your only son Isaac (Oh, but Ishmael. No, said the Lord. He doesn't come into the picture, as we learned from Paul in Galatians. Your *only* son Isaac. How exclusive and particular God can be!) and go to the land of Moriah and offer him there as a burnt offering upon one of the mountains, as I shall tell you. So Abraham rose early in the morning (this is the point of our Bible study: he did what he was told. He believed what God said) saddled his ass and took. . . .'

Verse 10: 'Then Abraham put forth his hand and took the knife to slay his son. But the angel of the Lord called to him from heaven and said, Abraham, Abraham. And he said, Here I am . . . . Do not lay your hand on the lad, or do anything to him, for now I know that you fear God. . . .'

Verse 15: 'And the angel of the Lord called from heaven a second time and said, By myself (and the writer to the Hebrews takes this up) I have sworn, says the Lord (I love this) because you have done this (Abraham believed and obeyed) and have not withheld your son, your only son (Think, if that man, having received the promise that he was going to be the father of many nations, lived until he was a hundred and his wife ninety-nine without any child except this Ishmael fellow, and then God gave an incredible miracle and then said, 'Go and kill him'. You could not conceive of greater faith and obedience than that in all the world. Put yourself in his place. Use your imagination. Why was he so willing? Well, first because God said it. Read the rest of the passage, it is wonderful) I will indeed bless you and I will multiply your descendants as the stars of heaven and as the sand. Your descendants shall possess the gate of your enemies and by your descendants shall all the nations of the earth bless themselves (or be blessed) because you obeyed my voice.'

Note, 'possess the gate of your enemies'. Post-millennial people say, 'Ah, this is something that is going to be fulfilled on the earth before Christ comes, that the Jews will be God's evangelists to the world.' God appointed the Jews to be his evangelists to the world, and they failed; *not* in David and Solomon's day, when the kings and the queens came to see the glory; what I call primary evangelism, drawing them. This happened again when Daniel and Ezekiel in Babylon, and Ezra and Nehemiah, Esther and Mordecai, lived the life. But mostly Israel failed to be God's evangelists, although again it was Israel who became God's evangelists to the world in the apostles; weren't they all Jews – Luke apart? But this is not the fulness of the promise. It seems to me that the Jews are yet to be God's evangelists to the rest of the world. God will have them be that, yet. This is the matter we are discussing, but we are coming on to it.

With regard to Genesis 22, look at Hebrews 11:17. This is a wonderful climax. There are passages in the Bible that take your breath away, they are so wonderful that the truth is inexpressible! 'By faith Abraham, when he was tempted, offered up Isaac and he who had received the promises was ready to offer up his only son, of whom it was said, through Isaac (and never Ishmael) shall your descendants be named.' Look at this: 'He considered that God was able to raise men, even from the dead.' Abraham two thousand years before Jesus Christ believed that 'God was able to raise men even from the dead. Hence figuratively speaking (I know there are things to be said about that, but I want things to be simple because we are reading Scripture, we are not listening to me) he did receive him back.' It is a figure, so says Scripture, of the resurrection.

You see, the whole point about that is that these men believed the impossible, over and over again.

All right then, what say you? Do you believe that there is a future for Israel of this sort? That is one question. You have to go and make up your mind on that, and ask the Lord to help you see it, if he will. Remember again Handley Moule's quotation in his commentary on Romans. Handley Moule was a gentle soul and his writing is characterised by grace, gentleness and balance. I doubt if you would find anything else as dogmatic in him as this. This man was deeply convinced about the future of Israel. And the practical effect of this is that, if it is true, the next thing to look for, towards the coming of the Lord, is the conversion of the Jews!

If you want a programme (I don't like programmes!) you have three suggested things: the conversion of Israel, possibly a revival after that, and certainly, the apostasy. You can leave out the middle one if you cannot believe or understand that – I have had difficulty myself with these verses in Romans 11:12-15. But as a programme the conversion of Israel and the apostasy at the end seem to me to be clear. But whether there is room for great expansion of the gospel to the Gentiles after the conversion of Israel so near the end – a-millennialists have believed we would be so near the end that there will be no time for anything more before the resurgence of evil as an aggravation of Christ's coming – that is my question, and I think it ought to be your question too.

Now, read again these verses in Romans 11:12,15. If the trespass of the Jews in rejecting Christ means wealth for the Gentiles (and of course it must mean spiritual wealth; what else in the world could it mean in this context? Because here we are, a crowd of Gentiles, who have been saved because the Jews refused Jesus; it is as simple as that), it is by this move that God has ordained that the Gentiles should be saved. And if the Jews' failure to respond and recognise Christ as their King means wealth to the Gentiles how much more will their (the Jews') fulness mean!

Now, 'fulness' in that whole context can only mean the coming of the Lord to them and to a much greater number of them, not necessarily to every Jew in the world. But how much more significant will be the coming of a much greater number of them to the Lord Jesus Christ, submitting to him and being incorporated in the church – not a separate company – how much more will their full inclusion mean! Full inclusion of the Jews mean to whom? To the Gentiles is the implication, if you are not going to make nonsense of the second part of the sentence. 'If their trespass means riches for the world and their failure means riches for Gentiles, how much *more* (what? More riches for the Gentile world) will their fulness mean.' Isn't that what it says?

Look at verse 15: 'For if their rejection (this is God's rejection of them because they rejected his Son, Jesus) means the reconciliation of the Gentile world, what will their acceptance mean (God rejected them, now he is going to accept them as a people) but life from the dead' (for them? That does not follow: it unbalances the sentence. It is for the Gentiles).

Ah, but somebody says, this is the end of the age, this is referring to the resurrection at the coming of Christ. That is a view that can be held. John Murray in his Romans commentary spends several pages dealing with the view that this means the resurrection at the coming of Christ, and gives lots of reasons against the view that 'life from the dead' means the general resurrection at the end of the age, on two counts. He says that while it is true that the word used for 'life' can refer specifically to the resurrection and frequently 'the dead' refers to the literal death, yet these same terms are also used in the figurative sense of spiritual life and death. He gives many quotations, about twenty or thirty to support what he says, and that is not unimpressive. His second point is this, that if Paul meant the resurrection, one wonders why he did not use the term occurring so frequently in his Epistles and elsewhere to designate this event when referring to both the resurrection of Christ and that of men (1 Corinthians 15:12); he has about a dozen quotations for that. So he says:

For these reasons there is no place for dogmatism respecting the interpretation so widely held that the resurrection is in view. The other interpretation, that of unprecedented quickening for the world in the expansion and success of the Gospel has much to commend it.

Now, this is a man that I should think almost all reverent Christians not necessarily agree with, but respect. He goes on:

The much greater blessing accruing from the fulness of Israel (v.12) would more naturally be regarded as the augmenting of that (reconciliation) referred to in the preceding part of the verse. Verse 15 resumes the theme of verse 12 but specifies what the much greater blessing is. In line with the figurative use of the terms 'life' and 'dead' the expression 'life from the dead' could appropriately be used to denote the vivification that would come to the whole world from the conversion of the mass of Israel and their reception into the favour and kingdom of God.

There is one other difficulty there. When you come to verse 25 some people see a difficulty in understanding 'fulness'. Read verses

25,26: 'Lest you be wise in your conceits, I want you to understand this mystery, brethren: a hardening has come upon part of Israel until the full number (RSV) of Gentiles come in.'

John Murray says you cannot, you must not translate this word in the Greek 'fulness' with the meaning 'full number' as if it necessarily meant 'full tale', or 'full count'. And he shows why. Because the word 'fulness' in v.12 cannot mean 'full account'. The point that people make is that if the Jews will not be saved until after the fulness of the Gentiles, and the fulness of the Gentiles means every Gentile saved without exception, then how can there be a great revival bringing in many Gentiles after the Jews are saved? It is a difficult point. But I must bring it up so that you can think about it.

Now how far have we got? Just one other paragraph, not very long, from Murray, on verse 12:

The argument of the apostle is not the restoration of Israel; it is the blessing accruing to the Gentiles on Israel's 'fulness'. The 'fulness' of Israel, with the implications stated above, is presupposed, and from it is drawn the conclusion that the fulness of Israel will involve for the Gentiles a much greater enjoyment of gospel blessing than that occasioned by Israel's unbelief. Thus there awaits the Gentiles, in their distinctive identity as such, gospel blessings far surpassing anything experienced during the period of Israel's apostasy, and this unprecedented enrichment will be occasioned by the conversion of Israel on a scale commensurate with that of their earlier disobedience. We are not informed what this unprecedented blessing will be. But in view of the thought governing the context, namely, the conversion of the Gentiles and then that of Israel, we should expect that the enlarged blessing would be the expansion of the success attending the gospel of the kingdom of God.

To draw to a close, the question we are to ask (and there could be no more practical question with regard to our existence as a Christian group and to our witness, service and warfare in the world) is, What we are to expect? What are we to look for? If God is saying this, our expectation should be absolutely tremendous; have you thought about this?

Here is a prophecy or prediction, if you like, for what it is worth. I see three possibilities for the future. I do not believe the six thousand years to the end of this century lead to the next thousand years (21st century) as a millennium in the sense that some do. But, in view of the population explosion and all the scientists say about the running down of resources and about the need for conservation one tends to think of the end of the century as of major significance for world history. But notwithstanding it all, there are still larger problems and questions. This is a hunch. I am not basing it on any of these things. One still sees the end of the century as possibly – this is why I want to live to the end of it – significant. I see three possibilities for Christ's church in the world before the end of the century.

First – and I put them like this – Christ may come soon. If Christ comes before, or at the end of, or around the turn of the century – I say to myself, well, the Jews had better hurry up and be converted! I will say no more about that.

Second, looking at the world as it is today I see the possibility of a new Dark Age. Think of this, which never ceases to astonish me: after the resurrection of Jesus Christ and the establishing of the New Testament church at Pentecost, and the mighty works of the apostles and the Holy Spirit in these early centuries, the world saw a thousand years of darkness – the Middle Ages, the Dark Ages and the rise of Islam in the midst of it – Mohammed would never have been, as prophet, if the Christian church had been aflame during these centuries, from the second to the sixth. Think of it. Before the Reformation and the missionary expansion at the end of the eighteenth and the beginning of the nineteenth, Livingstone and Moffat and all these people – Carey, Morrison – why did that take eighteen, nineteen hundred years to take place? Have you ever asked yourself that? How was it that God permitted a thousand years of such darkness? A few lights of course, but the darkness! The world could go on for thousands of years yet, and God could have another Dark Age in store for our sins! I hope with all my heart not, but it is a possibility because the world is getting very dark. Of course the light shines the brighter in the darkness and we thank God for that.

The third possibility, and here I am linking all that I have been trying to show you from Romans 11, is that of a great revival on the scale or dimension of, although possibly very different from, the Reformation. These three are the possibilities. There may be others, but these I have thought long about.

Now, if it is to be the third (not that I don't want the Lord to come!) one would love to be involved in preparation for it, whether one lived to see it or not. I love the verse in Hebrews 11:13, 'These all died in faith.' Just to put one's head on a pillow and die, saying 'Lord carry on.' I think that is beautiful, absolutely beautiful. If it is revival, in what sort of expectant spirit shall we prepare? I answered that in the first of these studies. I talked about the Greek word for 'occupy' which is *pragmateuomai*, be pragmatic. To occupy until Christ comes is to be pragmatic, to be practical. I said the church's task was two-fold, and the two folds belong together, evangelism and edification. If there is going to be evangelism, you have to build up a church that will go out to evangelise.

If I may just give a little of my own case, one of the things that has caused great concern through the years is that sometimes people come from afar to our church having been recommended to come, and seeing a handful of people, they say, Is that all? Two ladies came from Canada one day and sat down and muttered to one another, 'This can't be the place.' In kindness they said by the end of the service that perhaps it was. But you see, one of the reasons for that is that the Lord scatters the people almost before they seem ready to go. Our congregation is all over the face of the earth, evangelising, and people charge us constantly with not being evangelical and not preaching the gospel. You know, this is the refrain – although I think it is dying out – 'That is not the gospel.' If you don't give half a dozen *clichés* you are not preaching the gospel. The whole Bible is the gospel.

Occupy, be practical, be involved with evangelism and edification. But I am asking, in what spirit of expectancy do we do that? The expectancy of faith, believing that there is a word from God? I ask you to read these verses in Romans 11 and pray over them, and many more. You see it was such positive, hopeful, sanguine attitudes like that which produced these mighty men of the seventeenth century, then Whitefield and Wesley, and then the 1859 Revival.

Turn lastly to Mark 11:20-24. 'As they passed by in the morning they saw the fig tree withered away at its roots and Peter said to him, "Master, look! The fig tree which you cursed has withered." And Jesus answered them, (and this is the broadside I want us all to receive as we go) *"Have faith in God."*' What matters is not what good men I've been quoting say, of one view or the other, but what our Lord says, 'Have faith in God. Truly I say to you, whoever says to this mountain, "Be taken up and cast into the sea, (and that is a ridiculous suggestion in a way. What would be the point of putting a mountain into the middle of the sea? Jesus, I think, deliberately uses a ridiculous illustration. Isn't it fun! Don't you think there was the suggestion of a smile at the corner of his lips when he said it yet he was desperately serious?) and does not doubt in his heart, but believes that what he says will come to pass" (now you have first to believe that God said it; it is not what we say. You know you sometimes hear in a prayer meeting, 'O Lord, save many souls tonight', when possibly that person's faith scarcely rises to one. That is just blethers. It would be more in order to say, 'O Lord, I have nearly faith for one soul to be saved tonight.' That is more like it. And if you have nearly faith for that, that may mean the Lord is wanting to give you faith. It is not something we generate in ourselves) it will be done for him. Therefore I tell you, Whatever you ask in prayer, believe that you receive it, (and this implies and must involve God intimating it to you) and you will.'

Faith must be based on God's prophetic word. Christ has spoken: 'I will build my church and the gates of Hades shall not prevail against it.' Are we part of that, or not?

Now, to close, I read this from Iain Murray (with no apologies!):
The glory of Christ has indeed been declared on the earth in past ages. In the apostolic age. . . the Reformers and Puritans and the eighteenth-century Church knew his power and longed with

Charles Wesley that. . . 'the world might taste and see the riches of His grace'.

He goes on: 'The same was true in revivals of the last century' (the nineteenth). Then he quotes the Ulster minister who said,

> It were worth living ten thousand ages in obscurity and reproach to be permitted to creep forth at the expiration of that time and engage in the glorious work of the last six months of 1859.

And the last century was not like the century before and the century before wasn't like the century before that. And that century wasn't like the century before that, which was that of Luther and Calvin. Iain Murray goes on,

> But this world, according to the word of prophecy, has not seen the last of such wonders of salvation; there are reserved for the future such evidences of the efficacy of the blood of Christ that the Apostle, as he anticipated them and contemplated the grandeur of the whole plan of God, exclaimed 'O the depths of the riches both of the wisdom and the knowledge of God!' There is no hope for the world apart from revivals, but it is not in revivals that the faith of the church is to be rooted. Christ himself is the object of faith. The same faith which looks for his final appearing must also trust in his promised presence as the nations are evangelised. The Church, being united to him in whom the Spirit dwells without measure, will be built; she can no more be deprived of the Spirit's aid than can the finished work of Christ – upon which the mission of the church proceeds – be undone. When, therefore, the people of God find themselves with little evidence of spiritual prosperity, they are not to conclude that henceforth the church can only be a dwindling minority in a pagan world (and how much we are tempted to believe that: the evidence is before our eyes, empty kirks and pews and so on), nor are they to suppose that they may suspend working until there be some new outpouring of the Spirit. (I think that is very sensible. People are looking for sensation so much of the time). Rather their present duty is to exercise a fuller confidence in the word and person of the Son of God. In so doing they will not find the Spirit who glorifies Christ to be absent.

Test it, test it! Believe, believe and see – it works, or rather, he works!

'Christians', says Luther, 'must have the vision which enables them to disregard the terrible spectacle and outward appearance, the Devil and the guns of the whole world and to see Him who sits on high and says: "I am the one who speaks to you."'

Then Iain Murray gives a last sentence:

When Christ is thus the object of faith, then will his promise always be fulfilled, 'Nothing shall be impossible unto you.'

Last Wednesday our dear brother, Alistair Kennedy, gave us a Bible study in Aberdeen and a word about his years in Africa and particularly his work with the Worldwide Evangelisation Crusade in Senegal. It took them, he said, a little time to see that God was calling them to work in the French-speaking universities of Africa. What Alistair told us then I had not heard much about, except through their circular letters which we greatly appreciated, of the bitterness and the hardness of the people, and their hatred of Jesus. What he told us about the cost of serving in the midst of that situation! But he had a flannelgraph and he gradually placed names of the little Bible groups (G.B.U.'s) all across the middle belt of Africa until the black velvet was nearly covered. How many years did that take? Ten years – a daunting task at first. But,

Faith, mighty faith the promise sees,
And looks to that alone!

I give you this last verse to fortify and challenge you on your way: Romans 14:23. Don't bother turning it up, I can read it for you: 'Whatsoever is not of faith (talk of living positively and daringly!) is sin.' Now, go and live by faith!

THE LORD FROM HEAVEN

The Person and Work of Christ – 1

The first thing that strikes me in this title is the preposition 'from'. Why the Lord *from* heaven? It suggests a movement; and a challenge to my ability to present to you moving pictures of eternal truth in such a way as to allow that truth to flow directly into your minds and hearts and out through your finger-tips and your lips to God and to others! Anything less is barren theory, and barren theory is inexcusable in Christian theology. Those who make God sound dull may have heard of him and read of him, but they can surely never have met him! Once you have met him, in Jesus Christ and through his Holy Spirit (already I have invoked the Trinity, and that to me in itself is inexpressibly thrilling), life can never be dull.

We must start from the Trinity; for I could never begin to speak about the second person of the Trinity without setting what I have to say in the context of the Father and the Holy Spirit. It is impossible to understand any one person of the Trinity, except in the context of the wonderful, marvellous, mysterious inter-relationships between the three. Both the *Westminster Confession of Faith* and the *Thirty-nine Articles* declare that, 'In the unity of the Godhead, there are three persons, of one substance, power, and eternity; the Father, the Son, and the Holy Ghost' (*Thirty-Nine Articles*), or, 'God the Father, God the Son, and God, the Holy Ghost' (*Westminster Confession*). The Father is of none, neither begotten as the Son is, nor proceeding, as is the Spirit. The Son is eternally begotten of the Father – there never was a time when the Father existed without the Son; the Son is as eternal as the Father, and is therefore equal with him in power, glory, and eternity. The Scriptures are very clear that the eternal Son is very God; nor does the fact that Christ is the second person of the Trinity detract from his deity, nor the fact that he became man. His place as the Lamb on the throne of God (Rev. 7:17), is proof of that. What is said of the Godhead in the *Confession*, is true of him: 'To him is due from angels and men, and every other creature, whatsoever worship, service, or obedience, he is pleased to require of them.' He is not only the exact replica of the Almighty, reflecting completely the effulgence of his glory, but he bears the very stamp, impress, matrix, or sovereign superscription of his image (Heb. 1:3). He is co-Creator with the Father. 'In the beginning was the Word, and the Word was with God, and the Word was God. He was in the beginning with God; all things were made by him, and without him was not anything made that was made. In him was life (not only life-bearing life, but life-giving life, (1 Cor. 15:45), and the life was the light of men. The light shines in the darkness, and the darkness has not overcome it' (Jn. 1:1-5). This is what we celebrate in Edward Caswall's hymn, 'Lo, within a manger lies, He who built the starry skies.' He was made flesh of our flesh, and truly took our manhood upon him, and was like us in every regard, sin apart (Heb. 4:15).

We will come back to this. But let us get on to the third Person of the Trinity. The Holy Spirit who eternally proceeds from the Father and the Son (both confessions use practically the same words here), is of one substance, majesty, and glory with the Father and the Son, very and eternal God.

You see, the nature of the Son of God is inevitably bound up with his incarnation, and his humanity. It is here that the early church steered a steady course through the turbulences of potential heresy, to preserve both the deity and humanity of Jesus Christ without detracting from either. The glory of the Holy Spirit is seen in this steering the church safely through such hazards, as well as in preserving the Scriptures of truth.

Look at the wonderful balance of the doctrine of the deity and humanity of Christ expressed in the *Westminster Confession of Faith*, chapter VIII, on Christ the Mediator, 'The Son of God, the second person in the Trinity, being very and eternal God, of one substance, and equal with the Father, did, when the fullness of time was come, take upon him man's nature, with all the essential properties and common infirmities thereof, yet without sin; being conceived by the power of the Holy Ghost, in the womb of the Virgin Mary, of her substance. So that two whole, perfect, and distinct natures, the Godhead and the manhood, were inseparably joined together in one person, without conversion, composition, or confusion. Which person is very God and very man, yet one Christ, the only Mediator between God and man.'

The *Confession* continues, 'The Lord Jesus, in his human nature thus united to the divine, was sanctified and anointed with the Holy Spirit above measure; having in him all the treasures of wisdom and knowledge; in whom it pleased the Father that all fulness should dwell.' Now that, of course, describes a unique being, Jesus Christ. But when his humanity is so strongly emphasised it naturally makes us think back to man – the crown of creation – and to his constitution. It is plain that although he was made of the dust of the earth, yet he alone, of all God's creatures, was made in the image of God. If God made man in his own image, and then in the second person became man himself, is it not likely that the second person of the Trinity (in heaven before anything was made) was really the prototype or original pattern of man? So it was the prototype that became the antitype, the ideal copy of his own original.

As we run through the Old Testament, we ought to keep in mind the pre–incarnate and eternal Son. In the Old Testament, the Lord appears sometimes in angelic and even human form to specific and chosen men, for example, to Abram at Mamre, or to Joshua as captain of the Lord's host (Gen. 18; Josh. 5:13ff). Such background thinking, it seems to me, is exceedingly helpful when we come to look at the first biblical reference to the second person of the Trinity in Genesis 3:15. If you see this (as Luther did) as a high peak of biblical revelation, you will be able to stand on it and scan the whole Old Testament revelation right through to the coming of Christ. In a sense, you can summarise the whole Old Testament clearly and concisely, not to say, integrally, from that one verse. For it was from the point at which God challenged the Devil (following the fall and enslavement of man) that God revealed his strategy to deliver man from Satan's power. The late Professor Donald Mackay, I think, suggested that in Genesis 3, following the account of the Fall, God issued a new creative fiat, in respect of a new world in which man's relationships to the world, to his fellows and to God, not to say the Devil also, are radically altered. Interesting though it is, I do not want to discuss that, but to stress the major importance of God's declaration in Genesis 3:15. God says, 'I will put enmity between you (Satan) and the women (the first human being to become involved in sin), and between your seed and her seed; he (Christ, as Paul makes plain in Gal.3:16) shall bruise your head (that is, defeat him), and you shall (be able only to) bruise his heel.'

That prophecy of conflict between Satan and the woman's seed looks a long way forward, to Christ himself; but the enmity is established right away by God! We are right therefore, surely, in looking all through Old Testament history for signs of that enmity. The value of that approach to the Old Testament is that we can read it all very simply as related to Jesus Christ. It would, of course, take us a long series of studies to cover anything like that ground. We can look at only a few representative illustrations of faith in chosen men, as evidence of their enmity against the Devil. But we must also notice the Devil's attempts to daunt, defeat and destroy such men of faith, lest, of their issue, should come at last that seed of the woman destined to bruise the serpent's head.

Both the Devil and men of faith get busy, almost at once, with Abel, whose offering was acceptable to God, by faith. Cain's was not, with the result that Cain slew Abel, and we have the first murder, even fratricide. Then we have the account, still in Genesis 4, of the so-called advances in civilisation that came with Cain's wicked seed. That is significantly interwoven with the first case of bigamy in Genesis 4:19 and the second murder. Then in chapter 5 we have a new seed set to replace Abel's; a believing seed, of which came men like Enoch, who walked with God, Methuselah, and Noah. Noah's name suggests comfort or relief; perhaps his parents hoped that his life might alleviate somewhat the curse of the ground following the Fall (Gen. 3:14, 21). Noah's father said: 'Out of the ground which the Lord has cursed this one shall bring us relief from our work and from the toil of our hands' (Gen. 5:29). But the coming of Noah was itself an answer to the awful problems which had arisen among the early generations of man on the face of the earth, when human history was invaded by a new depth of evil, through the unholy marriages described in Genesis 6. Whether we regard the Nephilim as due to the direct intervention of demons, or of demon-possessed men, as Delitzsch believed, does not matter here. Either way, they lead to a new invasion of evil into the life of man. And we see similar (what we may call) 'experiments in evil' from time to time throughout the Old Testament. We know that the Devil tried everything as history progressed to foil and frustrate God's purpose of redemption by the seed. God's answer to the wickedness in Genesis 6 is the flood, with judgment to the wicked and salvation to Noah.

Then came the arrogant presumptuousness of man at the tower of Babel, and the confusion of languages there, by which God curbed the sin of man. Then came God's great new seed, Abram, and with him a new day, and a new race, the Hebrews. Then came Israel and the Jews, of whom came Jesus Christ. But notice something new in the way of evil, although there were signs of it in Noah, in his lapse after the flood, when the horrid races of Moab and Ammon were produced through Noah's incestuous unions with his daughters. Evil in God's chosen race! We see it singularly in the fact of Abram's imperfect obedience in not separating himself sufficiently from his kindred, and, therefore, getting stuck half way to Canaan at Haran (*cf*. Gen. 12:1-3, and Acts 7:2-4). The Devil was certainly busy trying to keep Abram out of the promised land. Later he was obviously busy contrarily, in getting him to pass right through the land and come out at the other end of it in Egypt (symbol of this present, evil world). There he landed in such trouble that Abram had to hurry out of Egypt back to Canaan.

But the most striking attempt of the Devil to foil God's purpose through Abram, was in getting (impatient) Sarah and Abram to try to effect God's purpose of a seed to produce the many nations promised (Gen. 12:1-3). Sarah gave her maid, Hagar, to Abram, to produce a seed by her. They did, but what they produced was the Arabs (or many of them) who have proved to be a thorn in the side of Israel ever since, and, one fears, will be almost to the end of time. When God indicated to Abram that it was time for the Almighty to send the promised seed, Abram plausibly offered him the boy Ishmael, as if to say, 'But you were slow, Lord; we've got a seed already, won't Ishmael do? We thought you'd forgotten!' 'No' said the Lord, 'this Ishmael shall not be your seed, but that which will be produced by your own aged bodies. And I will establish my everlasting covenant with that seed, Isaac.'

What we are saying is something that you can verify, in whole worlds of Old Testament studies during the rest of your life (as I have been doing for the most of mine), by seeing how the Old Testament is dominated by the coming of Christ, who as both divine and human is the embodiment of God's one everlasting covenant of grace, made first with Noah, then with Abram, Isaac and Jacob, then with Moses (Ex. 6), and then singularly with David and Solomon, the dual royal type of Christ to come, both as victor and peacemaker. God was preparing his seed for the coming of Christ while the Devil was trying desperately to prevent him coming. As this conflict unravels, we see emerging the pattern of this coming one, who is to be prophet (like Moses, and possibly Samuel), priest (like Aaron), and King (like David and his line). That is why we learn so much about Jesus Christ from the Old Testament, because the seed of faith residing in God's chosen people is naturally prefiguring him all through the Old Testament ages, and with increasing clarity and definition.

The promised line is preserved all through the Old Testament ages, and the pattern of things to come emerges ever more clearly despite the Devil's ardent attempts to destroy. Take the massive attempt of the Devil through Haman to exterminate the Jews in the kingdom of Ahasuerus (who reigned from Ethiopia to India), which was foiled by the man of faith, Mordecai, and his adopted daughter and niece, Esther. God is working on a long-term plan, in which the great One to come is prefigured and typified in some of the men of faith, like Joseph, Moses, Samuel, David, Isaiah, Jeremiah, Zerubbabel, Nehemiah and Daniel.

This is very clear in that group of Messianic psalms, 22–24. In Psalm 22 we have the psalmist, David, describing so many of the details of Christ's crucifixion, not unlike the de-humanisation of the suffering servant in Isaiah 52:14: 'his appearance was so marred beyond human semblance, and his form beyond that of the sons of men.' Then we come to praise for his resurrection at v. 22 and onwards. In the shepherd psalm (Ps. 23) we have the psalmist in the valley of the shadow of death, fearing no evil. He is anointed with oil and fed at a table in the wilderness, in the presence of his enemies, along with the promise of the Lord's goodness and mercy following him all his days, and the assurance that he will dwell in the house of the Lord for ever. Then we have Psalm 24 which contains the famous ascension passage, 'Lift up your heads, O ye gates, that the King of glory may come in. Who is this king of glory? The Lord of hosts, He is the king of glory.' All thoroughly messianic!

And could anything be more Messianic than Isaiah 53, with the story of Christ's rejection by men (which looked like his rejection by God)? 'He was wounded for our transgressions, bruised for our iniquities, his chastisement makes us whole, and his stripes heal us; for the Lord has laid on him the iniquity of us all. It was the will of the Lord to put him to grief. But it is also the will of the Lord to prosper him. He will receive a portion with the great. He shall see of the fruit of his travail, and shall be satisfied.'

All this prophetic purpose is contained in that one great verse of Genesis 3:15, where all the seeds of the divine intent, the suffering it is to cause and the eventual triumph, are contained in germinal form. If Jesus Christ, when he comes, is not the God-Man as predicted in these terms, then he is not Messiah. But he is; and this is the frightening sin of the Jews: they had been given clear portraits of their Messiah in the Old Testament. The trouble is that they did not put all these portraits together, like the police do when they make an identikit picture; else they would have seen that the Suffering Servant and the coming King of glory were one and the same person. They should have seen that, given the human situation (that of a world gone astray from its maker), the man (the seed of the woman) who was going to retrieve that ruin successfully, could only be such a person as combined these seemingly diverse, almost contradictory attributes. In fact, it was the very features which made them reject him (namely, that no King of Israel could ever be conceived as hanging on a tree as a guilty felon) that fitted him for, and necessarily constituted him, the only, and the right being and man for the job.

You see, given the situation as it was in the Fall, the one who was foreshadowed in the types and prophecies of the Old Testament was the very one who alone could save them. The only conclusion one could possibly come to in the light of that wonderful fitness of Christ for his task (so beautifully portrayed throughout the Old Testament), was that God knew what he was doing from the very start. Thus Genesis 3:15 prepares us perfectly for all that is to be.

In view of that, the sin of rejecting him when he came is so heinous, that only God's judgment of the Jews could do justice to it. It is Christ, or chaos, for them, as for us. And this is the heinousness of the sin of the world, and of Christendom today. It does not want a radical Christ, one who will deal with the dire human situation as it is, but opts for one to heal the hurt of the daughter of his people lightly, or slightly (Jer. 8:11).

The reason why people reject Christ is that he takes their plight too seriously. He is like the surgeon who says, 'My dear, you must come into my ward at once and have an operation: you have a malignant cancer which will take you away shortly, if it is not taken way from you.' 'Oh no', is the response, 'it is only an ulcer: a little medicine will heal it.' But the situation is far more serious than that.

Will a little social tinkering solve mankind's problems in Ulster, for instance? In our day, as well as in other days, this is so ridiculous that God has to bring mankind to the brink of ruin to show us that the disease is deep, and that only Christ can thread through the human situation from the throne of God to earth and back again. He alone is fit to deal with it, because he sees it as a heavenly, or spiritual problem. It is the problem of created spirits gone wrong and spoiling all the rest of God's creation, especially man, the key to the whole situation.

You may well think, as I have described it, that man is not the key, but that the Devil is, and it is a matter of killing the spider, not clearing away the cobwebs, if you see what I mean. But man is the key, for if God dealt too soon with the Devil, the king-pin of evil himself ('the whole world lies in the evil one', 1 Jn. 5:19), man also would be destroyed, whereas God wants to save man!

God did not need the cruel, human death of his Son to procure the destruction of his enemy, Satan. God could snuff him out at any moment, without the slightest trouble. But (to put it in modern parlance), if we were to attempt to shoot the kidnapper or hijacker too soon, what would be the risk to his victims or hostages? You would at all costs want to extricate his captives safely! Wouldn't you? To do that might cost the earth. But see how this is accomplished in the case of man enslaved to evil. The thing the Almighty goes for is the deliverance of man. When that is accomplished, (potentially, but kindly; it takes the rest of human history to complete redemption in all the successive generations of man), only then will God finally deal with the king-pin, the enemy, who is defeated potentially at the cross and, as the Revelation makes so plain, will with all his lesser associates be cast into the lake of fire.

But what I am asking you to see is how long and costly is the process of redeeming man! Yet it is only such an explanation (or interpretation) of redemption that satisfies both the intellect and heart. Otherwise one accepts the partial explanations that certain carefully (too carefully) selected portions of biblical truth impart, and yet one may never think the whole process through as a divine unity. If I can get you to think the whole thing through afresh, I am more than well rewarded for trying.

You may not believe this, but I am sure it is true: one of the reasons why Christians fall away when they become engrossed in their careers or their courtship and family life, is that they have seen the Christian gospel as a mere ticket for a secure after-life, and as a mere holding operation, and not as a whole world of grace. I was recently on holiday and was amazed as I attended church here and there to find how unexciting good evangelical preaching made the gospel sound! But see the Christian life as a romance, or as a warfare, with a long campaign, and the one thing it can never be is boring. Shall I tell you why it is not boring? Because the whole thing is lived in the presence of what I would call a realistic 'hide-and-seek' Saviour, who is constantly drawing us on. Then he seemingly leaves us high and dry in a tedious or tiring situation in which we do not know the moment when he is going to appear from behind a chair, or a tree, or a great rock in a weary land, to say, 'Hello there; how are you getting on with that task I set you?' Then with such an exciting God you may have a session of sheer bliss, in which he just pours the delights of his love – his personal, detailed, and huge care for you – upon you, as if he had nothing else in the whole world to do. Then you feel thoroughly ashamed that you doubted him in the dark, or in the seeming darkness and emptiness of your bare patch. And on it goes, and the one thing you never think of is boredom! When you think that this interest, excitement, and quality of surprise is to go on for ever, upstairs, only unimaginably heightened, you begin to think, 'Why have I been let in for anything as wonderful as this? What have I done to deserve a part in such an everlasting purpose of bliss and glory and love and joy?' You have done nothing but sin heinously, and land yourself in such a mess that you needed a compassionate and loving Saviour to take you out of it, and transport you into the delights of his love.

Of course, all this is totally involving. I recently heard a sculpture teacher on television who was interviewing candidates for a rather special course for budding sculptors. He said to one fellow, 'It's not a job, or an occupation, it's a whole life: you have to devote yourself to it utterly.' Now, I could believe that of any such vocation. But that can end in one's life becoming what often appears increasingly narrow, because almost everything else has to be sacrificed for it! It is true that before Christ reveals his best to us we have (to put it plainly) to put him first. But to choose Christ as our life is not like choosing banking, or high-class carpentry, or medicine, or engineering. It is to choose the key to all the rest of life, which affects the quality of all these, for a Christian banker, or carpenter, or doctor, or engineer, ought to be living in these vocations at the highest level or pitch of satisfaction and fulfilment.

Now, all this may sound more like an old-fashioned gospel appeal than one of a series of studies on the person and work of Christ! But this is just what the person and work of Christ will do for you. He will place you in two totally new worlds of reference. In relation to this natural world and that spiritual one he will say, 'Now find your unique place in relation to both of these, a place which has to do with your part in the perfection of the whole universe.' Until you find your God-appointed place, God will not be satisfied. But of course, you will. That is why you are here, this week, because God has something to show you about yourself in relation to the eternal Christ which is going to set your feet far more firmly on him, the rock.

Accept this opportunity as just for this purpose, and, I tell you, you will look back to these few days all the rest of your life, as of major and lasting significance. It is certainly my prayer, and it is a particularly warm, personal and affectionate prayer, I assure you, that this may be so.

'Now to him who by the power at work within us is able to do far more abundantly than all that we ask or think, to him be glory in the church and in Christ Jesus to all generations for ever and ever. Amen' (Eph. 3:20-21).

THE LORD FROM HEAVEN

The Person and Work of Christ – 2

I tried in the last study to relate Jesus Christ to both his 'eternal' origins (if I can use that phrase) and his 'historical' origins in the Old Testament.

I want to return to this for a little, first because it is vastly important in itself, but also because there is such vast ignorance of the Old Testament these days. Indeed, I would dare to say that even a good deal of the Old Testament studies offered to Christian folk are preoccupied with apologies, trying to defend and uphold our position and justify our views as conservative evangelicals against professional detractors from the Word of God. The result is that we are seldom given the Old Testament (in relation to Christ and the Christian church and its earthly and heavenly future) in a way that does not oblige us to be constantly looking over our shoulders to see what the infidels and semi-infidels are thinking. Of course we must answer them, but not spend our lives doing so! My opinion, for what it is worth, as a strategist, on spending our time on that is that one largely leaves the semi-infidels to get on with their job, of cutting up and mincing the Word of God into a heap of scarcely recognisable particles or fragments, and gets on with the real job of teaching those that are teachable; for that, in time, yields fruit and is yielding fruit which will, in time, deal with and put in their place professional detractors from the Word of God.

This is not to malign Old Testament scholars, or scholarship. A working pastor, like myself, owes more to them than can ever be said (I am thinking of people like E.J. Young, R.K. Harrison, J.A.

Motyer, Derek Kidner, *etc.*), but pastors have to begin where *they* end, having drawn from them what is of use for the building up of Christian souls. That naturally means leaving out a lot that is obviously of purely academic interest. Young ministers need some training in using academic books, pastorally, and this is simply a matter of gaining what help these men offer, as a preparation for the real work of making the Old Testament live; and not only live but point illuminatingly and wonderfully to Christ.

Jesus Christ, then, is that Eternal One who was with the Father in the beginning. The necessity of his coming is seen from the moment of the Fall (as Gen. 3:15 testifies). His identity is foreshadowed in ever clearer and more promising terms right through the Old Testament, until it points inexorably and inevitably to him. That sounds like a *build up*; but if you trace the story of Christ's coming through the story of Israel (which you must, since in his human nature, he is a product of that race), then you must also see the progress towards his coming as a *run down*. It was at the lowest ebb of Israel, as we said last time (and in a sense a run down of the whole known and inhabited, or at least, civilised world), that he came.

Both of these ways of looking at it can be helpful – as a build up and a run down. Towards the time of Christ's coming, in the history of the world at that time, the Hebrews, Greeks and Romans all had their turn. The day of the ancient Egyptians, Assyrians, Babylonians, and Persians was long past and over. On the other hand, the cultures of the Hebrew, Greek, and Roman nations (with comparative peace throughout the civilised world, and Roman roads stretching far into the Middle East) made the most propitious time for the Saviour of the world to come.

Our first study traced the rise of God's chosen people, from one man, Abram, to its peak in David and Solomon, and then the decline as Israel fell further away from God, and landed in captivity; and then, as oppressed and occupied people in their own Jerusalem (the royal family of Judah having become peasants). But you can also read the history of the world throughout the Old Testament ages as a gradually rising graph, with Christ coming at the climax. Paul does that, when he says to the Galatians: 'When the fullness of time was come, God sent forth his son. . .' (but that is much more from the heavenly point of view).

This Eternal One, foreshadowed through so many ages, at last came. But how did he come? Well, the angels certainly made a fuss of his coming, as we read in Luke. They had a celebration concert! But there does not seem to have been much fuss on earth. An innkeeper was hard put to it to find emergency accommodation; a few shepherds had an extraordinary experience; an old man and an old woman had certain intimations, Simeon and Anna. And, of course, there were Mary and Joseph. But until the wise men came from the East, there was practically no fuss in Palestine over the birth of Jesus.

Now it is this tension between the 'to-do' in heaven, regarding this birth, and the lack of it on earth, which has to be knowledgeably held, if we are really to understand the nature of what is involved in the person who came, and what he came to do.

This tension, of course, is part of a greater tension, whose diverse elements are the greatness of God on the one hand, and the humility (not to say humiliation) of his Son in his earthly life and death on the other. Part of that greater tension concerns the place of Adamic man in the divine economy. Made in the image of God (although formed of the dust of the earth) he became the enemy of God through Satan and through his own folly, and yet, through redemption, he is destined to sit with Christ, the Son, on his throne, and judge the world and angels, at the right hand of the Father. The bringing together of these, and all other associated 'opposites' (as they seem to us) provides food for concentrated and amazed thought enough to occupy us, not only throughout our earthly life but, I believe, through all eternity.

So we are really going to get down to the homely simplicity and the poverty of the circumstances of Jesus' birth. Indeed, what Mary and Joseph had suffered for misunderstanding in the gossipy village of Nazareth before they set out for Bethlehem, has not often (in my experience) been assessed. The pure virgin who was the legitimate female heir to the throne of Israel (you can see that in Matt. 1 and

Lk. 3) arrived at the outhouse, where her son was soon born. His conception was by the Holy Spirit. In the first study we mentioned the controversy which surrounds virgin births. It has been suggested that the diabolic counterpart to this birth is found in the vile marriages in Genesis 6. This is held by those who believe that the fallen angels (*cf*. Jude 6; 2 Pet. 2:4; 1 Pet. 3:19, 20) directly impregnated these women and thus produced the super-creatures of Genesis 6, perhaps, also, the giant sons of Anak, and such as Goliath. It could have happened again and again, after the flood had swept away all the original giants.

Whether this is the case or not, certainly, the miracle of Mary's conception is something which must fill us with a reverent awe, which Luke chapters 1 and 2 do everything to encourage. The embryo that grew in the virgin's womb was in every way natural, as was the babe, when he was born (like us, in all respects, sin apart, Heb. 4:15). Yet he was absolutely unique in this, that he was conceived through the power of God the Holy Spirit. We come back again to the *Westminster Confession of Faith*. He took upon him 'man's nature' – he was born of a woman – 'with all the essential properties and common infirmities, yet without sin'. 'So that two whole, perfect, and distinct natures, the Godhead and the manhood, were inseparably joined together (a man for ever) in one person, without confusion' (*i.e.* not each nature fused with the other and so confused that a third kind of nature was produced). This person, who is possessed of two, whole, perfect, and distinct natures, the divinity and the manhood, and who yet remains one person, is a mystery which neither Jews of old nor the Romans would accept, and many since have not been able to stomach it, because it leaves them with an element of mystery that they want to *solve* to their own satisfaction.

Cerinthus and the Gnostics got over the difficulty by assuming that Jesus was an ordinary man, born of Mary and Joseph, and that the divine Christ descended upon him, after his baptism, and left him before his suffering and death. They believed that God could not become man, because humanity partook of matter which they believed to be essentially evil. But matter is not essentially evil; it was dragged into evil, through the Fall (I Jn. 4:1-3). At different times, some have stressed the divinity of our Lord's manhood, at the expense of his humanity (Apollinarianism); and some have done the opposite, and have stressed his humanity, at the expense of his divinity (Nestorianism).

The burden of the biblical testimony was at last formulated in the Definition of Chalcedon (451 AD) in such a way that the two natures in one person was guarded: the 'one and the same Christ, Son, Lord, only-begotten, recognised in two natures without confusion, without change, without division, without separation; the distinction of natures being in no way annulled by the union but rather the characteristics of each nature being preserved and coming together to form one person and subsistence, not as parted, or separated into two persons, but one and the same Son, and only-begotten God the Word, Lord Jesus Christ. . . .'

Our next consideration is how the second person of the Trinity, the eternal Son, very God and very man, developed his human personality, from infancy to childhood, and thence to manhood. Some people find great difficulty in conceiving what the nature of our Lord's boyhood was. Perhaps the very possibility of a perfect boy is inconceivable to them – even more inconceivable than a perfect girl! One of the hymns speaks of the 'sinless boy'. All we know is that at the age of twelve he showed remarkable knowledge and insight, enough to amaze and doubtless embarrass the Jewish doctors of the law at Jerusalem. We also see that when he realised that he had caused Mary and Joseph profound concern, although he emphasised that he had been engaged on his Father's business, he went with them, and readily and completely submitted to them, presumably until he was thirty.

But why should this idea of a 'sinless boy' seem so incomprehensible? If sinlessness is *essentially* unnatural for a boy, then it is inconceivable. But how could sinlessness seem unnatural, when God made Adam and Eve sinless in the first place? We talk of their 'original righteousness', and although I do not know who can expound that completely satisfactorily, it must be a valid concept. Not only so, but holiness, or righteousness, or signs of grace in human nature as we may know it, or blamelessness, as we may call it, do not seem unnatural, do they? Nothing lights so sweetly and naturally upon a person as grace. The testimony of those who have met with great saints is often just this, that they have been astonished how simple, human and natural they were. Indeed, I never forget what the late Cassandra of the *Daily Mirror* once said about meeting Billy Graham in a pub in London, during the Harringay campaign: he said he would 'not have believed that goodness had such a cutting edge'; but it was goodness, sweet and gracious gentlemanliness, that Cassandra said had that cutting edge.

Jesus, as a little boy, would have been completely unconscious of his goodness, and it would have seemed perfectly natural to him, and doubtless seemed so to others, until they also longed for and sought to covet such goodness. Given what we *know* of who Jesus was, the record of him, at the age of twelve, seems perfectly natural, with nothing spooky, mysterious, uncanny, or other than human about him at all. Jesus was a man. He too lived by faith. But what of the development of his mind? Well, some have said that it was not until after his baptism, and some say long after that, that he really understood his calling and destiny. I would think, myself, that all supposed theories which limit Jesus' mind beyond the age of twelve, when he obviously knew that he needed to be about his Father's business, are dangerous. I do not necessarily mean that in his early teens he fully understood all his destiny – why, in his earthly life, he admitted that the day of his coming again was not known by him but only by his Father. Naturally, his consciousness developed with his childhood and boyhood, but I would be inclined to assert his pretty full understanding earlier rather than later in his life! Let us err on the reverent side!

Now, to come to the three years of his ministry, and his passion and death (not to say his rising). John the Baptist, having effected his preparatory work of proclaiming the kingdom and bringing many to repentance in Israel, began to retire and recede, and Jesus proceeded to the place of his baptism. By that baptism he identified himself with us in our sin, the Holy Spirit anointing him as our sin-bearer. Obviously it pleased his Father that he did this, as the prophet Isaiah tells us: 'it was the will of the Lord' or 'it pleased the Lord to bruise him: it is he who has put him to grief' (Is. 53:10). When the symbolic dove descended upon Jesus at the River Jordan (not tongues of fire as on the disciples at Pentecost, for they were sinners, whereas there was no sin in him) he heard his Father's voice declaring: 'This is my beloved Son in whom I am well pleased' (Matt. 3:17) – 'pleased,' note, not only as an equal person within the Trinity, but pleased with him in his willingness to come down, and be our Sin-Bearer (see also Heb. 10:5-9, where Jesus' dedication to the will of God is emphasised in the quotation from Psalm 40:6-8). How close that identification of Jesus with our sin really is, is stated in the starkest and most daring terms by Paul in 2 Corinthians 5:21, 'God made Christ to become sin for us, who knew no sin, that we might become the righteousness of God in him.' Nothing could be plainer. There is no room for pious shock at the daring of the language, for the few words in the original Greek are strung together with the greatest simplicity, stating that God made him to become sin, who knew no sin.

Now in a sense, we are anticipating ourselves here, because we are only at our Lord's baptism. But the implications of that baptism take us, at once, to the cross. It is as well to state here and now the three reasons why Christ came, as seen in his actual work and ministry.

Chronologically, you would say, he came, like his forerunner, John the Baptist, to proclaim the kingdom; that it was at hand, and men of Israel (in the first instance, Rom. 1:16, Eph. 1:12) were to repent and believe that the true reign of God was here. He took this over from John, and used precisely the same language, not putting himself on a par with John, but associating himself with his forerunner.

Then he offered the healing powers of the kingdom to his own people, the Jews; for he was one of them (his genealogy being carefully traced through early tribal and later royal lineage, and then, last of all, through that line during the humiliating later ages, Matt. 1, Lk. 3). He came primarily to them as God's evangelists to the Gentiles (see Isa. 42:6, 49:6). In connection with that, as I say, he offered them the gracious powers of the kingdom in his healings. They loved bodily healing and took it greedily. But they would not have his words about the kingdom! They might repent in crowds when thundering John the Baptist spoke, and they might make the long, weary journey of nearly thirty miles to the Jordan to be baptised in that remote place, but they would not repent for 'gentle Jesus meek and mild'. So much so that after John was in prison, from reports of the gentleness of Jesus' ministry, John himself sent to ask if he really were the Christ. For John made a national impact, whereas Jesus was concerned with both narrower and wider concerns, with the individual and then with the Gentiles (Matt. 11, 12) and the whole world (Isa. 42:6, 49:6). They would have his healing and his miraculous bread, but not his saving words. So he left them.

Those are two of the things he came to do, to proclaim the kingdom, and heal; and then to teach his disciples, largely the twelve.

Lastly he came to die. Without this, the rest were futile, for this underlay all. I want to sum up a lot at this point, by summarising what, for many years now, I have called the three dimensions of the cross of Christ (although I recognise that the death and rising of Christ is infinite, because he is infinite). It seems to me that we do not really know or understand all that the Lord came for unless we understand this: he came to do three things in one: to deal with sins, sin and Satan.

First he came to take away our sins, that is, to blot them out of God's sight or knowledge by fully bearing the penalty, the guilt and the shame for them, as if he himself were the sinner. That is why 'he opened not his mouth', when accused before Herod and Pilate (Is. 53:7). He accepted the guilt, as our substitute. Many do not believe that it is possible for a sinless man to bear the sins of others; they say it is immoral. But it is God in human flesh who did this. May God not do it, and it be right? And is it not a Godlike thing for him to do (it is so amazing), to stand in for us so that we go free? Do you see why he stood in? If we were to suffer for our sins (the things we have done wrong) we would die in them, because 'the soul that sinneth it shall die', and that eternally!

But he, dying for us, being personally sinless, dies with our sins and comes up without them (annihilates or obliterates their guilt and shame by bearing their punishment, even to death). Death could not hold him, since death is the result of sin, and he had none (Acts 2:24). That is the first thing (see Is. 53:6, and Jn. 1:29 for that in two stages: 'laid on him. . . takes away. . .').

The second thing is this (and Jn. 1:29 touches on it): he not only died *for* our sins, but *with* the root of what brought forth the fruit of our actual, overt transgressions, namely the sin in Adam's nature, of which we partake, since the Fall. Theoretically, this is distinct from Jesus dying as the substitute criminal and guilty one. That was Jesus getting rid of all the rubbish we had accumulated around our lives. But it was these lives *themselves* that were wrong. It is spiders that produce cobwebs; if you do not want cobwebs, then you must kill spiders because they produce cobwebs. And Jesus killed the spider, that is to say, our sinful nature (remember he was baptised, as if he were a sinner needing to be cleansed) and died our (that is Adam's) death. He, therefore, slew Adam, the one who brought sin into the human race, because he (Adam) became tainted with Satan's unsaveable taint (the Devil is unsaveable, because pure spirit gone wrong cannot be saved, and could never want to be saved). So the only thing God could do with rotten Adam was to kill him and begin again with a new man. Paul calls this new man the last Adam (1 Cor. 15:45).

This is where we begin to see the benefits of this work of Christ for us. For when we receive the Spirit of Jesus Christ, at regeneration, we receive the Spirit of one who died to Adam's sin, and who by that Spirit gives us his death to our Adam (Adam as in us) as a divine fact and potency. This is what Paul is labouring to bring out in Romans 6. He does not suggest that after conversion sin is dead in us; we know that is not true. But to all who receive Christ, by repentance and faith, is given Christ's death to their sin, because we could not die that death to sin safely. He, alone, came up from that death because he had no sin to hold him in death.

I like this way of putting it, because it simplifies what some preachers and teachers make very, very difficult indeed: God plants the seed of Christ within us (see 1 Jn. 3:9, *sperma*), and that seed, in germ, contains, as a complete and final and finished work (Rom. 6:9-11), Christ's death and redemption to our sin nature. This is what John means when he says that 'No one born of God commits (that is, practises) sin' (1 Jn. 3:9). The new life of God within the soul cannot sin. But since it is at first only a seed it has to grow to take possession of the whole life in its holy power. But all that Christ gained by his death for our sin nature is contained in that Holy Spirit seed, so that Paul can boldly say that we, new, born-again Christians, are 'dead indeed unto sin'. While there is another baggage, relic or remnant remaining there, of course (see Rom. 7:17, 20), the new Christian 'I' is dead indeed to sin. That is what has been given us. We have it, if we are Christians at all. Do you think it is too good to be true? Ah, it is too good not to be true! This is the fact, which we have to swallow. But when we have swallowed it like wonderful medicine (it will never do us good, handling it, and looking at it, and arguing about it), we shall prove that it is not only true, but because it is the truth of God we shall prove that it works!

These are two dimensions of Christ's death. In these, he deals with the fruit of sin and the root of sin planted deep within us. But there remains another dimension which, in so much teaching concerning the deepening of Christian life in the convention movement, is either left out altogether or its vital dimension is largely ignored. I know why it is: it is a major and strategic work of the enemy to draw away attention from him, because this dimension concerns him. This is the dimension of Christ's death as the final defeat of Satan.

I made a lot of Genesis 3:15 in the first study, and this is the direct link with that verse. When you thread through the whole of the Old Testament, from Genesis 3:15 to the death and resurrection of Christ, you establish a connection, which is as clear and plain as anything could possibly be. For that Genesis verse prophesies and promises the defeat *of Satan*. It says nothing specifically about sin at all, although that, of course, is implied and included – but about the defeat of the Devil and, naturally along with him, all his crew of demons (and fallen angels if they are different).

Notice how important this is. In fact it is so important that it is impossible to deal with it worthily at the end of this study. It must therefore spill over into the next study after which we will get on to the practical implication of all Christ's work for us, particularly in the life of sanctification (the normal life).

The third dimension of Christ's death, his defeat of Satan, embraces the other two (*cf.* Gen. 3:15), because it goes to the root of the trouble with regard to sin and evil. If sins are done away, and evil extirpated from the human heart by the slaying of old Adam, but Satan is left on the rampage, he could do the same again – or worse! So, in thinking about Christ's work on the cross, we must pay close attention to this third dimension, and then see its application to the life of sanctification, and also our training, as soldiers in Christ's warfare against all evil.

Paul is so sure that this third dimension is determinative and regulative for us as Christians, that in the famous warfare passage in Ephesians 6 he declares that we are to be strong in the Lord (that is, wearing the whole armour of the Lord). He says, we wrestle not (our contending, RSV) is not against flesh and blood, but is against a whole world and kingdom of evil principalities, powers, hosts of wicked spirits and rulers of the present darkness of this fallen world. We are not fighting merely against sinfulness in ourselves, either in root or in fruit. Rather, we are engaged against an extended campaign and strategic plan of the enemy to take over the whole universe, and especially man, the crown of creation.

What would have been the use of Churchill and Eisenhower nibbling away at this group of Nazis, here and there, in different parts of the occupied continent of Europe, or North Africa, if they ignored the fact that there was a whole hierarchy of evil residing in Berlin and at Berchtesgaden, who planned to take over the whole of Europe, and even the whole world? But we must pursue this theme further in the next study.

Let me sum up Christ's work thus: he came to deal with sins, sin and Satan; all of them. All of this is pertinent, not only to our everlasting destiny but also to our daily walk as Christians in the world. You cannot be the Christian you ought to be unless and until you know all this thoroughly. You must take a very strong grip on it. If you are doubtful of it all, and are one of those simple Christians whose knowledge of the Christian life is largely confined to forgiveness and justification, and you know little about the ongoing life of sanctification in Christ, and growth in grace, and of the warfare that is only possible for strong, mature, balanced Christians, then let us talk about it, and let us prepare to take a grasp of it as we try to expound it, God helping us!

THE LORD FROM HEAVEN

The Person and Work of Christ – 3

We turn now to a study of the work of Jesus Christ as that work applies to us as Christians. We cannot quite do that without taking in the cosmic significance of Christ and his work. It is this understanding which makes for stature in Christians and gives them spiritual and psychological poise. They know themselves as redeemed men and women and as belonging to the most important series of cosmic events in the universe. In Christ they become king-pins or lynch-pins, pivots or fulcrums of a situation which involves all worlds, and all constellations, not to say all ages of the whole universe. All that happens in time and space depends upon what God purposed to do, and did, for man in Jesus Christ. He is constantly working out from the completeness of that almighty potential day by day in the lives of his saints; and in a lesser, tragic sort of way in those who refuse to be saints, along with those horrid angelic forces implacably and eternally opposed to him.

What has already been said serves as virtually a long introduction to this, in order to show the significance of man in relation to the whole range of created things and beings. Man alone, of all creation, receives the image of God, and Satan attacks him, in his attempt to frustrate the Lord in his exalted plans for man; so what happens to man is definitive and regulative for everything else that happens in the whole wide world.

You see this plainly if you turn to Romans 8:19-24. Among other things, these verses state that the redemption of the natural creation waits (that is the scriptural word, in vv.19, 23) for the full redemption of man (that is full redemption with resurrection bodies, when Christ comes back in power and great glory). So that man is the key and what God does concerning man is the key to the understanding of the whole universe, including the reason for creating it.

But what is the Almighty's chief end in creation and redemption? It can be put in the most spacious, comprehensive, yet domestic terms, thus: God, in three Persons, the divine, happy, blessed, eternal family if you like, in need of nothing, being altogether self-existent and self-sufficient ('not standing in need of any creatures which he has made', (*Westminster Confession of Faith*, II.2), desired to add to his family (if I may put it like that) a bride for his Son. But, as Adam proved, looking for a companion amongst the animals, there was none of the lesser breed to satisfy him (Gen. 2:18-24); God sought a worthy bride for his Son and so made man of the dust of the earth (do you ask why?), but also in the image of God. Do you think that if Adam and Eve had eaten of the tree of life, instead of the tree of knowledge of good and evil (Gen. 2:9, 16, 17) they would have been incorporated into the eternal and pre-incarnate Christ? But, because the Fall intervened, the redemption of man became the greatest thing in the universe both as to its achievement and its end. If man, therefore, has not only to be redeemed from the sin into which he fell through Satan, but has to be redeemed from Satan himself, then all Christ's work to that end we must apply to the lives of believers everywhere, and especially to ourselves as believers now.

To my mind the most important thing in all this is to see that questions of sin and evil, however domestic, however personal, hidden, and peripheral we may mistakenly think them, along with all seemingly more major questions related to the main things in our life, like the new birth itself, our growth in grace, and our life's vocation and service and warfare for the Lord – all these must be related to the whole kingdom of evil and its strategy. For just as nothing is unimportant, as far as our life in Christ is concerned, so nothing is unimportant as far as the malign strategies of the whole vast kingdom of evil are concerned. You see, if I take a practical example: you may sin some so-called venial sin, privately, which sin you may have committed over and over again. You are sorry about it, in a sense, and hope it does not happen again, but there is no deep repentance. In the meantime, it may seem to have had no effect upon your life with God or your service and warfare for him. But one day you are faced with a situation which turns out to be of major importance for the rest of your life, and because you are in a state of spiritual defeat you are unable to cope with it properly; you fluff it, and flounder. Then what do you say? – that it was 'unfortunate'? Not if you are a trained and instructed Christian. You recognise that the whole kingdom of evil was watching over you, to condition you to that sin over and over again so that, quite unwittingly, you might commit it on that significant occasion and, therefore, miss God's strategic best for your life. I am not putting two valuations on the heinousness of any sin, but stressing the strategy behind sin.

Take an historical example of this: there were certain things in David's life that led to his sudden downfall in the matter of the sin with Bathsheba. The whole thing happened so comparatively innocently. David was not with his army at the season for battles against Israel's enemies. He was lounging complacently in his palace at Jerusalem when he saw the unclothed figure of this beautiful woman and he ultimately sinned with her, and even had her husband murdered to expunge, as he thought, his sin. But what lay behind all this? Just that, as God prophesied to Israel through Moses (read it in Deut. 28, 29), the spiritual downfall of Israel and their banishment to captivity, after many lesser trials, followed their turning away from the Lord. And, of course, as we know from the story of Solomon, David's son, that turning away took place through the sexual sins of these kings and their successors (see 1 Kings 11:1-13).

What we are saying, therefore, is that the Devil, lulling David to sleep, morally and spiritually, in his prosperous middle-age, suddenly swooped on him one fine day and made him sin that sin with Bathsheba, which rendered the remainder of his life completely useless to God, and full of disappointments (read the rest of David's life story right through 2 Sam., from 11-24 right into 1 Kings).

Not only so, but if you read 2 Samuel 12 (along with 1 Kings 11) you will see that God's pronouncement concerning David's sexual exploits was to affect the life of Israel henceforth: 'the sword shall never depart from your house' (2 Sam. 12:10). You see what I mean by demonic or diabolic strategy? We never know (among all the sins we may so complacently sin, or mildly deplore) when the Devil is about to pounce upon us if unguarded, and single out one sin to lead to a disaster which will mar a whole life. Like the Fall itself, it may even affect the whole of mankind. Do you think that it was in Eve's mind at all that she was doing something elementally and dimensionally disastrous to the whole human race when she consented to the serpent? Never. But it is given to us to see not only how heinous sin is in God's eyes, whether there be swift chastisement for it or not, but to see also that all temptation is part of a major campaign of evil, to get us down, not so much because the Devil hates us but because he hates God and would do anything in the world to spite him for not letting Satan unseat the Almighty and take his throne.

Some may think I am stressing the strategic side of all this far too much for your practical help. But we will never make real practical advance until we understand this biblical perspective. How pathetic it is almost to have to grub for what people call the simple gospel in the Word of God, when those blessed and wonderful gospel rudiments are but the first elements in a whole strategy of redemption which involves us, however modest and simple Christians we may think ourselves to be, in events which are not only world events, but events of eternal importance. One thing I believe is impossible for those who take in the mighty sweep of God's plan of redemption, as I am trying to trace it, is a continuing sense of inferiority, or what we glibly call inferiority complex. You cannot go on feeling inferior if you know that you are thus involved in world events or in events of eternal significance.

For instance, if you had felt in 1959 and 1960 that you had even a small part to play in the fall of Khrushchev and (as they still say) in his conversion, when he had fallen from power – it is even possible that his fall from power was due to his alleged conversion. If you had a part in the intercession which cried to God to save us from the menace of Khrushchev (think of the Cuban crisis!), and then God acted, you cannot feel yourself to be of no importance however humbly you bow before the Lord. You are part of his effectual army, by which he rules the worlds (Rev. 2:26, 27), a rule which is given to us in Christ by his work on the cross.

But I go too fast and too far. I want first to relate this third dimension of Christ's work on the cross to the life of sanctification, and before I do so to the life of Christian service and warfare, and of broad Christian strategies.

The first two dimensions, I said, were sins and sin. The essence of what may be called the Keswick message, or the message for the deepening of spiritual life, concerns the second dimension, the fact that in Christ we are dead to sin and alive to God (Rom. 6:11). This is the life of holiness we are not only called to live but are furnished with the power to live by the Holy Spirit. The divine potency of Christ's death and resurrection is given to believers so that they have the resources in Christ to live a new life. But it is the experience of many who take their stand upon this mighty truth (and Bunyan tells us all about this in *Pilgrim's Progress*) that the more they assure themselves that their regenerate selves are dead to sin and alive to God, the stronger temptation seems to come, and the living of the holy life becomes a right royal battle. This puzzles people and they are daunted by the sheer fierceness of the struggle. On the one occasion when I spoke at Keswick on this, in 1952 (and was ticked-off by the next speaker for it), I had a little queue (of young folk mostly) waiting at the side of the tent to see me afterwards. Their presence simply confirmed what I had just said, namely that there was another element to living the holy life which had heretofore escaped them and often left them bewildered and even in despair.

The answer I gave, and give again, is exactly the answer of John Bunyan centuries ago (but, of course, it is in the Word of God first). The enemy of souls himself creeps into this situation of struggle and lurks there, unseen and unknown. He masquerades as the mere dregs of the old, fallen nature, stirring up what the *Confession* calls mere 'remnants' of sin, until they become seemingly impossible to control and quench. On the other hand (pushing us to another extreme) he stirs up a pietistic and legalistic desire to ignore Christ's provision and supersede it by our own efforts.

Now, it is just this situation that the teaching of Romans 6 by itself (although it is one of the most important and one of the greatest chapters in the New Testament), does not help with, because it is not dealing with it. But I believe Romans 7, or part of that chapter, deals with it, although Satan himself is not mentioned there by name. What happens, when people seek to live by the truth of Romans 6 about being dead to sin, is that Satan deceives them into trying to die to sin in their own strength, instead of drawing upon the divine resource of Christ's finished work. This, of course, leads to legalism, and the harder they try in their own strength to be holy, the less successful they become, because Satan comes in on the legal effort.

It stands to reason that if we try to deal with inbred sin, when the real problem is Satan or one of his demonic agents, then we are barking up the wrong tree and are dealing quite unrealistically with the situation. It is as simple as a workman using the wrong tool or the wrong method to do a job. It is like trying to speed in second or third gear; or to use a poultice when surgery is needed. The resource God has given us to deal with sin is Christ's death, as a divine, inward potency of the Spirit. The resource God has given us to deal with the personal intrusion and intervention of Satan, or his demonic agents, is quite another dimension of Christ's same death – that dimension by which, on the cross, he defeated him and brought him to the end of his attempts to destroy Jesus by trying to make our Lord sin before he died. But Jesus, in that unique, elemental struggle, outlasted Satan and, I believe, vanquished him, ere he died. And then, having finished his work, he regally bowed his head and dismissed his spirit into the care of his Father.

It was precisely this discrimination – detecting the difference between sin and Satan – that Jesus exercised when Peter objected to his telling the disciples about his coming death. Our Lord turned on Peter, and addressed him: 'Get thee behind me, Satan!' Was Jesus calling Peter 'Satan'? Hardly! Rather, he was detecting Satan lurking in the folds of Peter's sinful flesh. The Devil had used Peter's lips to speak almost blasphemous words.

I can hardly get people to see the implications of this, or to take them seriously. There seems to be an intractable reluctance among evangelicals to take Satan seriously. Not so John Bunyan, of an earlier era. Would that there were more like him!

These, then, are my three dimensions of the cross of the Redeemer, the Lord from heaven. He delivers us from sins, from sin and from Satan – fruit, root and brute! But all this must be understood in relationship to our own Christian lives. There is so much to say here. For example, these three dimensions, expressed negatively in relationship to the whole range of evil, might also be expressed positively, in terms of the inflow of grace that follows our deliverance from evil, such as: peace flowing from the forgiveness of sins; love flowing from an experience of death to sin and self; joy flowing from victory over the Devil in our personal lives.

Had we time, we could take the third dimension and, using Ephesians 6:10-18 with other passages, show that there are three stages in our training to be soldiers of Christ. David learned a lot about this when he was running from Saul, as the Psalms indicate.

First, there is the lesson of strategic retreat, when we learn to run into Christ for shelter in the evil day. Then, second, there is standing our ground against the enemy, when we learn to wear all the defensive armour described by Paul. And, third, there is Christian attack, using the weapon of all-prayer along with the 'sword of the Spirit, which is the word of God'. This is exactly what Jesus did when he used such Scripture as Deuteronomy 6 and 8 against the onslaughts of Satan. He hurled great rocks of Scripture at him!

That leads us into thinking about what it means to draw upon the resources of spiritual victory which the Lord of glory has placed at our disposal by his own victory over all evil. But first we must see what this victory is in terms of ultimate strategy.

The universe, formerly governed by the Devil, a fallen and discredited ruler (always under God's sovereign will, of course), is now governed by the Man, Christ Jesus. The whole world will be judged by him (Acts 17:31). It is under his control. Think of that: a Man controls everything! And this control he has gained for us. He had no need to gain it for himself, since he already 'upholds the universe by the word of his power' (Heb. 1:3). It was *for us* – in order to incorporate us into his divine plan, that we might gain the mastery of evil – that Christ fought and won the battle against Satan in our flesh.

When Jesus says that 'all authority in heaven and earth' is his, he speaks as a resurrected, immortal Man. I do not find anywhere in Scripture that he bequeaths that authority to us. However, when he speaks of binding the strong man (Satan) in order to plunder his goods (Matt. 12:29), he goes on to say that those who are not *with* him are *against* him, and those who do not gather with him, scatter. It seems to me this implies several important points. First, Christ himself has gained victory for us over the whole kingdom of evil. Second, he has not given us executive control over his new dominion. We cannot be entrusted with that at the moment (even our prayers need to be mingled with the pure and perfect incense of Christ's prayers to bear fruit, see Rev. 8:1-5). It is only in his name, according to his will, that we receive the power of faith to do exploits for him. And this, surely, has to do with living, praying and waging war within the realm that Christ has established through his death and resurrection.

We cannot share in the justificationary aspects of Christ's death – we are furthest from him in that ('There was no other good enough to pay the price of sin; He only could unlock the gate of heaven and let us in'). But we do share in the sanctificationary aspects of his death. In fact, in union with him we die his death after him – and never so much as when we enter into his death regarded as an absolute and invincible resistance to Satan. This, I think, is part of what Paul meant when he spoke about completing what was lacking in the sufferings of Christ for the sake of his body, the church (Col. 1:24).

This is the second area where we come into major conflict with the Devil, when we contest the hold he has on other people's lives once his sway over our own life has been broken by grace.

I must forego the pleasure of bringing these studies to a close by painting a picture of the Lord returned to glory and reigning at his Father's side when all things will be consummated. Rather, I want to say something about the Lord from heaven as he is now, waiting for us to get on with the work he has made possible here and now. Let me do so by giving two illustrations from the Old Testament, which draw, in a proleptic fashion, from the victory of Christ still to come. They are both well known.

In Exodus 17:8-12, Moses controlled the battle against the Amalekites when he lifted up his hands in prayer. He shared in the costliness which Christ was later to know. He died deaths for others in the one and only death of Christ that was yet to be. So it must be with us, as we pray for individuals, groups and whole communities and nations.

The second illustration is in Daniel 10, which should be interpreted in conjunction with the insights into the conflict in the heavenly sphere in Job 1 and Ephesians 6:10-20. Here, Daniel was exercised about the future of his own people. He was brought into a divine agony in prayer for them. This went on for three weeks, but nothing seemed to happen. Then an angel came to comfort him, and to tell him that his prayer had been heard in heaven from the moment he had uttered it. Why, then, was his answer so long in coming?

What was happening was this. God wanted to send an angel to Daniel to give him prophetic insight into the future of God's people the Jews. But the demon prince, or demonic guardian angel that presided over the kingdom of Persia, intercepted God's messenger and prevented him from carrying the message to Daniel. But Daniel was praying, and what he was doing in prayer (all unknown to himself), was calling in the archangel Michael who has a special care for Israel. When Michael came, he engaged the demon prince of the kingdom of Persia and the angel was released and completed his journey. Daniel received the message and was encouraged by it!

We need to learn to think of our own lives in this context. We do not wrestle against flesh and blood – either our own poor human nature still beset with the remnants of corruption, or that of others. We wrestle against spiritual combatants, against principalities, powers, world rulers of the present darkness and against the spiritual hosts of wickedness in heavenly places.

You see (and this, I assure you, is complicated), what happens on earth in relation to divine and diabolic strategies is determined in the heavenly places. There the battle between the kingdom of God and the kingdom of evil has been intensified and radically altered since all authority is now in the hands of a Man who represents the saints of God. But, what is determined 'up there' about 'down here' is determined by what the praying saints do, or do not do, down here. Control has been vouchsafed to us in Christ, to affect the future history of man by waging war with the hostile powers in the heavenlies which must still be dealt with by each successive generation of warrior Christians. And this will go on until every knee shall bow and every tongue confess that Jesus Christ is Lord, to the glory of God the Father!

This is what the Lord from heaven came to do. Let us give thanks for him, and for his victory, by entering into our share of it, to his glory, to our blessing and the blessing of the peoples of these islands and far further afield even than that!

LAW AND GRACE

The best introduction to the subject of the Law and the gospel within the Covenant of Grace is surely the relevant chapters of the *Westminster Confession of Faith*. They provide a comprehensive statement of the ground we wish to cover: Chapter VII, 'Of God's Covenant with Man', and Chapter XIX, 'Of the Law of God'.

Chapter VII: Of God's Covenant with Man.
The distance between God and the creature is so great, that although reasonable creatures owe obedience to him as their Creator, yet they could never have any fruit of him as their blessedness and reward, except by some voluntary condescension on God's part, which he has been pleased to express by way of covenant.
II. The first covenant made with man was a covenant of works (sometimes called by others a covenant of 'innocence' or 'nature' or the 'Adamic administration'), wherein life was promised to Adam, and in him to his posterity, upon condition of perfect and personal obedience.
III. Man by his fall having made himself incapable of life by that covenant, the Lord was pleased to make a second, commonly called the Covenant of Grace: whereby he freely offers to sinners life and salvation by Jesus Christ, requiring of them faith in him, that they may be saved; and promising to give to all those who are ordained to life his Holy Spirit, to make them willing and able to believe.
IV. This covenant of grace is frequently set forth in the scripture by the name of a Testament, in reference to the death of Jesus

Christ the testator, and to the everlasting inheritance, with all things belonging to it, therein bequeathed.

V. This covenant was differently administered in the time of the law, and in the time of the gospel: under the law it was administered by promises, prophecies, sacrifices, circumcision, the paschal lamb, and other types and ordinances delivered to the people of the Jews, all fore-signifying Christ to come, which were for that time sufficient and efficacious, through the operation of the Spirit, to instruct and build up the elect in faith in the promised Messiah, by whom they had full remission of sins, and eternal salvation; and is called the Old Testament.

VI. Under the gospel, when Christ the substance was exhibited, the ordinances in which this covenant is dispensed are the preaching of the word, and the administration of the sacraments of Baptism and the Lord's Supper; which, though fewer in number, and administered with more simplicity and less outward glory, yet in them it is held forth in more fulness, evidence, and spiritual efficacy, to all nations, both Jews and Gentiles; and is called the New Testament. There are not therefore two covenants of grace differing in substance, but one and the same under various dispensations.

Chapter XIX: Of the Law of God.

God gave to Adam a law, as a covenant of works, by which he bound him, and all his posterity, to personal, entire, exact, and perpetual obedience; promised life upon the fulfilling, and threatened death upon the breach of it; and endued him with power and ability to keep it.

II. This law, after his fall, continued to be a perfect rule of righteousness; and as such, was delivered by God upon mount Sinai in ten commandments, and written in two tables; the first four commandments containing our duty to God, and the other six our duty to man.

III. Besides this law, commonly called Moral, God was pleased to give the people of Israel, as a church under age, ceremonial laws, containing several typical ordinances; partly of worship, prefiguring Christ, his graces, actions, sufferings and benefits; and partly holding forth various instructions of moral duties. All which ceremonial laws are now abrogated under the New Testament.

IV. To them also, as a body politic, he gave sundry judicial laws, which expired together with the state of that people, not obliging any other now, further than the general equity of them may require.

V. The moral law for ever binds all, those persons justified as well as others, to obedience to them; and that not only in regard to the matter contained in it, but also in respect of the authority of God, the Creator, who gave it. Neither does Christ in the gospel any way dissolve, but much strengthen this obligation.

VI. Although true believers are not under the law as a covenant of works, to be justified or condemned by it; yet it is of great use to them, as well as to others; in that, as a rule of life, informing them of the will of God and their duty, it directs and binds them to walk accordingly; discovering also the sinful pollutions of their nature, hearts, and lives; so that, examining themselves by it, they may come to further conviction of, humiliation for, and hatred against sin; together with a clearer sight of the need they have of Christ, and the perfection of his obedience. It is likewise of use to the regenerate, to restrain their corruptions, in that it forbids sin; and its threatenings serve to show what even their sins deserve, and what afflictions in this life they may expect for them, although freed from the curse threatened in the law. The promises of it, likewise, show them God's approval of obedience, and what blessings they may expect upon its performance, although not as due to them by the law as a covenant of works: so that the fact that man does good, and refrains from evil, because the law encourages the one and deters from the other, is no evidence of his being under the law and not under grace.

VII. Neither are the aforementioned uses of the law contrary to the grace of the gospel, but do sweetly comply with it; the Spirit of Christ subduing and enabling the will of man to do freely and cheerfully what the will of God revealed in the law requires to be done.

It will be seen from the foregoing chapters of the *Westminster Confession of Faith*, 'Of God's Covenant with Man', and 'Of the Law of God', that the Law was given in the context of grace. However, the tensions between the Law in the Old Testament and the gospel in the New, are so real and serious, that it is important for a satisfying study of the subject to distinguish the different uses of the Law.

The Reformers defined three distinct uses of the Law:
1) the political or civil use;
2) the tutorial use, to bring man to Christ;
3) the didactic use, as a rule of life for believers.

The Lutheran and Reformed views differed as to the priority of these three uses. The Lutherans stressed the second use, to bring man to conviction of sin, to drive him to Christ. They admitted the third use of the Law as a rule of life for believers, but held it with a certain reserve, since Paul says believers are 'not under the law'. It is useful, they said, only in so far as they were sinners, 'and', says Louis Berkhof, 'they treat it only in connection "with human misery"'.

The Reformed view, while doing full justice to the second use, placed the principal emphasis upon the third use, that related to sanctification.

Luther placed great importance upon such evangelical passages of the New Testament as Galatians 3:10-29; Romans 3:20; 4:15; 7:7; whereas Calvin held that this use of the Law was 'accidental' to its true purpose. It is our view that while acknowledging the civil use of the Law and the Law's function of driving people to Christ through condemnation, confusion readily arises through an undue emphasis upon the second use. It tends to drive a wedge between the two Testaments, obscuring their solidarity as together setting forth the one Covenant of Grace, revealed in Genesis 3:15, following the Fall. Most misconceptions concerning the Law in relation to the gospel of grace seem to arise from stress upon the second view of the Law as a preparatory instrument to lead men to Christ.

Calvin says we must see the Law in relation to Christ; and he sets forward Christ's threefold relation to the Law as follows:

(1) We see his active obedience to the Law, in that he who made it, and gave it, came under it (Gal. 4:4), kept it, and reversed Adam's breakage of it, thus fulfilling it for us.

(2) We see his passive obedience to the Law in his bearing the brunt of its condemnation of the sinful sons of Adam, taking their penalty upon himself.

(3) Then, having fulfilled it, personally, and borne its brunt, he comes by his Spirit to write it on our hearts, so that we may do it and love it from our hearts, because it is the Law of him whom we love.

We look first at the relation between the Law and the gospel in its justificationary aspect.

The *Westminster Confession of Faith* says that within the one Covenant of Grace there are two administrations in the Bible, the Old Covenant (Testament) and the New. We must look at these more fully, but first we should note that our Lord stands in a natural relation to the Law as man. As God's eternal Son, equal with the Father in power and glory, eternity and divinity, Christ came from heaven and was made man, subject to the Law, whose formulation expresses both the character of the divine Trinity, and the divine demand upon man. He was made under the Law (Gal. 4:4) to satisfy the perfect justice of God in respect of the first Adam, who signally and heinously failed to do so in face of God's abundant goodness to him in Eden. Christ thus came to satisfy the perfect justice of God – first by living a life of perfect obedience to the Father's will, thus reversing Adam's sin, and repairing and restoring the bond broken by Adam. This he did on our behalf, in his active obedience which constitutes his federal relation to the Law as the new Head of the race, absolutely acceptable to God.

Christ's passive obedience constitutes his *penal* relation to the Law, and is concerned with his sufferings for us, by which he bore and thus removed our sins, subsequently by his Spirit affording us the power to share in his sufferings.

Christ also fulfilled the Law *ceremonially* according to the Levitical law, by becoming the embodiment and anti-type of all that the ceremonial law symbolised – the lamb, the blood, the shewbread, the oil, the incense and the ark. Everything in the Tabernacle and in the

Temple – its furnishings, how the priests dressed, and what they did – all spoke of Christ. The outward historical sign and dramatic deed of God through the earthquake at the death of Jesus – the veil of the Temple being rent from top to bottom – proclaimed these types as no longer necessary. The reality was here to fulfil all, and take away our sinful Adam by the cross, slaying him in order to give us his new nature.

Of course, within the one Covenant of Grace there are various dispensations. God made covenants with Noah, Abraham, Moses, David, and others, all pointing to Christ to come.

It will be clear from all this that the Bible does not begin with Law, but with God's gracious covenant promises. The lavishness of God's provision for Adam and Eve in Genesis chapters 1 and 2, is something to take away our breath, and make Adam's and Eve's sin appear all the more heinous and monstrous. One of the most important things to know about the Bible (almost before we begin to study it closely), with a view to understanding its message, is that God first reveals himself to man as *gracious*. It is grace that is revealed all the way through; and if we say that the Law is like a rather thinly spread sandwich between the grace of Genesis and the grace of the gospel, that is not to say that the Law is not of grace; it is.

We have the grace of God to Adam. This is given various names. The word 'covenant' does not appear in the first two chapters of Genesis, but that God made a covenant with Adam and Eve is plain. It is variously called the Covenant of Works (see *Westminster Confession of Faith* VII, 2), the Covenant of Nature, the Covenant of Innocence (Matthew Henry), and the Adamic Administration (John Murray).

There is a new dispensation after the Fall. Immediately after the Fall there is the promise of the Redeemer (Gen. 3:15). Then, there is God's covenant with Noah before the Flood, and after it; God's covenant with Abraham, found particularly in Genesis chapters 12, 15, 17, the last including the covenant of circumcision. God's covenant with Moses is found in various places, particularly Exodus chapter 6. Then comes God's covenant with David (see 2 Sam.

7:12-21; 1 Kings 6:11-13, *etc.*). Yet all these covenants, except the first (the so-called Covenant of Works), with their different dispensations, are embraced within the one covenant of God's Grace; for the Old Testament is full of the gospel.

Think of this: every one converted through the ministry of Paul, Peter or any of the apostles during the first years of the Christian church, as far as Antioch (the second headquarters of the church), into Asia Minor and to the other Antioch, Ephesus, Troas, across the Aegean Sea to Greece, Macedonia and Achaia, and right on to Rome and beyond – every one was converted through the preaching of the gospel *from* the Old Testament, since there was no other. The first part of the New Testament to be written was Paul's Letters, from the late AD 40's to the 60's; then the gospels (Mark's was very likely the earliest, said to be from round about AD 70), and right on to the other Epistles, including John's and the Book of the Revelation towards the end of the first century – these probably spilling over into the next century. So, the saving Word then preached was from the Old Testament.

Yet the apostle Paul did not find the lack of explicit formulation of New Testament truth a hindrance. When he sought to declare the gospel in its purest essence (in Rom. 4 and Gal. 3), he went right back to early Genesis, principally to chapters 12 and 15, and showed the pure grace of God in his covenant promises to Abraham. But look at Hebrews chapter 11. The Old Testament saints from Abel, Enoch, Noah and Abraham, were saved by faith in Christ prophetically revealed. How could they be saved by Christ before he came? They were saved in prospect of his coming, faith projecting itself forward into the future with certainty, as Hebrews 11:1-3 shows.

Of course our salvation was not completed in history until Christ came, died, was raised from the dead and ascended into heaven. Our salvation is grounded in the death and resurrection of Jesus Christ. That is why Paul, when he went to Corinth, said that he was determined to know nothing 'except Jesus Christ and him crucified' (1 Cor. 1:2). But the sacrifice of Christ is an eternal reality in the heart of God – 'the Lamb slain from the foundation of the world'. That is why the *Westminster Confession of Faith* says that in the Old Testament dispensation, 'under the Law' the Covenant of Grace was 'administered by promises, prophecies, sacrifices, circumcision, the paschal lamb, and other types and ordinances delivered to the people of the Jews, all fore-signifying Christ to come, which were for that time sufficient and efficacious, through the operation of the Spirit, to instruct and build up the elect in faith in the promised Messiah, by whom they had full remission of sins, and eternal salvation; and is called the Old Testament.' (VII, 2).

The efficacy of the sacrifice of Christ, therefore worked backwards effectually to save the Old Testament saints. This may be seen from three New Testament references:

(1) Romans 3:22-24: Paul, expounding the core of gospel truth, says, 'For there is no difference; for all have sinned, and come short of the glory of God; being justified freely by his grace through the redemption that is in Christ Jesus.'

(2) Hebrews 9:15: 'And for this cause he (Christ) is the mediator of the new testament, that by means of death, for the redemption of the transgressions that were under the first testament, they which are called might receive the promise of eternal inheritance.'

(3) Acts 17:30, 31: 'And the times of this ignorance God winked at; but now commands all men everywhere to repent; because he has appointed a day in which he will judge the world in righteousness by that man whom he has ordained; whereof he has given assurance unto all men, in that he has raised him from the dead.'

So, it is clear that the Old Testament saints were saved by faith in the promised Messiah, their faith being their 'evidence' (Heb. 11:1).

Paul refers to this promise in Galatians 3:18; but he then goes on to ask, 'Why then the Law, when Abraham was saved by faith in the promised Messiah?' The answer to the question is that the Law 'was added because of transgressions.' Or, as the New English Bible says, bringing out the sense wonderfully, 'The Law was added to make wrongdoing a legal offence'. The Berkeley Bible says it was 'superimposed to show up sins in their true light'.

We must not forget that the Law was given to God's chosen, covenanted people, redeemed from Egypt by blood, an event which serves as the Old Testament type of Christ's sacrifice. In this aspect of the Law, God was not so much setting a standard for men to live up to – no one but Jesus ever lived up to it (Jas. 2:10) – but to show them how bad they were, in order to drive them to find mercy through the promised Redeemer and Deliverer from sin.

But here is the question: If the dispensation of the Law is part of God's Covenant of Grace, why does Galatians 3:11,12 say that the Law rests on works? 'Now it is evident that no man is justified before God by the law; for the righteous shall live by faith; but the law does not rest on faith, for it is he who does those things who shall live by them.' That would imply that while Abraham might have been saved by faith, Moses was not! The Moses who appeared with Elijah on the Mount of Transfiguration! Was he not saved? Hebrews 11:23 says Moses also was saved by faith. What, then, are we to make of the seeming contradiction? Deuteronomy 30, quoted in Romans 10:6-8, has the answer.

In Deuteronomy chapter 28, God had uttered threats and curses which would come upon Israel if they turned away from him, and this tone spills over into chapter 29. After these fearful things, which the beginning of chapter 30 seems to assume will take place, the Lord graciously says he will provide for their return to him in full repentance, when he will receive them, circumcise their hearts and those of their offspring, so that they will love the Lord their God with all their heart and soul, and live (vv. 2-6). None the less, the way is open to them to follow the Lord and be blessed *without* any of these horrid things coming upon them. 'For,' says the Lord, 'this commandment which I command you this day is not too hard for you, neither is it far off. . . . But the Word is very near you; it is in your mouth and in your heart, so that you can do it.' (vv. 11-14).

The Lord goes on immediately to say, 'See, I have set before you this day life and good, death and evil. If you obey the commandments of the Lord your God. . . .' Well! 'But if your heart turns away, and you will not hear. . . you shall perish. I call heaven and earth to witness against you this day, that I have set before you life and death, blessing and curse, therefore choose life, that you and your descendants may live, loving the Lord your God, obeying his voice, and cleaving to him; for that means life to you. . .' (vv. 15-20).

Does someone observe that the above chapter prophetically projects itself right through Israel's painful experience of sinning in the land, being taken out of it into captivity, and then returning to it? Yes, but even that does not invalidate God's gracious promise! Look at the many promises of life to Israel as early as Leviticus 18:5; Deuteronomy 4:1; 5:33. These contain no cynical offer, for it is obvious from Hebrews 11 that the Old Testament saints recorded there obeyed and lived. But how? Because the Covenant of Grace proffered and provided the ground of faith by which they did obey and live. When God said to Abraham, 'Look; I'll make your children as many as the stars in the sky,' Abraham believed God. It is as simple as that. He said 'Yes, Lord, I believe you will'. That was saving faith (Gen. 15:1-6).

This Covenant persists. In Moses' day the Lord said 'Now you shall see what I will do to Pharoah. . . I am the Lord'. The first thing the Lord did was to take Moses back to Abraham: 'I appeared to Abraham, to Isaac, and to Jacob, as God Almighty. . . established my covenant with them, to give them the land of Canaan. . . I have remembered my covenant. . . I will bring you out. . . redeem you. . . and I will take you for my people, and I will be your God. . . and I will bring you into the land' (Exod. 6:1-8).

The basis of the Covenant is God's unilateral (one-sided) declaration. Its ratification is not conditional on anything man does, or can do. God makes a Covenant with man and as soon as it is uttered it is in force. Man is, of course, required to obey the Covenant, but not as a condition of its being ratified or made valid. So God says to Israel in Moses' day, 'Look, you are my people, and I am your God, and there is nothing you can do about it except get the worst of me: you won't shake me off!' In Old Testament terms God is simply saying, 'You are my children, my chosen people, my Old Testament church, my Christians; and as Christians, you will live like this!'

But, you may say, in view of what Paul says in Galatians 3:11,12, and Romans 10:5 – that the Law does not rest on faith ('for he who does them shall live by them') – does that mean that only one who fulfils the Law perfectly, as in James 2:10, and as Christ alone was able to do, will be saved? What, then, would be the point of the

Covenant? But Paul says in Galatians 3 that the Covenant and the Law are against each other! Yes, but the word 'live' can and must have another meaning; these are the children of the Covenant, redeemed from Egypt by blood. The word 'live' was given to Israel in a sanctificationary context. That is to say, it was a word to those who were already God's people, and it was given to show them how they were to live day by day. It was a word to a saved people, to the church, to those within the fold, belonging to God. Whereas the word 'live' in the justificationary sense is a word to people just coming into the fold. For the word 'live' enshrines both the justificationary and sanctificationary senses; albeit it is here a word to people who already belong to God. The best help I can find for this is from Matthew Henry:

> Seeing God had showed himself so tender to Israel, and so willing to consider their frame and gratify them in what they desired, and was also ready to make the best of them; and seeing they had themselves desired to have Moses for their teacher, who was now teaching them; and seeing they had promised so solemnly and under the influence of so many good causes and considerations to hear and do so; he charges them to walk in all the ways that God had commanded them, assuring them that it would be highly for their advantage to do so.

The only way to be happy is to be holy!

Matthew Henry is taking the word 'live' there in the redeemed sense, in a regenerate, sanctificationary context; and he appositely quotes, 'Say to the righteous, it shall be well with them'. It is a word to believers. Hear Henry again on Leviticus 18:5, 'If you obey this you shall live'. He says:

> We have reason to thank God. . . that it is not so in force in the nature of a covenant, as that the least transgression shall forever exclude us from this life. The Apostle quotes this twice, as opposite to the faith which the Gospel reveals. (The twice is in Galatians 3:12 and Romans 10:5.) It is the description of the 'righteousness which is by the Law, the man that doeth them shall live – in them', and is urged to prove, that 'the Law is not of faith.' The alteration which the Gospel has made, is in the last word; still 'the man that doeth them shall live', but not live 'in

them': for the Law could not give life, because we could not perfectly keep it: it was 'weak through the flesh', not in itself; but now 'the man that doeth them' shall 'live by the faith of the Son of God'. He shall owe his life to the grace of Christ, and not to the merit of his own works; see Galatians 3:21, 22. 'The just shall live,' but they shall live 'by faith', by virtue of their union with Christ, who is their Life.

But then Paul quotes twice the words from Habakkuk 2:4 that 'the righteous shall live by faith' (Rom. 1:17; Gal. 3:11), which is the key to what we are seeking to find out. The context of Habakkuk is the impending invasion of Jerusalem by the Babylonians in Jeremiah's day. The Word is saying that the prophet will survive the invasion, if he trusts God. That is to say, he will be sanctified. He is already justified, he is the Lord's; but if he trusts in the Lord during the invasion he will be saved (preserved) in the sanctificationary sense.

This came literally true for Jeremiah. When the Babylonians came, the first thing the commander-in-chief said was, 'Where is Jeremiah?' Many were slain, many were taken captive, but when, rather sheepishly, they brought Jeremiah from prison, the commander-in-chief said to him, 'What would you like to do? Would you like to come with us to Babylon, or would you like to stay here? If you would like to stay here, I will see that all provision is made for you. I will see that the Commander who is to be set over Jerusalem after I have gone will attend to all your needs.' Why did he do this? Because Jeremiah trusted God that in an evil day he would 'live' – in the sense of survive.

When the apostle Paul, however, quoted Habakkuk 2:4 in both Romans 1:17 and Galatians 3:11, he gathered the flower of its sanctificationary context together and closed it up and presented it as a justificationary bud. (There is, of course, the implication of the earlier stage of the flower in the Habakkuk verse, since the Lord could not promise a *continuance* of life to his prophet if he had not given him life in the first place. This life he gave to believing Israel by calling them out to be his chosen people, and by leading them from Egypt, through the sacrifice of blood, and by the discipline of Sinai and the wilderness, into Canaan.)

There is, however, a third quotation from Habakkuk 2:4 in the New Testament, in Hebrews 10:37-39. There the writer seems to be unfolding the bud again and the context becomes more sanctificationary than justificationary:

'For yet a little while, and he who is coming will come and will not tarry. Now the just shall live by faith; but if he draws back, my soul has no pleasure in him.' But we are not of those who draw back to perdition, but of those who believe to the saving of the soul.

For those who do not draw back to perdition, but believe to the saving of their souls, are those mentioned in Hebrews 11, such as Abel, Enoch, Noah, Abraham, Isaac, Jacob and Moses. The sanctificationary 'by faith' therefore flows out of the justificationary 'by faith': they both belong to the one Covenant of Grace. But in God's dealings with Israel in the Old Testament it is assumed that they are the Lord's people and are therefore challenged to live their lives according to the quality of his Law.

This is no different from the challenge today. What is your assurance that you are a Christian? That your name is on some church roll? The Lord knows them that are his. But as far as we are concerned (the elders of the church in particular), we need to see signs that persons are in grace. This is the only test the church can apply to its people – the test that we are living according to what we profess.

None the less, as we well know from Israel's history, and indeed from that of the church, the Lord's people can stray or be carried far into the wilderness until it is almost impossible to recognise them as the Lord's! For while one of the most significant threads running through the Bible, from at least Exodus 6 to Revelation (21:3, 7), is the sovereign Word of God declaring that he has chosen this people to be his, and he will be their God yet; that declaration is also couched in more conditional terms in the Old Testament passages from which Paul quotes in 2 Corinthians 6:16-18:

I will dwell in them and walk among them. I will be their God and they shall be my people. Therefore come out from among them and be separate, says the Lord. Do not touch what is unclean, and I will receive you. I will be a Father to you, and you shall be my sons and daughters, says the Lord Almighty. (See Lev. 26:12; Jer. 32:38; Ezek 37:27; Is. 52:11; Ezek. 20:34, 41; 2 Sam. 7:14.)

God is therefore saying to his chosen people, Old Testament and New, 'I am your God and you are my people: now *live* as my people.' This is it in a nutshell! It runs right through the Bible, from God's promises to Abraham, through to God giving them the Law to live by, driving them back to him when they did not, and all pointing forward to and being gloriously fulfilled in Christ. We are saved by faith from beginning to end. By faith our sins are forgiven, being blotted out by the redeeming blood of Jesus; by faith we are taken into God's family and are declared to be righteous in his sight. But it is also and equally 'by faith' that we go on obediently to live the Christian life, drawing upon his power to fulfil his holy Law – not legally, in fear and in terror, but in love to Jesus.

Love involves obedience. A mother says to her child, 'Son, do you love me?' A father says to his daughter, 'Do you love me, my dear?' Then, do as I say. So it is in our relationship to God:

By this we may be sure that we know him, if we keep his commandments (1 Jn. 2:3).

By this it may be seen who are the children of God, and who are the children of the devil: whoever does not do right is not of God, nor he who does not love his brother (1 Jn. 3:10).

Every one who believes that Jesus is the Christ has been begotten of God, and every one who loves the parent loves the child. By this we know that we love the children of God, when we love God and obey his commandments. For this is the love of God, that we keep his commandments. And his commandments are not burdensome. For whatever is born of God overcomes the world; and this is the victory that overcomes the world, our faith. Who is it that overcomes the world but he who believes that Jesus is the Son of God? (1 Jn. 5:1-5)

So, the Ten Commandments were given to Israel in love, although, by and large, they did not return his love. They took the command to do right out of the context of love and put it into the context of Law. It was *they* who made the Law 'legal' in the bad sense, not God. He had said to them 'Love Me; and do as I say!' (for the word 'love' appears several times in Exodus 20 and Deuteronomy 30). But they did not love him, and obviously did not do as he said. They turned what God gave them by the grace of sanctification into an attempt to justify themselves, complaining that his Law was too hard to keep. Of course it was, and is, if we legalise it, and lift it out of the realm of grace. When he says to us, 'I will be your God and you shall be my child,' he is also saying, 'Now, behave like my child; for my grace is sufficient for you to do so.'

What God gave in a family context, sinners turned into an anti-family context. It is thus that many children turn their parents into task-masters and task-mistresses, because they do not believe that their parents really love them when they require obedience of them. They regard them as making rules for the sake of making rules, and only to have power over them. This can be true, and is doubtless too often true, but not where grace prevails. Christian parents must see to it, by grace, that it is not true.

It is certainly not true of God. He is no task-master. He is basically not a demanding, but a giving God, and reasonably demands only what he has given. Oh, that we might see it! 'My yoke,' he says through his Son, 'is easy.' All we have to do is receive. All we have to do is to lift our empty arms to him and receive him.

We have seen that the Old Testament injunction, 'Obey the Law and live', has a double aspect – justificationary and sanctificationary. We may say the same of our Lord's commandments in the New Testament (see Jn. 14:15, 21, 23; 15:10; 1 Jn. 2:3; 3:22, 24; 5:2, 3; 2 Jn. 6).

The truth is that although in normal New Testament sequence, and practically speaking, justification comes before sanctification (*cf.* Rom. 3-5 with Rom. 6-8), the Old Testament injunction, 'Obey the Law and live', is first given in a sanctificationary context, since the

Law was given to Israel following her redemption from Egypt. As already noted, this is true of Habakkuk 2:4, which Paul turns from its natural sanctificationary context to a justificationary aspect (see Rom. 1:17; Gal. 3:11).

Of course, as Luther would emphasise, as long as believers are sinners, they need the threat of the Law to drive them back to Christ in order that they might fulfil the Law by grace and not by self-effort. But the Law is primarily a guide to the loving and obedient, and the fulfilling of it is a measure of their love. Yet it is Paul (using Habakkuk 2:4 to point his justificationary lesson – that we are driven to Christ by the Law), who is also emphatic to say that the letter kills (see 2 Cor. 3:6; Rom. 7:5, 6). This is particularly true of awakened sinners (see Rom. 7:7-13).

But what of Christians? As far as they are concerned, the Law which powerfully drives men to Christ is weak, in that it has no power to effect what it enjoins (see Rom. 8:3; Gal. 3:12, 21). Only the Spirit can do that (see Rom. 8:4; 2 Cor. 3:6).

However, before we arrive at the glories of the Spirit-energised life expounded in Romans 8, we encounter its manifest struggles with the Law as seen in chapter 7. The Law has all the authority of God; it has the threat as well as the possibility of condemnation, but it has no inherent power, it is simply black upon white. God says, 'You must do this, and not that,' but the Law gives absolutely no power in the world to do good. Should we not then ignore the Law and turn our back upon it as useless because it has no effect? No; for the reasons set forth in Romans 7 (from verse 14 onwards) which, many godly scholars agree, deals with Christians.

Let us begin with Romans 7:13, a good jumping-off place: 'Did that which is good, then, bring death to me?' No, don't blame the Law; it is holy, just and good (v.12): blame sin; sin working death in me through what is good. The point in verse 13 is that sin dares to use what is good to work death in me, 'so that through the commandment sin might become utterly sinful,' by exposing the enormity of the offence.

What divides 7:14 from 7:13 is the fact that up to the end of verse 13 we are in the past tense, whereas verse 14 is in the present tense. That is significant. 'We know that the law is spiritual; but I am carnal, sold as a slave to sin' (NIV). What does 'carnal' mean? Unconverted? Not necessarily. Christians can sometimes behave carnally (see 1 Cor. 3:1-3; Heb. 5:11-14). Can you say of a Christian that he is 'sold as a slave to sin'? It doesn't say he sold himself to sin. The word 'sold' goes back to the Fall, for it is still true that we are sold to sin while we remain mortal (see vv. 17, 18, 20, 25).

This fact leads on to Paul's discussion of the struggles of the Christian. He says, 'I do not understand what I do. For what I want to do I do not do, but what I hate I do. And if I do what I do not want to do, I agree that the law is good' (Rom. 7:15,16, NIV). You see what this means? This is a Christian struggling to keep the Law, but surely glimpsing a life beyond the Law.

Paul goes on, 'As it is, it is no longer I myself who do it, but it is sin living in me. I know that nothing good lives in me, that is, in my sinful nature. For I have the desire to do what is good, but I cannot carry it out. For what I do is not the good I want to do; no, the evil I do not want to do – this I keep on doing. Now if I do what I do not want to do, it is no longer I who do it, but it is sin living in me that does it' (Rom. 7:17-20).

So, says Paul, 'I find this law (or principle) at work: when I want to do good, evil is right there with me (see Gen. 4:7). For in my inner being I delight in God's law; but I see another law at work in the members of my body, waging war against the law of my mind and making me a prisoner of the law of sin at work within my members' (Rom. 7:21-23).

Then Paul cries out, 'What a wretched man I am! Who will rescue me from this body of death?' (Rom. 7:24). And he answers instantly, and shouts out: 'Thanks be to God (for deliverance) through Jesus Christ our Lord!' (Rom. 7:25).

But when does this deliverance occur? Some might want to say, on believing and receiving Christ. But then, what of the second sentence of verse 25? That is surely a surprising come-down from the cry of triumph! To be realistic about the whole passage and the struggles admitted, we must assign the deliverance, certainly in its fullest extent, to our future resurrection. Calvin and the Reformers, Matthew Henry (although he gives two views), and John Murray, all hold that this is the meaning of the cry, that the hope, joy and thanksgiving there expressed, point forward to the believer's resurrection, as if to say, (as verse 25b implies) the struggle will go on until death.

It is therefore in that context that Paul is saying that although we give thanks to God that when this mortal body is done away we shall have deliverance from this body of death, at the moment, until I die, 'I myself in my mind am a slave to God's law, but in the sinful nature a slave to the law of sin' (v. 25b).

However, the solution to the problem of the struggles of the Christian believer, from the sanctificationary as distinct from the final point of view, comes only in chapter 8: 'Therefore, there is now no condemnation for those who are in Christ Jesus' – full stop! This complete statement is sanctificationary. Yet this is not held by every one. Martyn Lloyd-Jones held that Romans 8:1 reverts to Romans 5:1 and that Romans 6 and 7 are a parenthesis. He says chapter 8 is not about sanctification. But this cannot be so. The fact that Paul says there is therefore 'no condemnation' surely indicates that he has moved on from the subject of the guilt of sin (chapter 5) to that of the power of sin.

We may therefore go on to read the following verses in Romans 8 – full and rich and involved as they are – with remarkable clarity of understanding, for they do indeed set forth the present glory of life in the Spirit; whereas the Law (v.3) was powerless to work sanctification within us.

Is there no place then for the Law in the sanctified life? Yes! For since the Law was first given to the Old Testament church at Sinai following redemption by blood from Egypt, although it is powerless in itself, none the less by the Spirit it is necessary as a rule of life. This whole area has already been fully and eloquently set forth in the *Westminster Confession of Faith*, 'Of the Law of God', XIX 5-7 (quoted at the beginning of this study). What do you think of these passages? How are we to hold the Law in such a fine tension? The answer is, by the obedience of faith, which comes by grace alone. But is there not great danger of bondage to legalism? There is, for sin and Satan are constantly seeking to use God's holy Law, on account of our weakness, to condemn Christians, both in respect of sins they have committed, and those they have not (*e.g.* false accusations, see Rev. 12:10).

What, then, is the answer to the danger? It is the obedience of faith which works by love (Gal. 5:6). This is the point of such passages as 1 John 1:1-4; 4:10-12, 17, 18; 5:1-12, the theme of which is 'Love which loves to obey.' As the line from the hymn says, 'Love will make obedience sweet.'

When the apostle Paul, following our Lord (Matt. 22:35-40) says that love is the fulfilling of the Law (Rom.13:10), he means that the Christian does not think of himself as imprisoned by the Law as a restrictive code of conduct. Rather, he is energised by the Spirit to love both God and his neighbour. The Law as a rule of life needs to be followed, not with a servile spirit, but with submission and loving obedience. True, at first, young Christians, if they have not been brought up under the gracious umbrella of a Christian home or church, may need to keep close by the rule of life found in the Decalogue; but even so, they must see to it that it is informed and empowered always by love of Christ, lest they come under sinful and even Satanic bondage to the letter which kills. John says, in essence, 'Love God and obey his commandments.' This is why Paul says there is no law against the fruit of the Spirit. For when we love God, we do what pleases him. That cannot be wrong.

It is interesting that the Jewish *Shema* says 'Hear, O Israel: the Lord our God, the Lord is one. Love the Lord your God with all your heart, and with all your soul, and with all your strength. These commandments that I give you today are to be upon your hearts. Impress them on your children. Talk about them' (Deut. 6:4-6).

Christians also (equally, but with fuller assurance) ought to take the Law sanctificationally in the obedience of love. Jesus says, 'As the Father has loved me, so have I loved you; abide in my love. If you keep my commandments, you will abide in my love, just as I have kept my Father's commandments, and abide in his love' (Jn. 15:9-10). This is altogether a family matter.

Interestingly enough, that is exactly what Professor Francis Lyall said in a Bible Study on Redemption (Gilcomston South Church, Aberdeen, 28 March 1973):

> The basis of the idea of Redemption is a family matter. Redemption is carried out for a person by one of his family. This is the source and grounding of the Christian confidence. Salvation is not a business transaction: it is an act of grace by our Elder Brother, by those who love us far better than natural relations, by those who love as love is meant to be. This is why there is certainty for us. We trust our family.

A family matter, then; for God's Law is deeply embedded in his own heart, which is the heart of the divine, Trinitarian family, the Father, the Son, and the Holy Spirit. The Law of God in its primary form, the Ten Commandments, expresses the character of the holy heart of God before it is enjoined upon man as a set of ruling principles. It gives explicit pointers to the infinite perfections of the Almighty's nature.

One wonders how to show this in short compass. The three chapters in Revelation, in which the angels and the redeemed speak of God and the Lamb ecstatically, will give some idea of the glory of the being and character of God.

> Worthy art thou, our Lord and God, to receive glory and honour and power, for thou didst create all things and by thy will they existed and were created. (Rev. 4:11).
> Worthy is the Lamb who was slain, to receive power and wealth and wisdom and might and honour and glory and blessing. . . . To him who sits upon the throne and to the Lamb be blessing and honour and glory and might for ever and ever. . . . Amen! (Rev. 5: 12-14).
> Blessing and glory and wisdom and thanksgiving and honour and power and might be to our God for ever and ever! Amen! (Rev. 7:12).

In these places the lists of words expressing the illustriousness of the Almighty contain the epitome of his perfections, which the Father shares with his Son and the Holy Spirit, not only in eternity (Jn. 17:5,24), but, more poignantly, on earth (Heb. 5:8). The glory of the Son's relationship with his Father on earth is that, having knowledge of all they shared and still share in heaven, the Son is able to submit himself to unspeakable human testing, and yet remain perfect, in loyalty and love. It is the gracious rule and regulation of this law of love that the Son seeks to teach his own disciples.

It is a law which began to operate in the bliss of man's first estate in the innocency of Eden, beautifully expressed in Genesis 2: 15-17:

> The Lord God took man and put him in the garden of Eden to till and keep it (a delightful occupation!). And the Lord God commanded the man saying, 'You may freely eat of every tree of the garden; but of the tree of the knowledge of good and evil you shall not eat, for in the day that you eat of it you shall die!'

Thus we have the gracious provision of the positive law upon which man might build a satisfying life. Being a creature not yet tested, a negative law was given, a 'Thou shalt not', to test his obedience and submissiveness. There was a failure in this regard, however, which evoked, so early and graciously, that Covenant of Grace which began with Genesis 3:15, 'I will put enmity between you (the serpent) and the woman, and between your seed and her seed; he shall bruise your head, and you shall bruise his heel.' The enmity which God gave to the seed of the woman was obviously the enmity of faith – which gift of God may be said to operate the law of God in the heart of man.

We see this law in operation in the action of godly Abel offering an acceptable sacrifice to God (Heb. 11:4). It is a mark of faith, as the actions of God's chosen men, unfolding through the following chapters of Genesis and right on to the Psalms, show. This belongs to a spirit and attitude of mind and heart which delight in the law of God. We see the beauty of this frame of mind in all subsequent acts of faith, knowing, as we do, that they spring from the creative Word of God as he bestows his favour on whom he wills.

But Noah found favour in the eyes of the Lord (Gen. 6:8).

Noah walked with God (Gen. 6:9).

Noah built an altar to the Lord (Gen. 8:20).

Now the Lord said to Abram, 'Go from your country. . . .' So Abram went (Gen. 12:1, 4).

And behold, the word of the Lord came to him. . . 'Look toward heaven, and number the stars, if you are able. . . So shall your descendants be.' And he (Abram) believed the Lord; and he reckoned it to him as righteousness (Gen. 15:4-6).

Here we have the buoyant response of the chosen objects of God's grace to his Word of command and commission. They are suddenly on the divine wavelength, and from then on life becomes gloriously purposive and satisfying, whatever the cost to themselves.

Thomas Mann, lecturing on Wagner, quoted these words: 'Admiration is the only response to greatness. The power to admire is the power of the capacity to receive.'

As far as this conveys truth relative to the operations of faith as admiration and awe, leading to obedience, it is exactly what we find in the Psalter, from the very first Psalm:

Blessed is the man who walks not in the counsel of the wicked, nor stands in the way of sinners, nor sits in the seat of scoffers; but his delight is in the law of the Lord, and on his law he meditates day and night (Ps. 1:1, 2).

And from the long Psalm:

I will delight in thy statutes (Ps. 119:16).
Thy testimonies are my delight (Ps. 119:24).
Lead me in the path of thy commandments, for I delight in it (Ps. 119:35).
For I find my delight in thy commandments, which I love (Ps. 119:47).

I revere thy commandments, which I love, and I will meditate on thy statutes (Ps. 119:48).

Let thy mercy come to me, that I may live; for thy law is my delight (Ps. 119:77).

If thy law had not been my delight, I should have perished (Ps. 119:92).

Oh, how I love thy law! It is my meditation all the day (Ps. 119:97).

How sweet are thy words to my taste, sweeter than honey to my mouth (Ps. 119:103).

Trouble and anguish have come upon me, but thy commandments are my delight (Ps. 119:143).

My soul keeps thy testimonies; I love them exceedingly (Ps. 119:167).

I long for thy salvation, O Lord, and thy law is my delight (Ps. 119:174).

We then leap to Romans 7:16:

Now if I do what I do not want, I agree that the law is good.

I delight in the law of God, in my inmost self (Rom. 7:22).

Of course, we know that the 'law' in these quotations stands for the whole body of Old Testament truth, revealed by God to his chosen people. But since the core of this Word is the ten principles of the Decalogue, we have no compunction in applying them to the Law as a rule of life for believers. And the marvel of this oft-expressed 'delight' in the Law of God is that it is evoked from fallen creatures upon whom the grace of God has lighted, who, sinners as they are, belong to a long processional line of God's chosen ones which stretches right through the Old Testament centuries. For the law of God's original covenant with man, made in the garden, was broken almost immediately, after which the royal battle of faith ('I will put enmity. . .') was joined. Yet, by Genesis 6:8, the favour of God is revealed, and in Genesis 12:2 the promise of blessing to Abram, upon obedience, is given.

There is also, of course, the threat to curse, upon disobedience, as in Deuteronomy 28. And, long before that, Israel's sins led them into Egypt as a family – and then out again by God's grace, now as a nation. Much later they were away for their sins to Assyria, and others, later, to Babylon. But the promise to bless, even in those limited circumstances, is not entirely withdrawn (see Jer. 29:11-14). The promise to bless, and yet to curse upon disobedience, and yet to bless again, is stated clearly in Deuteronomy 30:1-6 (as in vv.11-14). And it is clear that what Deuteronomy 30:6 says, that the Lord God will circumcise their hearts and the hearts of their offspring, so that they will love the Lord their God with all their heart and soul, that they may live, is the precursor of Jeremiah 31:33, which states that the Lord will yet write his Law upon their hearts.

Now, for God to write his Law effectively upon their lawless hearts, it must become, in a sense, incarnate in them, the Word becoming flesh and dwelling in them. This is exactly what the coming of the Holy Spirit of the incarnate, crucified, risen and exalted Jesus, did, and does. Jesus said of the coming of the Spirit at Pentecost, 'For he dwells with you, and will be in you' (Jn. 14:17).

This is the sum of the matter, that the blessed Trinity is involved in internalising God's holy Law in such a way that we become children of God, upholding it, loving it and delighting in it and, as loving brothers, sharing it within his family. 'If you love me, keep my commandments,' is the sum. There is no wedge between the loving and the keeping, or between the keeping and the loving: they are to be one, as the Testaments are, in one comprehensive Covenant of Grace.

We obey because we love, even if that love is greatly mingled with understandable fear of One so great and holy. Yet it is given us, progressively, to let that love become increasingly tender and strong. Walking in the paths of his righteousness, as the Shepherd Psalm says, will then be pleasure.